Trauma
& Evil

TRAUMA
&Evil

Healing the Wounded Soul

J. Jeffrey Means

with contributions by
Mary Ann Nelson

Warren —
Thank you for your
support & encouragement
from a distance!
J. Jeffrey Means

Fortress Press
Minneapolis

TRAUMA AND EVIL
Healing the Wounded Soul

The lyrics for "Don't Wash Me" appearing on pages 174–75 by David Butler are used with the songwriter's permission. Copyright © 1997 David Butler.

Cover design: Julie Odland
Book design: Zan Ceeley

Library of Congress Cataloging-in-Publication Data

Means, J. Jeffrey
    Trauma and evil : healing the wounded soul / J. Jeffrey Means ; with contributions
  by Mary Ann Nelson.
      p.   cm.
    Includes bibliographical references (p.) and index.
    ISBN 0-8006-3270-2
    1. Spiritual warfare. 2. Good and evil. I. Nelson, Mary Ann. II. Title.
    BT975 .M43 2000
    253.5'2 — dc21   00–062239

The paper used in this publication meets the minimum requirements of American National Standard for Information Sciences — Permanence of Paper for Printed Library Materials, ANSI Z329.48-1984.

Manufactured in the U.S.A.   AF 1-3270
0 4   0 3   0 2   0 1   0 0   1   2   3   4   5   6   7   8   9   1 0

Contents

Preface

Personal Journeys into Evil

AS WE BEGIN THIS JOURNEY from trauma into the realm of evil, we want to share our respective stories of wrestling personally with the presence of evil as an active force in the world. This seems particularly fitting since the material we are presenting grows out of the life stories that patients and colleagues have shared with us. In talking with colleagues, we have been reminded repeatedly that our experiences are similar to those of others who have embarked willingly and unwillingly upon this journey into the realm of evil. Sharing our stories and respective journeys with one another also helps alleviate the isolation and lack of confidence that can develop within us when life experience of any kind is not shared.

With these thoughts in mind, we would like to share how each of us became interested in such a disturbing subject as evil. As with most things in life that change us significantly, the evolutionary process has been slow but constant. While conversion may seem spontaneous at times, there is often a long and tedious preparation process that has operated behind the scene.

*   *   *   *   *

It took a long time for the reality of evil to break through my denial. This is not because I lived a sheltered life growing up. On the contrary, in my early life I experienced a fire that threatened my home, the explosion of a building right before my eyes, the death of both a close friend and my father from cancer, as well as the systemic evils of a patriarchal church and sexism in society, the horror of the Vietnam War, racism, and the other critical issues of that era. As an adult, I have been exposed to violence, abuse, wars, and other atrocities on a daily basis through the sensationally driven news media. In the inner city of Milwaukee where I was the principal of an elementary school, I witnessed the effects of abuse, violence, and prejudice on children and families. I also was held at gunpoint, robbed, and left locked in a freezer. And yet, somehow, these experiences did not break through a denial system that kept me believing that people are good and the world is basically a safe place. Or perhaps I believed somehow I could change it and make it all better if I tried hard enough.

I have always believed that we and those to whom we minister are about co-creation of our world, as well as one another. So it was with my breakthrough about evil. It began a number of years ago when in both my professional and personal life I had my first encounters with persons who suffer from multiple personality disorder (now referred to as dissociative identity disorder). Their shared experiences confronted me with evil in a way that finally broke through my denial system. These persons had experienced extraordinary abuse at the hands of their parents and others known to them. The enormity and pervasiveness of this evil overwhelmed me. Initially, I was extremely fearful of it. For the first time in my life, I felt basically unsafe in the world, and my faith in a loving God was shaken. Since that time, I have struggled to name and understand evil, to understand God in new ways, and to discover how I want to respond to evil.

In 1990, on our drive back from a dissociative disorders conference, Jeff Means and I began talking about evil. At that time, we each identified a personal need to address the issue. We also saw a need for persons of faith to deal with these issues, since few people in our circles of colleagues seemed to be talking about evil at that time. I believe strongly with theologian Elizabeth Johnson (1990): "If God is there, resisting evil and willing life wherever people are being damaged, then followers of Jesus must enter into that same solidarity" (126). I also believe that to name something correctly gives us a certain amount of power over it, even when that means recognizing evil in all its ghastly reality. When I can name evil in that way, it also makes me clearer about the fact that it is in dedication to "life . . . more abundantly" (John 10:10) that I am committed.

It seems to me that it is reckless to think of evil as something "out there" and as something over which I have no control. I believe each of us has a personal responsibility. Part of assuming personal responsibility has meant I have had to face the potential for evil within myself. I have learned that the line dividing good and evil cuts through the heart of every human being, including my own.

With my denial taken away, my eyes have been opened to see the world more clearly, my vision has been broadened, and I can recognize that things often are not what they seem. For example, in my work with a female inmate, I have experienced evil at a local prison. We are persuaded to believe in this country that evil is embodied in the prisoners whom we lock away. However, the evil I have experienced is not in the inmate, for she admits her wrongdoing and is repentant. The evil I am now aware of is in the prison system itself that treats these women in inhuman ways. Power and control are exercised with no concern for helping them change their lives so they can live responsibly.

In our terrified longing to be in control of the universe, instead of turning our attention to the seeds of evil within ourselves, it is easier to focus on "all-bad" scapegoats like inmates. Recognizing evil in other people is far easier that seeing it in ourselves and in the systems of which we are a part. I am learning that the more I am able to face evil within myself, the more I am able to be with another who has been a victim of evil or even a perpetrator of evil. As theological leaders, our task is to help the people of God understand the experience of evil in the world and determine a faithful response to it.

MARY ANN NELSON

*   *   *   *   *

The reality of evil began to creep into my world in a most unsuspecting way. In the early 1980s, I was supervising a counselor in her work with a new and perplexing patient. The counselor reported that this female patient often would dress and act in sessions like a school-age boy, would huddle before and after sessions in a small vestibule outside the counselor's waiting room, and would seem to change voice tones, posture, and personality during sessions.

What was most perplexing about this patient to the counselor was that her own emotional responses to this patient varied according to the type of self-presentation she offered during any particular part of a psychotherapy session. The counselor knew from experience that her countertransference reactions to patients ordinarily did not vary so much, and with such intensity, within the time period of one session. A sense of "unreality" also surrounded her work with this patient, as if the patient was not fully present at the session and was "somewhere else" at times.

After numerous supervision sessions and much research, we concluded the only working diagnosis that captured the many dimensions of this patient was multiple personality disorder. There was not a lot of acceptance of this diagnosis at that point in history, and it was not a diagnosis we thought we would ever make in our own professional practices. As a consequence, we were reluctant to use this diagnosis, and we were apologetic and defensive about it whenever we discussed this patient in consultation groups. Yet the longer the counselor worked from this diagnostic perspective, the more puzzle pieces fell into place. Over time, we became more and more confident in this particular way of viewing this patient dynamically and symptomatically.

A couple of years later, the counselor working with this patient moved. Since I was most familiar with the patient, with the patient's agreement, I began working with her myself. In order to become more familiar with the dynamics and treatment issues pertinent to these patients, I began attending conferences dealing with dissociative disorders and abuse. I can still recall the tremendous relief that came over me as I realized I was not alone in the type of work I was doing.

In 1989, Mary Ann Nelson joined our staff and slowly began working with a large number of survivors of childhood sexual abuse. A few of these patients she diagnosed with multiple personality disorder, and some of them came into therapy with that diagnosis already assigned. My own caseload also included several persons with dissociative symptoms, and a few with this particular diagnosis. In order to share our experiences with other colleagues, Mary Ann and I led an informal presentation on the topic of multiple personality disorder and object relations theory at a professional meeting in Chicago. Our preparation for this presentation helped us begin integrating object relations theory with our personal experience of working with this group of traumatized and dissociative patients.

Later in 1990, Mary Ann and I went together to a conference on dissociation. Mary Ann subsequently reminded me that it was on our trip home from that conference that we had our first conversation about evil. On that trip, we also talked about what we perceived to be a general lack of awareness regarding the horrendous impact evil has on the lives of people. In retrospect, the fact I had forgotten this conversation suggests I was not able to comprehend for very long the existential despair I felt as I listened to the abuse histories of these patients and what their stories meant for the worldview I had maintained all my life.

Mary Ann's jogging of my memory made me realize that at an unconscious level I was dealing with the fact that working with the traumatic influence of evil on persons was the most disturbing aspect of my work. This was also the first time, still at an unconscious level, I searched for faith resources to help me cope with what I was seeing and experiencing in my work with these victims of horrendous abuse.

I also became aware that I had not experienced this depth of despair since seminary days in the late 1960s. At that time, Christian theology was struggling to respond to the influential forces of the "God is dead" movement and logical positivism. Finding a way to respond seriously to those views, while remaining true to my own faith and beliefs, was one of the most challenging assignments of my life. (I am grateful to Professor Clark M. Williamson for his patience and support through this "dark night of the soul.") I have discovered reluctantly that coming to grips with the real presence of evil in the world requires the same level of personal struggle. Increasingly, I have come to realize that these "breakthrough struggles" develop at those points in our lives where existential realities meet, and seemingly conflict, with religious commitments and worldviews.

In reviewing my own intellectual and emotional process in confronting evil in the world, I have come to realize how difficult it has been for me to face the reality of evil and my own capacity for participating in it and even perpetrating it. My first response to patient stories about abuse, which I would later think of as an expression of evil, was one of skepticism and therapeutic neutrality. This stance continued as I moved into a stage of being "intrigued and fascinated" by this group of patients. While this was an "interested *in*" response, it was still an intellectual, distant, and detached relational stance.

This skepticism, neutrality, and detached fascination eventually gave way and was dismantled by an increasing supply of patient drawings and writings, as well as words, postures, and abreactions, that were a depicting and reliving of abuse experiences. In a short time, I felt overwhelmed, bewildered, and scared. I responded by intellectualizing and fleeing into my head. In a paradoxical way, this flight away from what was so disturbing led me to seek out education and guidance from others. In the process, I discovered I was not alone and that others felt the same way. With that bit of support and reality check, I could allow my patients' experiences to sink slowly in. As they did, they gradually broke down my defenses, resistances, very strong denial system, and ultimately my worldview. This was no small task and explains why it has taken so long to accomplish.

I had grown up in a home that emphasized being "good." Being a "Sunday's child full of grace" made me fit right in. Early on, I developed a sense that I had to be good in order to be accepted and loved. As a child, I took this view to the extreme and concluded I had to be perfect. Subsequently, a large part of my own struggle in coming to grips with evil has been the gradual, and at times not so gradual, breaking down of the defensive barriers in myself to accepting the "not always good" aspects of my full humanness.

In my home, I was never told exactly what "being good" meant, but it was clear to me it was important and expected. I did learn it meant not listening to, talking about, or looking at "bad" things—whatever that meant. In fact, my parents had a small stone sculpture of three monkeys lined up in a row: one with its hands over its ears, the next with its hands over its mouth, and the last with its hands over its eyes. I was told it meant "Hear No Evil, Speak No Evil, and See No Evil." At the time, that seemed as close to a family motto as I could decipher.

As an adolescent, I hated that sculpture for the lack of reality it seemed to signify and for the self-imposed restrictions its subtle message seemed to call forth constantly from me. I now have it in my study as a reminder of how powerful an influence those early messages were to me and how strong and unyielding certain views of ourselves and our resistance to seeing *all* of life can be. The statue also demonstrates to me how important it is to share with others what we experience in our outer and inner worlds and how critical it is to continually break the silence when it comes to evil.

As my systems of denial continued to break down, I began getting scared and even paranoid about a world I had hitherto believed to be basically safe and benevolent. This experience of "vicarious traumatization" is a common response among persons who treat those who have been abused and tortured. As disturbing as it is, this fear provides an existential taste and beginning understanding of the life experience of our patients. It is not insignificant that that fear has subsided as I have become increasingly clear that it is the presence of evil with which I am dealing. Naming our fears is an important step in overcoming them. As I now attempt to keep the reality and signs of evil in mind, I find myself less fearful but more in need of support and buttressing from professional colleagues I trust.

By 1993, Mary Ann and I had begun to formulate an understanding of trauma-related disorders, some of the faith questions they raised, and the importance of faith resources in working with them. We also had become clear about the vital role grief work plays in healing from trauma, and that it is evil with which we are dealing and not just trauma.

After sharing our ideas at a conference with colleagues, I began work on a paper that focused on reasons the church and pastoral counselors have ignored the subject of human-induced trauma and abuse and its impact on persons (Means 1995). While the subject of evil was not central to that discussion, the importance of understanding how evil worked was now at the forefront of my mind.

In the spring of 1995, Mary Ann and I presented a workshop for local caregivers on the topic: "Hear No Evil, Speak No Evil, See No Evil: Working with Evil in Our Midst." The following spring, we led a similar workshop at a professional meeting in Vancouver. Feedback from these workshops affirmed that we were working with important and helpful ideas. The idea for this book germinated during these projects.

I have always felt honored when persons I see for counseling and psychotherapy take the risks involved in sharing their life experiences and sacred stories with me in our work together. The therapeutic journey along what Scott Peck has called "the road less traveled" will take therapist and patient alike into dimensions of our respective inner worlds that have not yet been illuminated, yet nevertheless control much of what we do and how we think.

The personal journey I have just shared has had a great impact on the way I see what people present when they come to counseling. No longer do I think people bring only painful problems for which they seek healing and wholeness. Rather, I view these persons and their concerns as messengers who have been living in parts of the world I have no direct experience of and may never see, yet with which we all are intimately connected. When they come for help, these patients do not just bring problems to be solved. They also bring messages encoded within their many experiences of woundedness. To those caregivers who will listen, these are loud messages about what is happening to people in our world. These patients, and the messages they deliver, go beyond calling attention to their own specific life dilemmas. These messages also call our attention to larger cultural and systemic forces that hurt persons and require our attention. Many of the forces they describe are ones that tear people apart physically, psychically, emotionally, relationally, and spiritually. Such forces are best described by the term "evil."

J. Jeffrey Means

*　　　*　　　*　　　*　　　*

Those of us in caregiving vocations, no matter what our context, want to do our work effectively. To do this, we need resources and support from the communities in which we work. Much of what we do requires an ability to operate with the faith and assurance that we are not alone. When our professional and faith traditions are silent on an important topic such as evil, it is easy for us to feel emotionally dropped and unsupported. This is the very thing our patients feel when they have experienced the active presence of evil in their lives.

We hope the material presented here will make a contribution to the psychological and pastoral care literature about working with victims of evil and will be of help to caregivers who have shared struggles similar to our own. We also hope it will bring some clarity to this complex subject and be a resource to those courageous caregivers who, each in their own ways, confront the havoc evil creates and care for those affected by it.

Acknowledgments

This book could not have been written without the many clients who shared their experiences with us and confronted us with the presence of evil in our world and lives. They allowed us to receive their stories and walk with them along the often fearful and treacherous path of reclaiming their selves and souls. In doing so, they acted as catalysts, moving us from our denial to where we are today in our understanding of evil, its impact on persons, and our need to address it at individual and systemic levels.

Writing is a difficult exercise. Working with traumatic material makes the task especially excruciating. At many points and times, it would have been easier to stop this endeavor and walk away. That was not a choice. It was often as if we were called to this task, and it would not let us go until it was finished. In this very limited way, our experience parallels the experience of the survivors with whom we work in psychotherapy.

A project of this scope is not possible without sustained nurture and support provided by many people over a number of years. Our colleagues at Des Moines Pastoral Counseling Center and others, particularly those in the American Association of Pastoral Counselors, encouraged us to pursue our ideas about trauma and evil and put the content of our workshops on this topic into a book. Their feedback and support along the way were essential.

In this regard, we want to express special appreciation to Ellery Duke for helping to create a work environment that encourages persons to do what they enjoy and are passionate about. We also are especially grateful to Susan Pierce for her interest and help in critiquing early drafts and researching articles. Feedback from Susan Ackelson, Lowell Houts, Eileen Burtle, and Kathy Reid was also affirming. Jeanne Schossow's skill and attention to detail were helpful in the retyping of early drafts of chapters. Assistance from the Center support staff was critical at times and truly appreciated.

A special note of thanks is due other colleagues who reviewed early drafts and offered their critiques: David Hogue for the particularly helpful and sustaining academic review and critique he offered at a critical juncture in the process; Lallene Rector for her review and input on sections related to self psychology; Jim Poling for his encouragement of authors new to a task of this magnitude; and Ann McDonald for her review from the vantage point of a clinical social worker in a religiously based counseling center.

On a more personal note, I want to express heartfelt appreciation to my wife, Diane Glass, for her patient love and understanding through many early morning and weekend absences, and a constantly cluttered dining room table. Her supportive presence, constant encouragement, and beautiful piano playing have provided sustaining care and nurture for my spirit. I am also grateful to my two sons: Tim Means for his inquisitive interest, and Aaron Means for his love and support from a distance.

Lastly, we are especially grateful to Hank French, former director of Fortress Press, who recognized value in a complex manuscript that did not fit neatly into one subject area and had the courage to commit to its publication. Our production editor, Zan Ceeley, and the staff at Fortress Press have been delightful and creative workmates and guides in bringing this book to print.

Introduction

THIS BOOK ADDRESSES the harsh reality of abuse and neglect in our culture. Within psychological circles, this topic ordinarily falls under the rubric of trauma. Trauma is a broad topic that encompasses many forms, intensities, and degrees of hurt. Taking the form of physical, sexual, and/or emotional abuse and torture, human-induced trauma is a special category of trauma. This trauma is best described as an expression of evil.

Moving beyond trauma to evil helps us shift our thinking. It encourages us to consider the powerful forces within persons and our culture that set the stage for potential acts of cruelty against others, without losing sight of the tremendous impact that violence and abuse have on particular persons. Such a shift also moves us beyond the psychological and physical dimensions of life to which a focus on trauma can limit us, and into the moral, ethical, and spiritual dimensions.

Some psychotherapists and other caregivers may be reluctant to make this type of shift. However, focusing on evil, as described here, offers caregivers a way to understand and intervene in patterns of intergenerational abuse and neglect that provide a nurturing ground for the ongoing cycle of abuse and violence. It also encourages caregivers to take seriously the task of finding the personal resources, beyond their training in psychotherapy, that they will need for this demanding and complex work.

Our focus is on evil in contemporary American culture as it is manifested in and through abuse and violence perpetrated by persons against other persons (human-induced trauma). Our hope is that the thoughts

1

and perspectives offered here will be of interest and assistance to all caregivers who work with individual and social problems stemming from violence and abuse, regardless of their professional discipline or faith perspective.

However, it is not our intention to look at all dimensions of trauma and the healing process. Many comprehensive resources are available for caregivers who want a thorough grounding in this vast and complex subject. This book assumes a basic understanding of trauma theory.

Neither do we look exhaustively at the subject of evil. Rather, the perspective on evil presented here grows out of our work with persons in pastoral psychotherapy and our work with caregivers engaged in a variety of pastoral care settings. While specific examples of evil are used to illustrate the concepts presented, we are more interested in understanding the process dimensions of evil than we are in categorizing specific acts or experiences as evil.

The professional perspective from which we come at this task is that of pastoral counseling and psychotherapy. This means we are committed to integrating contemporary theories of psychotherapy and human development with resources offered by Christian faith and theology. We seek to do this in a manner congruent with our particular identities and the way we practice our respective vocations. This book is an attempt at that type of integration.

As psychotherapists who work with people in outpatient contexts, a good deal of our time is spent working with the internal mental worlds of those who come to see us. In this complex endeavor, the wisdom and traditions of theorists help us understand the richness and sacredness of these internal dimensions of persons from a scientific perspective. As *pastoral* psychotherapists, we are also keenly aware that we work not only with the minds of persons, but primarily with their souls. Because we believe with others that the soul requires "care" rather than "treatment" or "fixing" (Ashby 1997; Ashbrook 1996; and Moore 1992), and because the soul requires many forms of care, we have chosen to use the term "caregiver" throughout the book (and make note of specific groups of caregivers only when necessary for purposes of clarity). Likewise, the term "caregiver" keeps all providers of care on equal footing with one another as we work together to form a community of care in which to embrace those who seek our help.

The theoretical perspective from which we work is best described as object relations theory as it is informed by self psychology, trauma theory, and systems theory. This perspective provides a conceptual framework with which to understand the vital and dynamic relationships existing between the inner worlds of persons and the wider social and cultural contexts in which persons develop and live.

Most of our clinical work has been with individuals who have suffered some form of abuse at the hands of others. The concepts and case illustrations presented, however, seek to address issues pertaining to individual, institutional, and cultural dynamics as well. It is our hope that the concepts and perspectives gleaned from our work will be useful to anyone who deals with evil in American culture.

Although we have worked with an increasing number of male survivors, most of the survivors with whom we have worked in psychotherapy have been women. While we are acutely aware that many men are victims of abuse and violence, we have chosen predominantly to use references to the feminine gender. In addition, while what is presented will be most directly applicable to working with survivors and will be from their perspective, we believe much of the material here also applies to work with perpetrators, and some references to this will be made.

We are aware that those who read this book will come from numerous spiritual and faith persuasions. The theological and faith perspectives offered here are personal ones. Although we feel passionately about them, we do not intend to claim that they are universal or representative of the beliefs shared by a wide range of Christian persons of faith.

For both of us, the language, images, and traditions of the Christian faith are helpful guides and resources in our work. It is not our desire, however, to persuade others to adopt them, or to suggest they are preferable to other spiritual and faith traditions. Instead, we offer them as just one example of how two particular caregivers have made use of our faith traditions to provide us courage and a context of meaning for the work we do. We hope, however, to encourage those who read this book to do their own integrative work with the particular faith and spiritual resources that support and nourish them.

The following brief synopsis of the book is offered to further orient the reader as you prepare to take this journey with us. While each chapter contributes an important piece to the overall picture puzzle the book presents, for the most part they are freestanding.

The preface is a reflection on our lengthy personal journeys as we were increasingly confronted with the presence of evil in our world and in our lives. We look here at key experiences that blocked and expanded our vision and played an important role in moving us to where we are today in our understanding of evil and how it works to destroy people and community. At each point along this path, we were unaware of where we were headed. Only in retrospect can we see how each of our steps was leading us to a profound awareness of evil, its impact on persons, and our call to address it in some way.

Chapter one provides a larger context for the discussion to follow by introducing the subject of evil in juxtaposition to its relationship with sin and suffering. Building upon Ted Peters's seven steps toward radical evil, a spectrum of evil is presented to emphasize the need to develop awareness of less than radical expressions of evil. Such an awareness helps us more easily identify the potential for evil that lies within each of us, thereby eroding the illusion that evil is something "out there" and not a part of the personal life experience of every person. The idea of radical disconnectedness as a precursor of evil is presented.

Chapter two is an exploration of the many dynamics we use to keep evil veiled and unrecognized within our culture. We look at the many ways the impact of evil on persons is minimized and denied. In this chapter, we also present indicators that suggest the presence of evil.

Chapters three, four, and five build upon one another. In chapter three, we look at the nature of the self and our reliance on others for its development. The development of the self is presented from an object relations and self psychology perspective, and the processes of splitting and differentiation are introduced. In chapter four we look at trauma and the various defensive ways the developing self responds to trauma attacks. The confounding nature of these self defenses is also presented along with their social implications. The impact trauma has on our ability to develop the mental capacities necessary to relate to ourselves and others out of a respect and appreciation for the integrity of persons is also described. In chapter five we present a definition of evil, which is then placed in the context of how our created selves are called into being through our interactions with others. Our focus here is on evil as a process that divides persons within and against themselves and separates them from their necessary relationships with the world, others, and God. A distinction is offered between trauma and evil, and processes by which evil destroys the self and soul of a person are described. We also put forth the notion that it is the evil dimension within human-induced trauma, and not trauma per se, that is so destructive of persons, and that it is evil that makes healing from what we call "abuse" so difficult.

Chapter six focuses on caring for victims of human-induced trauma in a way that heals the divisions evil creates within persons as it wreaks havoc in their lives and creates the potential for the abuse of others. The important role played by mental processes such as dissociation, splitting, changes of state, and projective identification are explored theoretically, and practical applications are offered for working with individuals and couples affected by them.

Chapter seven continues the focus on caring for hurt persons. Two important dimensions of this work are highlighted. The complex process of helping persons with issues of guilt, shame, and self-blame is discussed, as is the task of working with the meaning-making process that runs like an underground stream throughout the entire healing process. Paul Hessert's view of how our preoccupation with meaning-making paradoxically moves us away from approaching life through faith is presented. This perspective is then used as a guide to help caregivers avoid the many "detours of forced meaning-making" that are unhelpful to persons in the process of healing.

Chapter eight addresses the important role grieving plays in healing from the profound losses human-induced trauma creates within persons. Walter Brueggemann's work on the relationship between the public expression of grief and hope is explored. The role grieving plays as marking a turning point in the healing process is presented, as is the view of grieving as a bridge between suffering and hope. This discussion is placed in the context of contemporary understandings of grief.

Chapter nine shifts the focus from the level of caring for persons to that of speaking out prophetically against evil at all levels within our culture. The traditional split between the pastoral care and prophetic roles is discussed, as is the need to reconcile it. The concept of "pastoral counseling as cultural critique" is presented as a bridge between these two traditional, but often separated, roles. Various faith resources offered by the church for victims, perpetrators, and caregivers are explored, and their potential as powerful healing agents is presented. Important dilemmas faced by the church as it seeks to be a healing resource for caregiving and a prophetic voice within culture are also discussed.

In chapter ten, the "traditional Christian" view of the cosmos as being in a struggle between God and Satan is explored. This split cosmology is juxtaposed with Elaine Pagels's historical research into the role of the *satan* in early Jewish and Christian thought, and implications for caregiving are offered. The dangerous result of the mutually supportive interplay between such a split cosmology and the psychological defense mechanism of splitting is presented, as are its implications for the mental health and development of persons. The subject of working with unintegrated internalized bad objects is reviewed, and the idea of viewing them as *satans* to be embraced and understood is offered as an alternative to traditional views of possession and exorcism. Suggestions based upon this view are offered for pastoral caregiving and church congregational life.

The closing chapter returns to a more personal note by focusing on the self of the caregiver. Here we revisit the metaphor of the wounded healer and look at the helpful and hurtful roles the wounds of a caregiver can play in the process of helping others to heal. We also look at important attitudes for caregivers to develop within themselves and to teach those whom they may be responsible for training.

Concerning the case illustrations presented throughout this book, in each illustration, names and identifying characteristics have been changed to protect the privacy of the people involved. Some of the cases we share here have come from our respective practices, some have been shared by colleagues from around the country, and some of the illustrations are a composite of various cases. All of these cases are presented to illustrate the concepts being discussed and are not offered as formal case studies.

Finally, we want to state that this can be a disturbing book to read. As you work your way with us through this complex subject, you will likely experience a wealth of emotions ranging from fascination and intellectual intrigue to a deep sense of despair. This is the nature of working with persons who have been abused and traumatized. It is more the case whenever evil is involved.

Part I

Theological and Sociocultural
Dimensions of Evil

1

Evil in a Larger Context

CAREGIVERS WORK ON A DAILY BASIS with the rending effects evil inflicts on the lives of people. At the existential level of day-to-day life, evil's unpleasantness makes it easy to flee into the intellectual detachment that the study of the problem of evil (theodicy) affords. We want to move beyond that detachment. For if we listen closely to the messages people share about the many ways evil has affected their lives, evil takes on a personal and present quality that affects us and beckons for some response from us.

Discussions of evil have traditionally taken place within a religious context that includes references to such related topics as sin and suffering. As we set the stage, therefore, for our own journey from trauma into the realm of evil, we want to place evil within the context of key topics generally associated with it.

The Church and Evil

One of the few places evil has been consistently mentioned has been within communities of faith. At the same time, the church and religiously committed individuals have tended to leave evil unacknowledged as a part of their own worlds and to ignore and deny the depth of evil's impact on people. When evil has been acknowledged, it too frequently is pushed outside. Peter Gomes (1996) states, "One of the great acts of transference in modern times is the transference of the responsibility for evil and sin from individuals to institutions and to society at large" (253–54). Ted Peters (1994) has suggested that mainline theologians have "lost interest in the internal workings of the human soul" (2), choosing instead to focus their attention on political and economic structures of oppression and systemic forces of evil as seen in various forms of discrimination. In Peters's words: "The evils of our world have been consigned to social forces beyond the scope of our own personal responsibility. Deep down, however, it seems to me that each of us is at least dimly aware of our own responsibility. But when our theological leaders abandon the task of helping us to understand the experiential dynamics of sin, we are left with a symbolic or conceptual void" (2–3).

We also push evil outside ourselves by lodging it in "evil people" who are then summarily dismissed en masse as if they have no relationship to the rest of us. The result of this maneuver is that we become co-conspirators in the very evil we seek to address, and we inadvertently contribute to the further polarization of society into good and bad forces. More importantly, we mislead ourselves into believing we are somehow immune to evil becoming lodged in ourselves.

When those of us in the church deny and ignore the potential for evil that resides in every person, we contribute to the church's failure to address evil in its most basic form and to provide leadership in confronting evil. When those of us in the church ignore evil in the world, we contribute to the church's failure to look at all of life, as well as to the church's collusion in propagating the delusion that the world is a safe and benevolent place. When the church fails to confront evil at any level, it ultimately robs those touched by evil of the faith resources for which they so desperately long.

This dilemma has not gone totally unnoticed by the church. For example, the 203rd General Assembly of the Presbyterian Church (U.S.A.), meeting in 1991, approved a "Study Paper on Family Violence." This assembly authorized the Stated Clerk of that denomination to print and distribute that document to each church, and further urged all its churches to study that paper and establish programs to respond to domestic abuse in their communities. The preface of that document opens with the following scriptural reference: "from prophet to priest, every one deals falsely. They have healed the wound of my people lightly, saying, 'Peace, peace,' when there is no peace (Jeremiah 6:13-14)" (General Assembly 1991, 1).

This document goes on to condemn the practice of making domestic violence and sexual abuse "women's issues," rather than issues of concern to the whole church. One result of the segregation of these important issues is that they remain outside regular activities of the church, such as theological education, scriptural reflection, liturgical practice, and even worship. Another result is that leaders of the church can more easily avoid addressing these issues "seriously and responsibly" (General Assembly 1991, 1). The preface to this document closes with a call to "those who have ears to hear, . . . (and) eyes to see," to act with justice and "create a community where the wounds of the people are healed more than lightly" (General Assembly 1991, 2).

Evil has also been a topic of concern in the international church community. The 1994 Seoul Congress of the International Religious Federation for World Peace devoted its attention to the presence of evil in the world. In an edition of the federation's newsletter, Thomas Welsh (1994) noted evil's "ability to emerge universally and with a certain degree of absolute equality" and that "evil is the great obstacle of true unity" (162). Welsh also observed that "one of evil's great accomplishments has been its ability to infiltrate our religious traditions, often undetected" (163). The subtlety of evil's snare was noted in this way: "evil cleverly infiltrates morality. . . . Moralists, both religious and secularist, representing one cause or another, fail to see how, in their own high-minded protest or crusade, they too have been co-opted even as they blush from the accolades poured out by admirers" (Welsh 1994, 163).

These examples suggest an increasing interest on the part of the church to recognize and correct its avoidance of this important topic. They also make it clear that much work still needs to be done, especially in terms of individuals and systems becoming more self-critical and reflective as they seek to address the presence of evil in their world and their own participation in it.

A Definition of Terms

Against this backdrop, we want to present some thoughts and ideas about issues of central importance to an understanding of evil. We will begin with evil itself.

Evil

Evil is not a topic that lends itself to easy definitions. One of the better and encompassing definitions is offered by James Poling (1996): "Genuine evil is the abuse of power that destroys bodies and spirits; evil is produced by personal actions and intentions which are denied and dissociated by individuals; evil is organized by economic forces, institutions and ideologies, but mystified by appeals to necessity and truth; evil is sanctioned by religion, but masked by claims to virtue, love, and justice" (110). The strength of Poling's definition is its breadth and the fact he identifies ways evil becomes entrenched in, and supported by, social structures and cultural values. While it is important to remain aware of the many ways evil is supported and sanctioned culturally, our focus in this book is most directly related to how Poling suggests evil is produced. More specifically, we will emphasize the divisive nature of evil, how it affects in such depth so many dimensions of a person, and how to heal the divisions it creates.

Sometimes when grappling with a concept, it is helpful to begin with how it is manifested in the extreme. Ted Peters (1994) defines the most severe form of evil as "radical evil" and indicates that it is symbolized by Satan and is engaged in consciously, for its own sake, and in an unapologetic way (9). Those who work with traumatized and tortured persons support this view. The worst forms of trauma are the "human intentional type," or trauma perpetrated consciously and intentionally by one human being on another.

Radical evil is the type of evil that calls out most loudly for attention, since it is so blatant and shocking that it overpowers normal defenses and breaks into our awareness. Focusing on this extreme form of evil, however, makes it too easy for us to rationalize that evil is not a part of each of us and our daily lives. When this severe form of evil becomes the measuring stick, it is too easy to disconnect from it personally. And yet, when we look in the mirror after some of our worst and most private moments, we know that evil is a potential even in ourselves.

A first step in changing our perspective is to think of evil in a broad enough way that everyone can identify with it. In a broad sense, evil can be defined as people hurting people. This view regards evil as initiated, perpetrated, and participated in by persons. Traditionally, evil perpetrated by humans has been considered under the topic of "moral evil," as distinguished from "natural evil," which pertains to events of nature that cause suffering, death, and destruction. We will be focusing exclusively on moral evil.

At the same time, it is important to note that the impact of natural events can be exacerbated by the acts of people. A government's blocking of relief aid to portions of its population devastated by years of drought and starvation, thereby compounding their suffering, would certainly be an expression of evil. In a more subtle way, the neglect and denial of the growing body of evidence demonstrating the vast and deleterious impact of human activity on the earth and the environments required to sustain life also contributes to the suffering of persons.

Human-initiated acts that result in and contribute to the suffering, death, and destruction of other human beings and life-sustaining environments are in a different category than naturally occurring events that destroy property and life. The capacity of humans for acts that transcend the biological determinism of nature sets us apart from the natural world even though we are integral members of it. This is also the trait that makes us the chief caretakers of the world. Lest we lapse into periods of irresponsible oblivion, the responsibility for evil must be kept in human hands.

The Spectrum of Evil

To keep our ears, mouths, and eyes open to the presence of evil in the world, one should think of evil in broader terms than radical evil. Developing a perspective that aids our understanding of how evil so easily infiltrates our personal and professional lives on a daily basis is also helpful. One way to do this is to think of a spectrum of evil that considers various dimensions.

Such a spectrum can be viewed as comprising three continua: unaware to aware, passive to active, and unintentional to intentional, which are depicted in figure 1. Each continuum has been given a heading that summarizes the main element it represents.

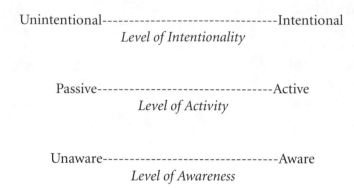

Unintentional------------------------------Intentional
Level of Intentionality

Passive------------------------------Active
Level of Activity

Unaware------------------------------Aware
Level of Awareness

Figure 1: The Spectrum of Evil

Starting from the base of figure 1 and moving upward, the first continuum represents the level of awareness at any given point in time, which includes awareness of ourselves and our context. Our level of consciousness is also reflected on this continuum as well as the degree of dissociation present, which can affect sensory input, our thought processes, the affective dimensions of ourselves, and our behavior (Braun 1988). Levels of repression and denial are also reflected on this continuum. This continuum is placed at the base of the figure since awareness is such a basic dimension and prerequisite for preemptive responsibility-taking.

The second continuum of passive to active represents the extent to which we energize ourselves for action or refrain from it. This decision to be active or passive in a particular situation can be influenced and driven by the level of awareness present. Thus in some situations, we may be passive because we are unaware of the need for action. In other cases, our awareness of possible consequences can lead us to remain passive rather than put ourselves at risk through some action on our part.

The third continuum represents the degree of intentionality with which a person moves in some direction to accomplish a desired goal, and also reflects the person's will or desire for something specific to happen. This of course will be affected by the extent to which there has been some level of awareness and the degree to which there has been the active investment of self in reaching some objective. It will also be affected by the limits of our humanness. Because we are not capable of understanding all the intricate and delicate connections between one aspect of life and another, the potential impact of our actions is always going to remain unknown to some extent.

The limit of our predictive knowledge is clearly seen in terms of the interconnectedness of all aspects of the environment. With good intentions, for example, flood control projects are built to protect people's homes and businesses. Only later does it become clear that this benevolently intended intervention causes more upstream flooding and subsequently results in continued loss of property, as well as the destruction of natural habitats of wildlife species already endangered. The very limits of our humanness means there will always be an unknown. One of the marks of maturity and integrity, however, is a willingness to risk action in the face of this unknown *and* a willingness to take responsibility for unintended consequences resulting from that action.

Referring again to figure 1, those expressions of evil that fall at the far right end of these continua are represented by blatantly cruel and often very public events such as the abduction and rape of a child. These are the types of events that usually capture the attention of the news media and other voices of society. Such events are litigated, often with much fanfare, and seem so clear-cut in terms of guilt and innocence. These acts are so shocking that they disrupt our normal routines as if to wake us abruptly from a sound sleep. Expressions of evil at this end of the continua would include examples of radical evil.

Any particular expression of evil is likely to be best described as falling at different points along each of these continua. For example, persons have been hurt by the intentional and conscious choice of persons to remain passive and do nothing. Over the years there have been numerous reports of people in apartment complexes watching out their windows as a person on the sidewalk below is robbed, beaten, and murdered while no one calls for help or chooses to intervene.

At other times persons behave in an active and conscious way, but the specific result may be very different than the intended outcome and, hence, quite unintentional. For instance, in the play *A Few Good Men*, two young U.S. Marines stand trial for participating in a prank that resulted in a fellow marine's death, a death that was accidental and unintended (Sorkin 1990). Their intention was to harass him in the hope of shaping him up to be more of a team player so that he did not make his unit look badly. At one point, the attorney for the two marines is frustrated by their refusal to consider a plea bargain. From their perspective, they are guilty of the death, since it was a result of their actions.

An awareness of these continua lifts up the complexity of particular situations. Continuing with the same example, these marines knew they were caught in a cover-up since their action was the result of carrying out an order. From their perspective, the fact their superiors refused to acknowledge issuing the order should reflect on those superiors and not only on themselves. In their view, they were being "good marines" for obeying the order. These men were caught in the bind of being good marines by intentionally carrying out an order that resulted in the unintended death of a fellow marine. Not carrying out the order would have spared their colleague but would have made them bad marines. When they are finally found innocent of the charge of murder but "guilty of conduct unbecoming of a marine," they are at the same time relieved and bewildered.

It is a mistake to assume that events clustering at the left side of these three continua are harmless to persons. As we shall see in succeeding chapters, the impact of severe neglect on persons is as damaging as acts that are more intentionally and actively perpetrated. In addition, the worst forms of human-induced trauma are those in which some violent act against a person is followed by a period of neglect and lack of support.

Examples of evil that cluster at the left side of these continua are also more a part of our daily lives, less obvious, and more easily overlooked. Until we become skilled at recognizing precursors of evil as they develop at this end of these continua, we will remain ineffective in dealing with evil. Focusing attention on recognizing early expressions of evil at this end of the continua increases our ability to see and accept responsibility for the many ways all of us participate in the propagation of evil.

Life requires the exertion of self. This self-exertion can be for good or evil purposes. The right end of the continua comprising the spectrum of evil presented here clearly implies an exertion of self, an exertion that can be for good or evil. The left end of these same continua focuses our attention on how the nonexertion of self can also lead to evil by allowing us to slip into it and become ensnared by it. Thus, again, both ends of this spectrum can lead us into propagating evil—one by means of exertion of self, and the other by nonexertion of self.

When the dynamics portrayed in this spectrum of evil are combined with forces described in the next section that set the stage for sin, or separation from God, it becomes clearer how those structures necessary for the propagation of good and evil are intricately woven into the basic fabric of life. In this sense the preconditions for evil always exist, whether it is evil that is expressed through the outright, blatant, and active abuse of persons, or the type of evil that results from subtle yet equally damaging forms of neglect and lack of action. It is our belief, therefore, that a great deal of the potential existing for the perpetration of evil can be transformed, thereby reducing the amount of evil perpetrated. This is achieved by working with dimensions within persons and systems that contribute to persons slipping into evil out of a lack of awareness, a passive and nonassertive stance toward life, and a lack of clear intention or will.

Sin, Anxiety, and Evil

When evil is viewed as perpetrated by human malevolence, it becomes easier to conceptualize evil as the result of sin. Within Christian religious circles, evil has been thought of as one effect or consequence of sin. Adam and Eve's act of free will disrespected a limit set by God and resulted in their expulsion from the paradise of the Garden of Eden. In this assertion of human will against Divine Will, humankind "fell" and became alienated from God.

When it comes to understanding evil, specific infractions, or "sins," are not as important as the state of being estranged from God that is referred to as "sin" (Tillich 1967, 2:46). Therefore, being in a state of sin predisposes us for committing sins. Peters (1994) describes the essence of sin as the failure to trust God in the midst of our anxiety (8). Søren Kierkegaard (1941) emphasized a similar theme of distrust but put it in terms of the fear and despair of not being ourselves while in the presence of God (123). Paul Tillich (1952) developed this theme by thinking of sin as the failure to exert "the courage to be."

These theological views suggest that sin, and by implication evil, are rooted in a lack of faith—an unwillingness to acknowledge our creatureliness and dependence upon a God of grace for whom and with whom all things are possible. From this perspective, we move into a state of sin, and drift into the realm of evil whenever we are tempted by anxiety and distrust to establish our lives on an independent (and seemingly more secure) basis apart from God. We do this because we lack the courage to take anxiety into ourselves and affirm ourselves in spite of it. In the words of Tillich (1957): "doubt is overcome not by repression, but by courage. Courage does not deny that there is doubt, but it takes doubt into itself. . . . Courage does not need the safety of an unquestionable conviction. It includes the risk without which no creative life is possible" (101). Anxiety, therefore, plays a central role in eroding our faith. For this reason, it is important to briefly discuss how anxiety's effect on us contributes to predisposing us to sin.

The manner in which anxiety affects our relationship with God, and hence our faith, is similar to the manner in which Harry Stack Sullivan (1953) believed anxiety disrupted interpersonal relationships in general (95). Sullivan maintained that as human beings our necessary environment is an interpersonal one. This is seen in our dependence upon interpersonal relationships for the satisfaction of basic needs such as food and nurture. Sullivan hypothesized that when anxiety enters the picture it disrupts these interpersonal relationships so crucial to our well-being. In turn, the felt level of confidence we have that our needs will be met within the bounds of those relationships wanes.

To cope with the disruptions anxiety produces, Sullivan proposed the existence within us of a "self-system." The function of this system is to find ways to reduce the anxiety present within our interpersonal relationships so those relationships can be maintained enough for our needs to be met (Sullivan 1953, 166–68). In many cases, this is done by sacrificing the expression of some aspect of ourselves for the sake of interpersonal harmony.

D. W. Winnicott, the British pediatrician and psychoanalyst, recognized this same dilemma but viewed the problem from a different theoretical perspective, one that went beyond a focus only on anxiety. He proposed that one way a person can cope with anxiety, fear, disappointment, and hurt in important relationships is by putting her "true self" into hiding and relating to the world and others from the safer position of a "false self" (Winnicott 1965). This "false self" may manifest characteristics perceived to be desirable to significant others but can also exhibit characteristics problematic to them. In either case, the chief function of the "false self" is to protect and shield the "true self" until such time as an environment or relationship is determined to be safe enough to risk exposing the "true self." In this context, sin may be viewed as that state of being separated from God, ourselves, and others out of fear that if we are known we will be found unacceptable and left ontologically and existentially abandoned.

Ernest Becker (1973) focused on the existential anxiety people experience when confronted with their own mortality and discussed the mental maneuvers we engage in to maintain the denial of death. In *Escape from Evil*, Becker (1975) suggested that evil results from the awareness of our mortality and our response to it. One such response can be the taking of life from others in an attempt to delude ourselves into thinking we have power over life and death. In his words, "People use one another to assure their personal victory over death. . . . Through the death of the other, one buys oneself free from the penalty of dying, or being killed. No wonder we are addicted to war (Becker 1975, 108).

Peters discusses the subtle and seductive power of evil that comes from its promise to help us cope with the anxiety we experience as creatures living in a natural world we do not control. He warns us in this way:

> Claimants to immortality and infinite power dance before us, inviting us to eliminate our anxiety by joining in the ecstasy of their dance. They are spouting lies of course, but the siren song of their invitation rises daily. When we accept the invitation, our interior soul becomes bound to the destiny of the exterior power, and that destiny is always death amid delusion. Faith grants integrity and a sense of direction in our essentially finite and limited life. It grants the courage to face down the pretenders to immortality because it trusts, despite our anxiousness, in the care of a transcendent God. (Peters 1994, 61)

Paul Tillich (1967) also warned of the danger in giving into such seductive forces by noting that we become demonic, or begin participating in evil, when we relate to something that is relative as if it were absolute (1:140). Coming at this same theme from a different perspective, Becker (1968) believed that the demonic emerges when we fail to take "critical control" of the institutions we establish. In these cases, we inevitably become manipulated by "impersonal forces" that operate beyond our control, but that we ourselves "actively and uncritically" foster (142).

Merle Jordan (1986) builds upon this same theme in the context of a person's life story. He reminds caregivers of the importance of listening to a person's story "in terms of what or who is perceived as the ultimate authority in the psyche of the person and how he or she experiences being defined or valued by that ultimate authority" (21–22). Jordan then reminds pastoral caregivers that one of their primary tasks is to "challenge idolatry: the worship of psychic false gods who usurp God's place at the center of the self and oppressively define people's identities" (23). Since a direct relationship exists between idolatrous faith and the inability to love persons whose ideas conflict with our own (Tillich 1957, 115), the ability to recognize and challenge idolatry (especially within ourselves and our institutions) is critical if we are going to respond to evil in ways that are healing.

The point these writers are making is that in our attempts to understand and respond to evil it is important to acknowledge our internal susceptibility to sin as rooted in a basic distrust that God will actually care for us and accept us. It is this anxiety and fear, distrust and unfaith that ultimately lead us to seek security on our own terms. Because this felt security is such a basic need, and so valuable and crucial, there is then the dilemma of where to place it for safekeeping.

One solution is to place it in the hands of some false god that promises the security we want but will ultimately fail us. Another solution is to keep it in our own hands and live behind a narcissistic defense in a delusion-filled world that continually feeds us with the untruth that we are self-sufficient creatures in need of no one and no-thing outside ourselves. Both responses put us in charge of that which we are incapable of securing. This reality has a way of eventually breaking in upon us. We can become so overcome by the massive and incomprehensible task of caring for ourselves that we and our lives can begin to disintegrate and fragment. The despair experienced at this point is extremely severe. It is also exacerbated by the dim, but ever present, awareness that "we did it to ourselves."

A Precursor of Evil: Being Radically Disconnected

Evil can be viewed as a chief result of sin, or estrangement from God. More generally it can be viewed as moving into an ever-increasing state of disconnection. Unhindered, such regression may eventually culminate in a radical disconnection not only from God, but from other people and our own uniquely created selves as well. This process is pictured in figure 2.

In Relationship with Self, Others, and God

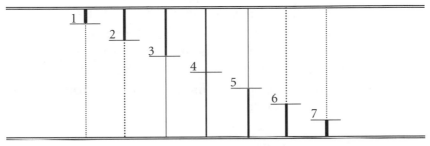

Out of Relationship with Self, Others, and God

Peters's Seven Steps to Radical Evil
1. Anxiety 2. Unfaith 3. Pride 4. Concupiscence
5. Self-justification 6. Cruelty 7. Blasphemy

Figure 2: Moving into Evil
[This figure uses Ted Peters's seven steps to radical evil in *Sin: Radical Evil in Soul and Society.* Grand Rapids, Mich.: Eerdmans, 1994: 10–17.]

In this representation, each step away from relationship with God represents one of Peters's seven steps toward radical evil. Sequentially, these steps are anxiety, unfaith, pride, concupiscence, self-justification, cruelty, and blasphemy or radical evil (Peters 1994, 10–17). When the last step is reached, we have retreated so far within ourselves and away from God and others that evil takes on a life, motive, and power of its own. In this position, we have only ourselves and our own internal processes from which to take our bearings. This leaves us unsupported and without the safety nets of alternative and corrective attitudes and opinions that relationship to others provides. In extreme cases, we can become delusional.

This gradual shift away from relatedness to God, others, ourselves, and even reality itself leads to an increasing isolation of oneself from the mainstream of life. It also sets the stage for an egotistical, out-of-control, and ultimately self-destructive approach to life. A high-profile example of this process was reported concerning former presidential advisor Dick Morris. In a news article reporting on an interview with Morris, the interviewer states, "he acknowledged that he had been egotistical and out of control before his precipitous fall from grace. He ignored his wife, ignored his friends, ignored the rules" ("Morris Is Remorseful" 1996). Morris is reported to have said of himself: "My sense of reality was just altered. I started out being excited working for the president. Then I became arrogant, then I became grandiose, and then I became self-destructive" ("Morris Is Remorseful" 1996).

The idea of evil being the result of ever increasing levels of disconnection can be viewed as an extension of earlier concepts. In his thorough review of the thoughts of Ernest Becker, Peters (1994) notes that Becker saw the source of evil as "rooted in humanity apart from the rest of nature" (47). Thus, Becker conceived of evil as an expression of what happens when we separate ourselves from the rest of nature and fail to recognize our relationship to it.

Separating ourselves from our human environment has the same effect, since as humans our necessary environment is an interpersonal one. While Becker did not directly root the cause of evil in individuals, he did locate it at the junction between an individual and an *impersonal* economic institution (Peters 1994, 48). This suggests that a key element in Becker's thinking was the impersonal or nonrelational nature of an institution's response to human need, as well as its (i.e., our own) nonreflective lack of responsibility (Becker 1968, 141–42).

The basic ontological structure of self-world proposed by Paul Tillich also supports this view. This structure and the ontological polarities that are an expression of it—individualization-participation, dynamics-form, and freedom-destiny—clearly reflect dimensions of "being a part *from*" and "being a part *of*" (Tillich 1967, 1:164–65). From Tillich's perspective, moving exclusively to one side of these polarities or the other is a violation of the basic structure of life and the natural relationship and corrective tension among these polarities. At the same time, Tillich's view recognizes that disconnection, as represented in the process of differentiation, is a natural part of being a creature in the world. By nature, we are separated from *and* connected to the rest of creation. Tillich reminds us of the importance of keeping these in balance.

Despite the idealized cultural myths of individualism and autonomy to the contrary, at a personal and intuitive level we humans know we are relational creatures and have been created that way. And despite our wishes to the contrary, this makes us dependent upon other persons. As newborns, we literally depend on others for our lives, and human children remain dependent on adult caretakers longer than other species of mammals.

Not only are we physically dependent on others, but we are emotionally and psychologically dependent on them as well. We are learning more and more about the intricate and complex ways our interactions with others provide a foundation for the structuring of our mental worlds and personalities (Parsons 1970; Stern 1985; Wolf 1988). Those interactions form the matrix upon which a sense of personhood and sense of self develop.

We are created to a large extent by the nature and quality of our early experiences with others, by messages we internalize about ourselves from interactions with others, and by the ways in which we are valued or not valued by people important to us. In this sense, we participate in the literal creation of ourselves and others through the interactions we have with them. Even at those points where we developmentally strive for differentiation from others, the result of that process on our developing sense of self is greatly determined by the responses we get from those from whom we are individuating.

Our religious and spiritual development is also affected by relationships with others. Research continues to support the long-held premise that one's image of God, or the way God is conceptualized, is influenced and formed by the nature and quality of her early interactions with caretakers (Rizzuto 1979; McDargh 1983; and Resch 1992). Thus, a child begins to develop her concept of the world and others, including God, by the nature in which she is physically and emotionally handled and responded to by the person(s) responsible for her care. For example, a child usually develops a concept of the world and God as trustworthy and responsive when her parents respond promptly and comfortingly to her cries of distress. Similarly, children reared in abusive and neglectful environments often conceive God as harsh, judgmental, and uncaring.

Various life experiences can disrupt one's developing concept of self, world, others, and God. They do this by disrupting the interpersonal environments in which the basic structures influencing one's attitudes and orientation to self and the world are formed. Experiences of human-induced trauma and neglect massively distort these interpersonal relationships, damage developing mental structures, and subsequently have a continuing deleterious impact on a person's development and interactions with others.

The effect of such abuse and neglect upon children is especially devastating. This is in part because a child's self-structure and defenses are weak and in the early stages of formation. Children also lack fully developed cognitive capacities, so they are even less able to understand what is happening to them than are adults in similar circumstances. Children are also more severely damaged by the tremendous power differential existing between themselves and significant adults.

The more anxious our lives are, the more we naturally resort to defensive maneuvers in an attempt to safeguard whatever developing sense of self and security we *do* have. Exposure to traumatic events makes these defenses even more crucial, and they become more entrenched. As the severity and duration of human-induced trauma increases, as support and nurture following traumatic experiences are lacking, and as outside support for our developing, yet fragile, sense of self decreases, those internal defenses we rely upon take on more importance.

Consequently, traumatic experiences result in people cutting themselves off emotionally and psychically from others and themselves. This pulling inside of well-developed defensive positions occurs to a far greater degree than the anxiety of being a dependent creature in the world would normally require. In this way, human-induced trauma naturally propels persons into a state of being radically disconnected, and also keeps them stuck in a state of social isolation from others and psychological isolation from themselves. Persons who have a history of being abused, neglected, and isolated in these ways are often prone to perpetrate similar abuse and neglect on others.

If one has radically disconnected from oneself and others in order to survive, we can begin to understand what a tremendous amount of courage is needed for some survivors to persistently seek out help— usually in the face of massive distrust. A woman in psychotherapy to resolve issues of severe childhood sexual abuse had been to many therapists over the years. One day she said, "The day I trust you will be the day I am ready to stop therapy." This was her way of saying that the basic issue she would be working on throughout therapy was that of trust.

The normal responses to the anxiety of living as a creature in an uncontrollable and unpredictable world is very different from the mortal fear, terror, and maladaptive ways of being and thinking in the world developed by persons subjected to evil in the form of human-induced trauma. Nevertheless, normal existential anxiety and mortal terror can both move persons further into a state of disconnection from self, others, and God. The more this state of disconnection approaches a state of radical disconnection, the more likely the results will be blatant psychopathology, pathological and/or sociopathic behavior, moral decline, and radical evil. Such a state of radical disconnection sets the stage for and supports the blatant use of others as objects whose only value is to be used for the meeting of truly selfish needs.

It is also the case that an existent state of disconnection can be further exacerbated and increased. This phenomenon is seen in socially sanctioned responses that lead to a further sealing-off of troubled and injured persons behind walls of social ostracism and avoidance. Even more blatant are the disturbingly tangible means of isolation and banishment seen in the concrete walls, bars, and barbed-wire fences used in the criminal justice system, or what Schlosser (1998) has called "the prison-industrial complex."

One of the ironies of human experience is that the increased sealing-off of one person or group, for the purpose of creating safety and security for another person or group, ultimately leads to the increased objectification of all parties, and to their mutual isolation from the basic elements and building blocks conducive to healthy human life. The more we isolate from one another, the easier it is for us to become critical and skeptical of one another. As we push one another further and further away, there is less and less empathic and nurturing human contact so necessary for healing change. This isolation further destabilizes individuals and social structures, leads to less safe and secure human environments, and increases the potential we will be a danger to ourselves and others.

Human beings are not created to develop outside of relationships with others who accept and care for them. When we do, our capacities to appreciate the diversity of life, to view the world realistically, to engage in meaningful relationships with others, and to develop and maintain a cohesive sense of self are severely compromised (Horner 1984, 283–84). If our own fears and defenses keep the God that creates and sustains life, and guides and nurtures us in the way of life, separated from us, we are left ontologically abandoned and to our own devices.

In such a state, we are easily overwhelmed by the magnitude of managing life on our own. With God as a counterpoint removed, humankind is left adrift and at the mercy of our own devices. This is similar to viewing perversions as resulting from the loss of a strong and coherent self, which subsequently leaves a person guided only by drives and impulses, and as an attempt to head off total self-fragmentation (Wolf 1988, 43). Paul Tillich (1957) described this same process this way: "The disrupting trends of man's consciousness are one of the great problems of all personal life. If a uniting center is absent, the infinite variety of the encountered world, as well as of the inner movements of the human mind, is able to produce or complete disintegration of the personality" (107). In this sense evil in its most radical forms can be considered an expression of "moral psychosis."

In summarizing this section, it is worthwhile to note the important relationship existing between the radical disconnectedness we have just explored and the spectrum of evil presented earlier. This linkage is suggested by Walter Wink (1986) when he states the following: "When we fail to bring a committed ego to struggles for choice, . . . then to a degree we place ourselves in the power of autonomous complexes of the psyche or idolatrous institutions in the world" (34). To the extent we are radically disconnected within ourselves, from others, and from God, we lack the information and the necessary checks and balances that true, informed, conscious, and ego-driven choice requires. The absence of a capacity to make committed choices, as well as the courage to implement those choices, further rounds out a scenario that produces a fertile climate for the propagation of evil.

Suffering

Suffering is often the effect of sin that people most intimately and passionately experience. Any discussion of evil must give attention to suffering, since suffering is the chief result of evil. Suffering will be more fully explored in chapter eight, but a few words are in order now.

J. Christiaan Beker was a faculty member at Princeton Theological Seminary and a prisoner of war during World War II, and he offers us some helpful ideas in understanding the way evil affects persons. Beker (1987) makes a distinction between "suffering at the hands of the power of death," and "suffering at the hands of human injustice" (57–79). Suffering at the hands of the power of death includes loss of life and property resulting from natural occurrences, such as drought, earthquakes, tornadoes, floods, and other disasters, as well as personal tragedy such as chronic illness. Beker believes the only comfort available for dealing with this suffering is the knowledge that God will ultimately prevail. The events that lead to this type of suffering are beyond human responsibility and guilt, and therefore beyond any strategy of human action. There is nothing for us to do to prevent this type of suffering, which Beker (1987) terms "tragic suffering" (68). Those not directly affected by it can offer assistance, aid, and comfort, and it is important to do so, but those directly affected must basically place themselves in the hands of God.

Suffering at the hands of human injustice is different. This type of suffering is the result of human-induced trauma and is open to human intervention to stop and prevent. In our experience, when suffering at the hands of humans becomes pervasive, systemically supported and reinforced, and overwhelming by design, as in cases of torture, sustained abuse, neglect, and the social segregation of groups, such suffering takes on the characteristics of suffering at the hands of the power of death. People in these situations begin to feel like there is nothing to be done and that only God can provide a solution. Since God does not intervene, their reasoning proceeds to the conclusion that God does not care, God is powerless, and/or God is absent.

In our work with survivors of severe abuse, this attitude is often present. Their belief is that there was nothing anyone could have done; the situation was hopeless. This conclusion, though false, is even more prevalent when a person's suffering has been compounded by persons and systems of influence that conspire to keep abuse active, hidden, and protected.

A Lack of Public and Prayerful Support for Victims of Evil

Within the church and the culture-at-large, there appears to be a clear bias in the direction of responding with public and prayerful shows of support and encouragement to persons caught in natural tragedies, illness and disease, or suffering at the hands of the power of death. These same responses, however, are not so forthcoming for persons who have suffered at the hands of human-induced trauma and injustice. Exceptions to this are cases of massive and overwhelmingly destructive acts of violence and murder. Examples of these include the bombing of the Alfred P. Murrah Federal Building in Oklahoma City, which resulted in the death of 168 persons, many of whom were children; the massacre of kindergarten children and their teachers in the quiet town of Dunblane, Scotland; and the more recent school massacres, such as in Littleton, Colorado.

In the least, the lack of support for persons who have suffered at the hands of other people, or have caused the suffering of others, points to our continued dis-ease with the subject of human-initiated suffering. At the worst, such a lack of support indicates that our attitudes (even within the church) have been infiltrated by our culture's warped sense of where responsibility for such events rests, i.e., with those who have been hurt. In ways such as this, those of us within the church, and those outside the church, continue to reveal our haunting discomfort with sin.

An additional factor must be considered in attempting to understand our resistance to supporting those who hurt, and have been hurt, by other people. The existence of human-initiated suffering reminds us of our own vulnerability, and reminds us of the potential perpetrator within each of us. In our humanness, we are terrified to acknowledge that, no matter how strong and alert we are, others always possess the power to victimize us and cause us suffering. We are equally terrified to acknowledge that no matter how good and upright we are there will always be circumstances that lead us to feel like hurting someone else and causing them suffering.

As we shall see in succeeding chapters, our massive dis-ease with human-induced suffering is a major hurdle with regard to our ineffectiveness in dealing with it and the expressions of evil it represents. In the next chapter, we take a deeper look at factors that keep evil veiled and unacknowledged within our culture, and then look at ways we can recognize its presence. In later chapters, we will revisit our reluctance to publicly acknowledge the suffering and grief of victims of violence and human injustice, as well as the sin and evil inherent in the acts that cause the suffering of others.

2

Unveiling Evil: Obstacles and Indicators

Obstacles to Recognizing Evil

AS CAREGIVERS WHO WORK daily with helping people face and adaptively respond to the impact of evil in their lives and the brokenness it creates, we are sooner or later hit by the question, "How can there be so much evil perpetrated in our culture while we remain unaware of it?" In order to recognize evil, this is the first question that must be addressed.

Consensus Trance

Two overarching concepts offer a perspective for understanding our lack of awareness and provide a direction for changing it. The first concept is Charles Tart's (1987) belief that "human beings are in a perpetual state of trance induced by the society they live in. He calls this state "consensus trance," or "the sleep of everyday life." These consensus trances are difficult to perceive because we grow used to things being a certain way. In Western patriarchal culture, for example, white males have been blinded to aspects of the world that hurt and devalue others because of generations of privileged status that reinforce the many consensus trances so entrenched and unyielding to change.

Every culture and subculture has its own set of consensus trances. In American culture, for example, violence is a way of life that is woven integrally into the fabric of society. One example is the film industry's enamored preoccupation with the horrific and visually overwhelming depiction of destruction, murder, and violence, often against women. Another is the gun lobby's "death grip" on Congress that perpetuates and glamorizes the ownership and proliferation of handguns and continues to support the ownership of assault-type weapons (see Diaz, 1999).

We remain oblivious to the chilling effect this undercurrent of violence has on our day-to-day activities until we move out of our culture and experience places where violence is not so predominant. A colleague recently shared how his twenty-five-year-old daughter took a spontaneous three-week tour of Europe on her own and returned telling him that she had never before felt so safe and free traveling on her own. She attributed this to the absence of a violent mind-set in the countries she visited and to the relative absence of handguns as compared to the number of such weapons in the United States.

Awakening from the consensus trances in which we are stuck as a result of living in a violent society is rare. It takes the shockingly sudden, senseless, and tragic death of an innocent tourist seeking directions in Miami, the death of innocent children and adults in a bombing, or the killing of a respected community leader caught in the literal crossfire of warring factions on a city street to wake us up—and then only temporarily.

In one such case, Phyll Davis was fatally wounded on her way home from work in the late afternoon when her car entered an intersection and was hit by the crossfire of a traveling gunfight between two groups of people with a grudge against one another. In a newspaper article following this tragedy, an emergency-room physician with experience treating the wounds suffered by perpetrators was quoted as saying:

> These are people that are not concerned about their own injuries. . . . They are so charged up to get revenge that they are not worried about charges being filed against them. They aren't even thinking about going to court. . . .
>
> We are raising a generation of kids where violence is their primary nature. Violence is not secondary or reactive. It is primary. That's a model shift in American society in the last twenty-five years. Before, violence was a means of protection. Now it is a primary motive. . . .
>
> We are producing predators. That is their life. (Abrams 1996)

In an editorial about community reaction to this incident in the same edition of the newspaper, the process of awakening from the "sleep of everyday life" and then falling back asleep was described this way: "Des Moines' emotional response has to be translated into practical actions; otherwise the city will fall into a well-worn formula. Step 1: Feel outraged. Step 2: Argue that Des Moines' small size and large spirit enable it to solve the problems that strangle larger cities. Step 3: Gradually slip back to business as usual" (Abrams 1996).

Sociocultural Dissociation

The second concept that helps us understand our inability to recognize evil is dissociation. Adam Crabtree (1992) refers to dissociation as "the partitioned assimilation of information and experiences." While dissociation can be utilized as an effective ego defense for purposes of individual psychic survival, Colin Ross (1991) has pointed out it can also function on a broader sociocultural level. At both the individual psyche and sociocultural levels, dissociative processes protect us from that which is overwhelming until we are strong enough to face the realities impinging upon us.

While dissociative processes can be helpful, they also prohibit us from learning and leave us destined to keep repeating unhelpful and dangerous experiences. This is a direct result of how dissociation works. That which is dissociated is left "un-associated" or "split-off from" and "sealed-off from" the rest of our experience. As such, it is not fully experienced and integrated with the rest of what we know. That which is dissociated is *in* us, but not available for learning. For all practical purposes, it is as if we never had the experience that is dissociated. Dissociation leaves us with no way to learn what we need to know to avoid similar experiences in the future. This leaves us culturally doomed, as individuals are doomed, to a constant and often intensifying repetition of similar experiences, much like we see clinically in a repetition compulsion—or as popularly depicted in the movie *Groundhog Day*. In this entertaining film, the main character awakens to the same day over and over again until he finally learns the lesson he has failed to grasp.

To overcome the restricted cultural consciousness that results from consensus trance and dissociation, Crabtree (1992) suggests using what has been learned in working with dissociation within individuals. In this regard he offers the following advice:

> When we work with dissociation on the level of the individual . . . we must listen to all the parts, all the alters, and let them bring forward their knowledge and experience. Only in that way can eventual integration take place.
>
> The same approach must apply when dealing with cultural dissociation. Those elements of the culture that have been alienated from the mainstream—the alter personalities of the culture—must be allowed to tell their experiences, give us their information, and describe their experiences. . . . These voices are alienated from the center, from the mainstream of our culture. Because of that, they may speak with a discordant or unpleasant tone. But just as with alters in an individual, we must tolerate those distortions to hear the central vein of truth in their stories. This is a demanding task, for it means being willing to listen to what the culture considers unspeakable. The task will be well rewarded by the retrieval of a lost treasure—the totality of human experience—from its state of cultural oblivion. (153)

In the work we do as caregivers, it is important to maintain contact with persons different from us. Doing so not only enriches our lives and provides us a more balanced view of life in general, but it also makes it less likely that we will succumb to the "sleep of everyday life" (Tart 1992). As a result of these two processes, socially induced consensus trances and culturally reinforced dissociation, evil is not always easy to see or recognize.

The Subtlety of Evil

In addition to the screens that consensus trances and dissociation provide to keep evil hidden, there are several other factors that support our blindness regarding evil. One such factor has been discussed in chapter one, where we proposed the idea that expressions of evil tend to occur along three continua that form a spectrum of evil. Expressions of evil reflected by one side of that spectrum are so subtle that evil goes unrecognized.

Evil also creeps up on us. This is most dramatically exemplified in the series of steps Peters offers that lead us toward radical evil. As seen in chapter one (and in figure 2), these steps begin with anxiety and move through the additional steps of unfaith, pride, concupiscence, self-justification, cruelty, and finally blasphemy or radical evil (Peters 1994, 10–17). Each of these steps takes us from the common to the uncommon in such small incremental moves that each one by itself can easily be overlooked or mistaken for something other than a move in the direction of evil. It is commonly agreed, for example, that the Holocaust evolved over time in such subtle moves and shifts that no one could have predicted it at the beginning of Hitler's reign. By the time events played out, however, it was difficult to entertain the possibility of a different ending scenario. In summarizing this process, Holocaust scholar Raul Hilberg (1987) states that this tremendously tragic act of evil was the result of "ordinary people doing extraordinary things."

Hiding behind Mental Illness and the Law

Another factor that keeps us blinded to evil's presence is presented by Kimberly Williams Crenshaw. An attorney who assisted in the representation of Anita Hill in her testimony before Congress, Crenshaw (1995) speaks of the central role played by the "denial of credibility" in the continued disempowerment of oppressed groups of people. She argues that this process is rooted in our cultural propensity for disbelieving victims, especially victims of sexual abuse. Two ways this denial of credibility is supported is in the process of converting evil into mental health language and legal language.

The presence of evil is denied when we pathologize its effects and those impacted by it. This process begins when we shift the focus from evil acts to the traumatic impact of those acts, and when we speak of "trauma-related disorders" rather than the terrorizing and torture of persons. Post-traumatic stress disorder (PTSD) is an example of such a disorder that appears alongside other mental disorders in the *Diagnostic and Statistical Manual of Mental Disorders* (DSM-IV) by the American Psychiatric Association (1994). Based upon presenting symptomatology, these classifications help describe the severity and type of response a particular person has had to life circumstances and trauma. By helping us clarify presenting symptoms, these categories can be of some help in guiding an intervention strategy to facilitate healing of a trauma wound.

The major problem is that while these classifications presumably categorize "mental illnesses," in all practicality these disorders get localized in persons who are then seen as "having a disorder" (Bollas and Sundelson 1995, 133, 139). Such a radical shift diverts attention away from what caused the trauma in the first place. It also contributes to overlooking the fact that a person's trauma-induced responses are *normal* human reactions to terror and evil. The end result is that victims of trauma-inducing acts are given the message once more that "they are the problem," and the person injured is further disenfranchised by labeling her/him as having a "mental illness."

Not only is evil missed when we nonreflectively use the lens of mental illness language and pathology, but also when it is viewed through the lens of law as it is practiced in our litigious culture. Instead of contributing to the resolution of the problem of evil, a preoccupation with suing those who hurt us contributes further to the propagation of evil by making the central objective that of locating blame. This inclination creates its own set of problems. It contributes to our thinking of one another as enemies (Tannen 1998), encourages us to dichotomize persons into the exclusive categories of "guilty" and "innocent," and de-emphasizes the integral part *all* persons play in determining what happens in our world.

Locating responsibility for what and who hurts others is important but not clear-cut. Recent investigations into the lives and behaviors of publicly elected officials seem to be endless in the seamless manner they are connected to one another. This phenomenon reflects the reality that any act or event that initially gets the attention of someone and results in triggering an investigation is actually the result of many acts and events participated in by many people over a period of time. The line separating the guilty from the innocent is increasingly recognized as fuzzy.

Hiding behind Language

To a great extent, evil is not recognized because it is named something other than what it is. This masquerade has worked quite well. The most basic elements of our culture, language for example, have been co-opted in this masquerade process. Nancy Cole (1995, an ardent advocate who has called attention to this tendency in language, indicates that the use of the word "stress" in the diagnostic category of "post-traumatic stress disorder" severely and unfairly mislabels a person's experience. That experience would be more accurately reflected by words such as "chronic fear and mortal terror." Cole goes on to argue that the linguistic manipulation of experience reflects an "active political and cultural bias," rather than "a benign, innocent misuse of words." She puts it this way: "When abuse is denied, whole aspects of reality are dismissed, erased and obliterated through *active*, highly charged, and opinionated processes. . . . Denial doesn't just *happen*; it is *required*. It is required by the individual to survive; it is required by the society to maintain the status quo" (Cole 1995).

Language and the use of words actively participate in the creation of the realities people live in, and they circumscribe those realities. Those who have been victimized become trapped by the very language used to describe their experience. An experience that "terrorized" them is suddenly referred to as "stress." This process contributes to the continued disempowerment of persons who have endured horrifying experiences at the hands of others.

Cutting Ourselves off from History

A further dynamic that contributes to a failure to recognize and name evil is the tendency to be so focused on the present that history is minimized and not integrated. As a result, we become cut off from our historical roots, as illustrated by columnist Ellen Goodman (1995) in her report of the death of Bessie Delany. The lives of Bessie and her sister, Sadie, are shared in a moving way in the book *Having Our Say* (Delany and Delany 1993). In her column, Goodman related some key moments in the life of these remarkable women. She noted that they were born to a free-issue woman (whose own parents, one black and one white, were not allowed to marry under Virginia law) and to a former slave who later became the first black Episcopal bishop. Goodman mentioned that Sadie was the first black home economics teacher in New York, and Bessie the city's second black dentist. She noted that they voted the first time women were allowed to vote, and that Bessie's strong will almost got her lynched when she was younger. Goodman (1995) ended her column this way: "This woman lived in a country that uses 'that's history' to describe last year's trend. We count generations by twenty-year spans. Today many regard segregation as a distant memory and cannot understand why anyone still harps on discrimination. . . . Now we have lost a sister. A human connection has been broken with a past that didn't seem so distant when she talked about it."

As persons die who were directly affected by the evil of their day, the more personal links between those events and ourselves are lost with them. There is something real and tangible in sitting with a person who actually lived a historical event that is never adequately captured in history books.

A resident in psychotherapy training experienced this phenomenon in her own family (Means 1995, 302–3). Her father had been in combat during World War II. She reported that he would sometimes tell "war stories" at civic and school events but was reluctant to tell those stories to his family. After years of wondering why, she finally realized that when he told these stories in the intimate and supportive context of the family he invariably would weep as he remembered those experiences. The sharing of his grief made those experiences real and tangible not only to himself once more, but also to those who weren't there who were moved by what they saw and experienced in his remembering. A living human connection with events of history and evil keep the devastation that evil wreaks upon human life alive and available for learning. When this connection is lacking, it becomes easier to disconnect emotionally from those events and see them as unrelated to ourselves and current affairs.

Being Scared-off by Evil

Lastly, we deny the presence of evil because we are terrified by the horrendously hurtful, cruel, and bloody kinds of evil people tell us about—if we are willing to listen. This was poignantly brought home during an interdisciplinary case conference involving a resident who was counseling for the first time a woman who had been sexually abused. As we worked with him, it became clear that he was resisting entering what he called the "psychic cave" of her sealed-off experience from which she was shouting for assistance. Because of his resistance, he was not providing her the support and guidance she so desperately needed, and he was not facilitating her working through the abuse and hurt that were continuing to impact her life. As he was confronted about this at one point in the conference, he stated tearfully: "I'm afraid if I help her move into her memories, I will have to go with her, and if I go with her, my view of the world as a basically good and safe place will be shattered. I'm not sure I can handle that for myself, or be able to think about the fact that my wife and kids may be more vulnerable living in this world than I can be comfortable believing" (Means 1995, 299).

As the more experienced therapists present listened to what this resident was saying, we were taken back to points in each of our lives when the barriers of denial were first cracked open by the reality of evil, and we became fearfully aware of its presence. Because dealing with the effects and power of evil is so disturbing, it is relatively easy for those of us who are more experienced at recognizing and naming evil to forget how difficult our own awakening to evil really was.

Indicators that Evil Is Present

If we are going to lift the personal and cultural screens that keep us from being aware of evil, we must be prepared to be as affected by what we see as the resident was in the last example. As we now lift those screens, what are the marks and characteristics of evil by which we can recognize it and name it for what it is?

People Are Hurt

The first indication that evil is present is that people are hurt, which can occur on many levels: intellectual, emotional, physical, psychic, relational, or spiritual. Evil can attack one's possessions, relationships, sacred objects and beliefs, character and self-esteem, physical well-being, and even one's contexts of meaning. While hurt takes many forms, it leaves a wound and a scar, and people are never the same. In later chapters, the many ways people are hurt by evil and the many losses evil produces in those lives it touches will be examined more closely.

The Integrity of Persons Is Disrespected and Disregarded

Evil disrespects and disregards the integrity of persons and tears them apart physically, psychologically, relationally, and spiritually. Evil is present when people are objectified and then used and manipulated, rather than related to as the valued human beings they are. One of the most blatant and disturbing examples of this was shared by a woman who, as a very young girl, was offered as the "pot" for her father and his friends to sexually abuse at the conclusion of the weekly poker games held at their home.

The violation of integrity is seen when particular aspects and dimensions of persons are valued and related to, rather then the whole person. This violation is clearly seen in the sexualization of women (Johnson 1992, 261) and the splitting of persons into parts for sexual and pornographic interest.

Disregard and disrespect for the integrity of persons can also be manifested in more subtle forms. Particular characteristics of a person may be lifted up and made the basis for opinions about them. This violation is seen in a wife's comment to her husband who revealed to her that he was gay. In the continuing discussions between them regarding what to do about their dilemma, she said: "Being gay is about sex! You just want out of your commitment to me so you can do what you want to do!" This comment reflects the lifting up of one dimension of gayness, the sexual aspect of one's preferences, and refusing to acknowledge other and more basic dimensions of one's personhood, such as the need for love and respect.

This same disrespect is manifested in a clinical approach to persons that fosters the assumption that knowing a physical or mental diagnosis provides enough information about them that further attempts at getting to know them are deemed unnecessary. It is unfortunately common in some settings to hear such statements as, "He's just a difficult patient" or "Oh, she's just another borderline." Not only are such comments a blatant example of the disrespect for persons in need, but they are also all too often used to justify more harsh and intrusive interventions or even to indirectly withhold or refuse treatment because someone is deemed "untreatable" or "too much trouble."

On a more subtle level still, personal integrity is violated when some-one's employment is terminated based of a redefinition of the job with-out first determining whether he/she may have, or be able to develop, the new skills required, and whether he/she has other attributes that might be of equal value to an employer. Similarly, there is a disrespect for the integrity of people when persons are moved in and out of jobs as if they are interchangeable parts with no respect for the network of rela-tionships and the synergy developed among people who work together.

Resources Are Removed

Evil isolates people from their resources. Sometimes this occurs in a physical sense by removing people from that which supports and nur-tures them. Evil can block people structurally by putting obstacles between them and that which sustains them. These structures can be physical, such as a locked door and chains, or less tangible as in the case of a mother having to work a shift that prevents her from providing the necessary care to her child. A parent refusing to compromise in meeting an ex-spouse halfway to facilitate visitation with children could be a fur-ther variation of this same theme. Another example would be a divorce property settlement that strips someone from so much of his/her mate-rial world that he/she feel like Joseph left in a pit by his brothers and forced into slavery.

Resources Are Invalidated

A further mark of evil is that the resources people do have are invali-dated, which can take many forms. In a domestic quarrel, one parent may devalue the other parent in the eyes of a child who developmental-ly needs an idealized image of her parents in order to feel safe and spe-cial. The faith resources of a person can be invalidated by narrow and bigoted faith perspectives that see only their particular brand of faith as "true." We recall, for example, a woman who received a letter from her pastor saying she was no longer a member of the church and was unwel-come to worship there. She had reluctantly started a divorce action when her husband, after years of mental and emotional disrespect and abuse, physically assaulted her and locked her out of the house. The pas-tor took this action with no attempt to talk to her and based solely on the husband's report of "her mental illness." This act by the pastor invalidated this woman's belief that God and the church would understand and support her, separated her from the resources of the church, and reinforced already entrenched ideas in her head that she was the problem and was of no value to anyone. Unknowingly, this pastor's action contributed dramatically to her subsequent psychological decompensation. In more blatant cases, torturers diabolically work to turn a victim's loving God into an absent, ineffective, and silent figure.

Persons Are Disempowered

Evil also disempowers people by finding ways to make what was potent and effective, impotent and ineffective. This is a more direct attack on the person than the removal or invalidation of resources, but similarly leads to a weakening of ability and spirit. At the individual level, this can take the form of intimidation, which produces fear and results in the narrowing of perceived options and the loss of hope. At a systemic level this may take the form of acts that contribute to the malnutrition and starvation of people, to the disenfranchisement of a person, group, or class by lack of voting rights in the political process, or to the economic rape of a person, people, country, or natural resource.

Persons Are Turned against Themselves

Evil also turns a person against herself so that self is used against self. The case of the woman who received a dismissal letter from her pastor comes to mind again. The psychological decompensation she suffered was successfully used by her husband to intercede with a psychiatrist of his choosing to commit her to the mental unit of a hospital for an extended involuntary stay, which further worsened her condition. Additional examples abound. Some patients report cults using induced hypnotic states to encourage a subject's dissociated hands and arms to do something hurtful to someone else. In such cases, the subject is encouraged to watch the hand that is hers but not hers (because it is dissociated from her). The end result is often extreme guilt, self-loathing, and distrust of one's self and motives. An incestuous parent may use a child's own natural bodily responses to repeated sexual stimulation to make the point that the child really "wants and enjoys" what is being forced upon her.

Survivors of such abuse report feeling betrayed by their own bodies. We have had patients say, "As a child I learned to breathe softly because even breathing could put you in jeopardy." Another patient's father was frighteningly cruel if awakened in the night. Terrorized that she would wake him during a trip to the bathroom, she would urinate onto tissues while trembling in the corner of her bedroom. Later in life she deemed this coping strategy so unusual that she saw herself as disgusting and wrong. In torture situations, a person's natural pain avoidance mechanisms are used to force him/her to divulge desired information or a confession, thereby leading to the false, but apparently clear, conclusion that "I wasn't strong enough."

Basic Human Needs Are Prostituted

Evil prostitutes basic human needs by making normal needs, desires, and reactions vulgar, dirty, or available for a price. An example of this is seen when people are forced to scrape together, in whatever way possible, the food, shelter, resources, and connectedness with others they need to survive, and are then disenfranchised because they have managed to survive in what others deem to be "unacceptable" ways. A jealous and controlling father who interprets his daughter's interests in an attentive and nurturing male friend as her "slutting around" would be an example of a normal and healthy need being made vulgar.

An example of this was shared by a female client who told of her finally mustering enough courage in high school to talk to her school counselor, a male, about her abusive father. After the counselor called the parent to request an opportunity to discuss some concerns that his daughter had voiced, the father confronted his daughter with the accusation that something sexual must have gone on between her and the counselor since "adult men are not usually interested in young girls like you." This woman reported she never sought help again from anyone until she saw a counselor in her late thirties who sexually molested her, thereby confirming her father's earlier messages, which remained active in her mind. Shockingly, this same father slipped his hand underneath his daughter's nightgown when she was forty years of age as she trustingly shared a motel room with him to lower expenses on a trip to see relatives.

Community Is Violated and Desecrated

Lastly, evil violates the integrity of community and desecrates it. Evil devalues, degrades, and destroys the interconnectedness among people, thereby besmirching the sacredness of the communal dimension of life. James Poling says (1996) evil denies communion and is "destructive to the web of relationships on which all life depends" (111). This desecration can occur at all levels of life. The communal nature of human life is contaminated and torn asunder when the forces of evil turn one segment of society against another, when dichotomous thinking patterns divide life and people, and when the sacred relationships developed among persons are belittled, defamed, or treated with disrespect. An example of disenfranchised grief that demonstrates the desecration of community comes to mind.

A woman discovered in the newspaper obituaries the death of a clergyman by whom she had become pregnant in her late teens. She had promised the man she would not divulge their secret to anyone so as to protect his career and standing in the church. She gave birth to a daughter whom she raised as a single parent. Over the years, the minister had stayed in contact with the woman until the girl's early elementary school years, when he suddenly stopped visiting. At no time during those years did they ever acknowledge to the girl that he was her father. The daughter later married and started her own family.

Upon learning of this man's death, the woman decided to tell her daughter who her father was and that he had died. After discussing the situation, she and her daughter decided to attend the funeral service the next day. The woman reported that as they made their way to and from the church pew they encountered some mutual friends of hers and the deceased man who knew of their liaison and also knew of the daughter. Instead of greeting them and welcoming them to the funeral service, she and her daughter were shunned, leaving their grief and loss unacknowledged and unsupported. With this lack of acknowledgment of her early and significant relationship with the deceased man and others there, the community they once shared was further desecrated.

A Case Illustration: Susan

The following case example is presented as a way of making some of the concepts presented in this chapter even more tangible by placing a number of them within the context of another actual life situation. This example will also further facilitate our transition to a more existential focus that characterizes the following chapters as they approach evil from a therapeutic and clinical perspective and look in-depth at the profound effect evil has on the self and soul of individual persons. This example is not unlike what many caregivers see.

When basic human needs are ignored, rejected, or invalidated by those in roles and positions to appropriately meet them; when the means by which these needs have been previously met are no longer available; and when prior abuse has already left one vulnerable for being exploited further, the stage is set for the possibility these needs will be prostituted. This situation places a survivor who has unmet needs in an incredible dilemma. She can either do without or seek the satisfaction of mobilized needs through some "illegitimate" source that leaves her increasingly divided from herself and ostracized from others.

While meeting needs in this way resolves the immediate existential experience of deprivation and abandonment, it produces numerous other difficulties. These include experiencing oneself as "bad" or "weak" for having such strong needs; experiencing shame and guilt for relying on "illegitimate" sources of satisfaction; experiencing a loss of self-respect for indulging in activities contrary to personal moral standards of conduct; risking the displeasure and misunderstanding of others important to her; and opening oneself to the continued abuse and victimization of perpetrators who are all too willing to selfishly use others for their own pleasure and purposes under the guise of being "helpful."

The clearest example of this we have seen is that of Susan, a fifty-five-year-old married woman who worked as a registered nurse in a large medical research hospital. This was Susan's second marriage. Her ex-husband from her first marriage was a drug addict, prone to physically violent episodes, who would exchange an evening of sex with Susan to get the drugs to feed his habit. While most of the men he brought home for this purpose were vulgar and violent men, one of the dealers to whom Susan was periodically given treated her with seeming kindness.

He impressed her with his apparent empathy as he would listen to her accounts of being violently beaten by her husband and would treat and touch her gently.

Susan's reactions to her time with this man were profoundly disturbing to her. On the one hand, she felt dirty and devalued by her husband's callous treatment of her as an object to be used and passed around as if she were a toy. On the other hand, she found herself feeling oddly comforted by the warmth and tenderness she most often experienced with this one kindly man. One night after a particularly severe beating at the hands of her husband, Susan escaped with her young toddlers and eventually succeeded in divorcing her husband.

Two years later she married Jim, a man who was a respected professional and treated her lovingly with warmth and respect. They had a mutually satisfying relationship for ten years until Jim suffered a severe heart attack. Although successfully resolved in a medical sense, this crisis left Jim terrified that if he became excited in any way he would die. He began distancing himself sexually and emotionally from Susan, viewing his erotic attraction to her as a potential threat to his life. He moved to the basement and abstained from all physical contact and shows of affection with Susan.

While Susan compliantly "understood," over time she became emotionally depleted and empty, depressed and hopeless. Although in the depths of despair, she drew the attention of a physician who had recently joined the hospital staff. Unhappily married himself, he and Susan exchanged frustrations about their disappointing marriages. One night while on duty, Susan found herself engaged in oral sex with the doctor. The last thing she recalled was hearing him say in a commanding, intimidating, deep male voice, "Meet me in the prep room." This pattern persisted over several months, leaving Susan in a desperately confused state of déjà vu and hating herself.

One night, despite promises to herself she wouldn't give in, Susan succumbed, as if automatically, once again to the doctor's command to meet. After it was over, she found herself on a riverbank contemplating the dark, icy waters as a welcoming solution to her dilemma. She was tired of the struggle and the private hell to which it condemned her. Seeing herself as a good and moral person, she could no longer reconcile being unable to control her intense urges for closeness and care, giving in to the intimidating commands of a man who basically used her as others had, and living with a husband who once treated her so well but now saw her as a threat to his life. As daylight broke, Susan called for help.

A Brief Review

Before moving to the next section, it may be helpful to review the material presented so far. In chapter one we placed evil in a theological context and in juxtaposition to sin, anxiety, and suffering. We also suggested that disconnectedness within oneself and in one's relational world is a major precursor to evil. In addition, we introduced three continua that play an important role in understanding evil: unaware-aware, passive-active, and unintentional-intentional. We suggested that to deal effectively with evil we must direct our attention to those aspects of ourselves and others that operate at the unaware, passive, and unintentional ends of these continua.

Regardless of whether abuse is perpetrated in a blatant and tornadic fashion, or in a more subtle and constantly eroding manner, it produces long-lasting effects. This is especially the case when that harm has been inflicted by someone who is emotionally important to the victim and is someone she has trusted and depended on for her survival and well-being. In addition, a great deal of damage is done to persons by individuals and systems that remain unaware of what motivates them and the impact they have on persons, that are passive, neglectful, or otherwise nonresponsive to the expressed needs of others, and that are unintentional about the harm they inflict. These are also the very types of individuals with which most caregivers work on a daily basis.

In this chapter, we have identified seven factors operating within our culture that conspire to keep evil's presence veiled, hidden, and denied. These factors contribute to our remaining oblivious to the destructive forces of evil that operate beneath the surface of our individual lives and that gain strength in the fertile ground of cultural and institutional unconsciousness that these same factors create. The value of this type of review is that it brings to conscious awareness the subtle, and not so subtle, ways we have of defending ourselves from the harshness and cruelty evil fosters within and among people. As a counterbalance, we have also identified eight characteristics of evil that can be used to identify its presence in particular situations. Our purpose in presenting this material is not to provide a means of categorizing this or that as "evil," but rather to help us develop an appreciation for the strength of our reluctance to face evil head-on, as well as an appreciation for the insidious ways evil threatens and destroys persons and community.

As pastoral psychotherapists, we work with many people who have been hurt by other people. For this and other reasons, we have said that we believe it is important to keep responsibility for evil in human hands. In the next chapter, therefore, we want to turn our attention to the internal mental worlds of individual persons. In this regard, we are most interested in those interpersonal processes that facilitate the structuring of those mental worlds and that call a person's self into being. An understanding of these processes is crucial if we are to have an appreciation for the devastating and far-reaching effects evil has on persons and if we are to develop therapeutic interventions that break the self-perpetuating cycle of abuse and violence that evil creates among persons.

Part II

Intrapersonal
and Interpersonal
Dimensions of Evil

3

The Nature of the Self: Its Development and Continuing Vulnerability

IN ORDER TO UNDERSTAND the profound effects trauma has on persons, and to set the stage for appreciating how evil is even more devastating, it is helpful to look briefly at what we know about the self, its development in relationship to others, and its lifelong dependence upon others.

A Definition of Self

Over the ages the self has been viewed in a multiplicity of ways by philosophers and psychologists (see Baldwin, 1987). Hamilton (1990) reminds us that "self" has meant such things as wind, breath, shade, shadow, soul, mind, as well as referring to a person and one's body (9). Daniel Stern (1985) suggests that while the self is difficult to define, our sense of self takes many forms: "There is the sense of a self that is a single, distinct, integrated body; there is the agent of actions, the experiencer of feelings, the maker of intentions, the architect of plans, the transposer of experience into language, the communicator and sharer of personal knowledge. Most often these senses of self reside outside of awareness, like breathing, but they can be brought to and held in consciousness. We instinctively process our experiences in such a way that they appear to belong to some kind of unique subjective organization that we commonly call the sense of self" (5-6).

Ernest Wolf (1988) refers to the self as a "presumed psychological structure" (23) that is inferred from the observation of the "emergence of a sense of selfhood during the second year of life" (11). As a "label for the psychological organization that gives rise to my self experience,"

Wolf describes the self as "metaphorical in nature" (13) and as having a history in the sense that it has stability over time (27).

In an attempt to maintain conceptual clarity, some writers distinguish "self" from "person." Atwood and Stolorow (1984, 34) state, "We have found it important to distinguish sharply between the concept of the self as a psychological structure and the concept of the *person* as an experiencing subject and agent who initiates action" (cited in Lee & Martin 1991, 187). This distinction will be adhered to in what follows.

It is important to underscore that while we are primarily focusing on "self" in terms of a psychological structure, our actual sense of self very much includes our physical or bodily selves. Our bodies are an integral part of our selves. If our body and self become separated from one another, our potential for wholeness is limited and we suffer in some manner.

Thus at one level the self can be viewed as a continually operating system that organizes experience (Lee & Martin 1991, 188). At another level, the self represents the essence of one's personhood and is a source of agency as a person initiates activity in the world. Winnicott (1965) spoke of a "central self" and defined it as "the inherited potential which is experiencing a continuity of being, and acquiring in its own way and at its own speed a personal psychic reality and a personal body structure" (46).

While the embryonic self is innate and ordinarily contains the capacity to organize experience, it requires a matrix of relationships within which to develop and mature to its potential. This means that *the structuralization of the human mind grows out of human relationships*. The development of a sense of self is one aspect of this structuralization.

Fairbairn and other object relations theorists offered an important corrective to Freud's early view that our primary motive in life is to seek pleasure. These theorists called us back to the realization that we are creatures who are more basically created to seek relationship (Fairbairn [1944] 1981; Guntrip 1969). Relationship and connection with others is more basic and necessary for our survival and development than is pleasure.

Despite this corrective, it is disturbing how entrenched Freud's earlier view continues to be in mainstream American culture, and how much we still believe it and rely on it as a misleading guide for our lives.

One example of how Freud's "pleasure principle" continues to guide our behavior is in the tragic irony of frequent geographic moves embarked on by those climbing corporate ladders. Many of these are fueled by the offer and pursuit of greater material wealth, security, and happiness, only to result in staggering losses of connection and relationships on the part of family members caught in the shuffle.

Included in the disruptions created by these migrations are the loss of connection and support from families of origin, extended families, and other parental support systems; friends; and trusted professionals who have come to know us over time. The consequent loss of naturally supportive, human, interpersonal resources has contributed significantly to the disintegration of the nuclear family we have witnessed over the past thirty years. This in turn has contributed to an increasing paucity of supportive relationships available for the development of a secure, strong, and cohesive sense of self in our children.

Self and Object

In spite of the vital importance of the self, it cannot come into fruition or continue to exist all on its own. Rather, the self requires the continuing presence of others in its life. Ashbrook (1996) states, "None of us is a person *until* we have been called forth by the responsiveness of others" (3). In a similar vein, John Shea (1997) notes, "The self is necessarily a self-in-relatedness" (260). This emphasis on the vital and irreplaceable role significant others have on the development of self, and the very structuralization of the human mind, is a major emphasis of object relations theory.

Object relations theory has done much to bridge the gap between the individualistically oriented views of early Freudian theory and more recent trends of focusing on the social systems within which individual persons develop and live. While systems theory has extended our horizons beyond the individual to the broader social milieu, its equally narrow and often rigidly defended perspective has contributed to a lack of interest in understanding the intricacies of human mental development. The externally focused approach to persons that behaviorism offers has also encouraged a lack of interest in the internal mental worlds of human beings, not to mention the increasing impact of the reductionistic lure of psychopharmacology. Object relations theory's continued emphasis on the interactions between one's mental development and an individual's network of relationships is perhaps this perspective's most important and continuing contribution.

One of the main stumbling blocks of this theory, however, has been its use of the term "object," which refers to "something invested with emotion" such as a person, place, thing, fantasy, idea, or memory (Hamilton 1990, 5-7). This has created two major problems. The first is that in most cases an "object" is a shorthand term for "significant other person." Some people react negatively to this language feeling it "objectifies persons." The insufficiency of our language pool, however, should not be the cause of rejecting a major theoretical perspective. In the hope of lessening the resistance of the reader to this theoretical language, the following historical excursion is offered.

Freud first used "object" in his study of perversions (Hamilton 1990, 5). As is commonly known, human beings form significant attachments to more than just other people. In the case of perversions for example, we have the capacity to become emotionally connected to personal articles associated with another person, and we can develop attachments to particular parts of a significant other, such as her/his feet. This observation demonstrates the human mind's capacity not only to objectify others, but also to mentally divide those others (objects) into parts. We can also do the same to our selfs. In the extreme case of particular perversions and fetishes, emotionally invested objects come to symbolize important needs, wishes, and fantasies associated with a significant other, and can take on tremendous importance with regard to arousing or soothing the individual attached to them.

The second problem the term "object" has created in people's minds is confusion related to lack of clarity about whether a particular object is internal or external. This confusion is a result of the fact that the term refers to both types of object. Also, by the process of internalization, *external* objects and our experience with them become *internalized*. This process of making the external internal by taking into ourselves our experience of the external world is what provides us with the basic building blocks for the structuralization of our mental processes. This internalized experience of ourselves with others in the world provides the framework around which basic mental schemas develop (see Piaget 1936; Flavell 1963). These resulting schemas in turn serve as guides and filters by which we perceive all that is around us and in comparison to which we evaluate all succeeding experience.

Each encounter we have with another person takes the following form: *self* connected to *other* (object) by our *affective response* in the interchange. As Hamilton (1990) points out, this is similar to the grammatical structure of a simple sentence consisting of a subject and object connected by a verb (6). When internalized, these experiences with others take the form of *object relations units*. Each of these units consists of *self and object representations* connected by the primary mediating affect.

As our perceived experiences of ourselves with others are internalized and transformed into mental representations, they are in essence objectified (or more accurately, subjectified). This ability gives us tremendous flexibility to organize, synthesize, and in other ways mentally manipulate experience. This same ability, however, also makes it easier for us to keep persons objectified in our minds, thereby making it easier to treat them with malice. Because object relations theory describes this normal human capacity to objectify and internalize experience, we can perhaps be more sympathetic to the practical usefulness of the term "object," as well as to its potential pitfalls.

Human beings, under normal circumstances, are born with the capacity for *whole object relations*. This means we are capable of perceiving and appreciating the whole of ourselves and others, as well as specific attributes and characteristics that comprise the whole. The extent to which this capacity is actualized is in large part dependent upon the extent to which significant others facilitate that development. If this capacity is not developed, we can become preoccupied with certain attributes of a person to the exclusion of all others.

In order to gain an appreciation for the importance of developing whole object relations, and in order to further emphasize the vital role we play in the mental, psychological, and emotional development of one another, a brief review of development from an object relations perspective is helpful. While this material is complex and some readers may not be familiar with it, it does impress upon us what miraculous creatures we are and the tremendous extent to which we depend on one another.

The Developmental Process

Margaret Mahler (1968) identified a number of different developmental stages based on studies of children interacting with their mothers (see also Horner 1984). The first stage Mahler identified was the autistic stage of development. During this time the infant is more self-absorbed than tuned into the outer world and other people. As the "sensory barrier" creating this initial "autistic haven" gives way, an infant begins the process of meeting those persons who will care for her. Attachment theorists have pointed out that infants are born with the natural drive to seek out and attach (or bond) to their caretakers (Goldberg et al. 1995). As Johnson (1985) points out, this meeting can be characterized by a warm welcoming, or the infant can be met with coldness, aloofness, and even displeasure and hate (55).

If the environment is empathetically warm, welcoming, sensitive, and appropriately responsive, the child and mother begin to bond. This bonding process involves what Kagan (1982) has described as "successive triumphs of 'relationship to' rather than 'embeddedness in'" (77). This process of attaching involves a dance of relationship-building that will continue throughout the newborn person's life. Mother and infant slowly become attached in a symbiotic state in which the infant begins to perceive mother and interact with her, but they are not yet fully differentiated from one another. As normal development proceeds, the child moves into the separation-individuation stage of development, which involves progression through ever increasing levels of differentiation, represented by the substages of hatching, practicing, and rapprochement. Successful progression through these developmental hurdles eventually leads the child to the last stage of development, which results in the achievement of object constancy and ego identity.

As a child moves through the developmental stages just outlined, she is concurrently involved in the process of internalizing her experience of self in relationship to her caretaker and formulating mental representations of those interactions. The development of these self and object representations is summarized in figure 3. The rectangular boxes represent the nature of self and object representations at each stage of development.

A. Undifferentiated Self-Object Representations
Symbiosis

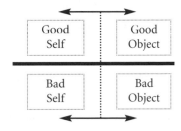

B. Split Self and Object Representations (Part-Object Relations)
Separation - Individuation

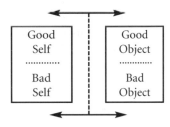

C. Whole Self and Object Representations (Whole Object Relations)
Object Constancy

Figure 3: Normal Development of Self and Object Representations

There are two important processes, according to object relations theory, that become focal points around which mental development proceeds and various developmental tasks can be conceptualized. These are (1) the *discrimination* and subsequent separation (splitting) of opposite affective states ("I feel satisfied and at peace" and "I feel frustrated and agitated"), and (2) the *differentiation* of self from other ("This is me" and "This is not me"). As we shall see in forthcoming discussions, both of these processes have significant relevance for understanding trauma and evil. These two processes, as well as those described in the following section, are also represented in figure 3. Splitting is represented by the horizontal lines. The degree of splitting is symbolized by the intensity of these lines. The differentiation process is represented by the dotted vertical lines. The degree of differentiation present is again reflected by the intensity of these lines.

Splitting and the Differentiation of Self and Object

As a child encounters the world and interacts with others, the child's affective experiences are divided (split) along the sensorimotor discrimination gradient of pleasure and pain. Something feels rewarding and satisfying (good) or something feels frustrating and dissatisfying (bad). As this discrimination occurs, there is also a beginning differentiation of self from object. The internalized mental representation of this more differentiated, yet still symbiotic, relationship is referred to as a *self-object representation* (the hyphen here symbolizes the incomplete differentiation). These self-object representations are depicted in A in figure 3.

As the child's continuing experience of her primary caretaker(s) becomes divided along this gradient, there begins to develop a "good self-object" and a "bad self-object" representation. Again, the terms "good" and "bad" are *not* used in a moral or judgmental sense, but rather to distinguish the basic affective quality of the experience of self in relation to other. These interchanges can be rewarding, satisfying, and pleasurable (good) or dissatisfying to the point of being frustrating and disappointing (bad). As development proceeds, more and more experiences are built-up around these two poles. Since the child has not yet developed the mental ability to entertain two so radically different feeling states at the same time, the defense mechanism of splitting comes into play. The beginning use of splitting is represented in figure A of figure 3, where the not yet fully differentiated self-object representations are split according to whether their primary affective quality is rewarding (good), or frustrating (bad).

This psychological process of splitting is helpful in keeping oppositely charged experiences separate and distinct. This separation of intensely opposite affective states provides the developing child with a useful mechanism for splitting-off powerful negative affect, thereby helping to create enough psychic calmness and safety to facilitate ongoing mental development. Without this ability, the child would be overwhelmed (traumatized) by the disorganizing potential of built-up masses of negative affect, and there would be no psychic sanctuary within which mental development could proceed. Therefore, this splitting of "good self-object" from "bad self-object" is adaptive for further mental development, and the use of this powerful defense mechanism is helpful and normal.

As development continues, the degree of differentiation between self and object increases. This differentiation also initially organizes around the feeling states of "feels good" and "feels bad." While increasingly differentiated, self and object representations remain split as "good self" and "bad self" in relationship with "good object" and "bad object." From the infant's perspective, these are still totally different selves and objects. For example, the mother/father with whom she feels good is experienced as different from the one with whom she feels bad, and the good self the child experiences is considered different from the bad self that is experienced. Since the self is still developing clarity, strength, and cohesiveness, and since the child is still dependent on the good graces of her caretakers for survival, it is too overwhelming, fearful, and confusing for her to conceptualize self and object as a *mixture* of good and bad. This stage is represented in figure B of figure 3. While not yet firmly established and distinct, here self and object representations are differentiated, and these representations form as separate (split) good and bad part-self and part-object representations.

When attempts to get needs met are consistently frustrated, or when life experiences are traumatically overwhelming, the integrative functions of the self are hindered. This can lead to an inability to integrate goodness and badness, leaving splitting as the primary operative defense. Early failure becomes an obstacle to eventually viewing self and others in a more holistic and integrated fashion. Such a failure has a destabilizing effect on future interpersonal relationships since it increases the likelihood that the splitting defense will be reactivated at times of psychological regression precipitated by stress or by the breakdown of more weakly developed higher-level defenses. Because it plays such an important role in the types of processes that are a manifestation of evil as we will be defining it, we will return to splitting in chapters six and ten.

If there is enough "good enough" mothering provided by empathic, nurturing, sensitive, and attuned objects with whom the child relates, over time the child develops the mental ability to resolve this split in her self and object representations. The critical factor here is whether there has been enough good experience of self and object to neutralize the bad experience enough so that integration can occur without the good getting lost in, or overcome by, the bad. A successful solution to this dilemma results in the resolution of the split between good and bad self and object representations and in the maintenance of clear yet flexible boundaries between self and other. With the resolution of splitting, self and object are now clearly differentiated from one another, and it is possible to comprehend self and other as capable of producing *both* positive and negative affective reactions in one another (see C, figure 3). At this point, the possibility of whole object relationships exists. There is no longer the need to utilize splitting as a defense to keep rewarding and frustrating experiences of self in relation to others rigidly separated. The continuing availability of splitting as a natural and defensively driven psychic posture is depicted by the dotted horizontal lines in C, figure 3.

This developmental leap into whole object relations sets the stage for attaining object constancy and self-identity. This includes the ability to remain emotionally connected to an object even if that object is not in physical proximity to self and even if experiences with that object are not always satisfying. It also provides the ground from which the child can learn to enter into social exchanges with others with a clearly differentiated and firm sense of self-identity that will continue to expand and develop throughout the rest of life.

As can be appreciated, this achievement of whole object relations, object constancy, and self-identity is no small task and is a major accomplishment for all parties concerned. The developmental ground is now laid from which a child can go on to engage with others in an intimate, intentional, and committed fashion; appreciate others for the unique and separate selves they are; support the autonomy and individuality of others, rather than be threatened by it; and be capable of such human qualities as mercy, grace, and forgiveness (Hamilton 1990, 109).

The tremendous dependence we have on our relationships with objects for the development and maintenance of our sense of self is summarized by Hamilton (1990) in the following way: "If there is no external object with which to compare one's self, there is no self and no stable sense of reality. . . . our very selves will disintegrate without external as well as internal objects, for the self is nothing except half of the self-object duality" (18–19). In a similar vein, Stern (1985) talks of the other as a "counterpart" to our sense of self (5). Winnicott made a related point when he spoke of there being no such thing as a baby or a mother, but only a mother-baby combination, since each depends on the other for existence and definition (see Giovacchini 1979, 329). In the words of Christopher Bollas (1987), "The mother's way of holding the infant, or responding to his gestures, of selecting objects, and of perceiving the infant's internal needs, constitutes her contribution to the infant-mother culture. In a private discourse that can only be developed by mother and child, the language of this relation is the idiom of gesture, gaze, and intersubjective utterance" (13).

Bollas goes on to describe the infant's subjective experience of the mother as a "transformational object," which is "experientially identified by the infant with processes that alter self-experience" (14). This emphasis on our primary objects serving a transforming function, rather than merely providing a source of pleasure or a means of relationship, anticipates what we will explore more fully in the following section on self-object experiences.

Daniel Stern's (1985) work with infants also clearly demonstrates the importance of this interplay between a mother and child and focuses specifically on its critical contributions to the progressive development of a child's sense of self. As the self of the child continually emerges and becomes more complex, this interplay changes and both requires and produces differing types of interaction. The developing self moves through these different "domains of self-experience and social relatedness" as it grows and matures (11).

For purposes of our discussion, the crucial element that is underscored by this complex material is the vital role significant others play in creating an environment conducive to the development and maintenance of the self. As we have seen, for healthy self-development to occur, these environments must provide the nurture, sustenance, protection, and social interactions necessary for the internal structuring of the self, for calling forth all the potential contained within the self, and for restoring the equilibrium and integrity of the self when it is depleted, battered, and hurt. These matters will continue to be the focus in the following section.

Selfobject Experiences

The work of Heinz Kohut has helped us more fully comprehend and appreciate the types of interactions we need with others for the self to develop in a strong and complete manner. Specifically, we require interactions with persons who function as *selfobjects*. Selfobjects are objects that provide the experiences needed to evoke and structure the developing self and to maintain the vigor and integrity of the self. These *self-evoking* and *self-sustaining* experiences are called *selfobject experiences* (Wolf 1988, 52).

These selfobject experiences are intrapsychic and subjective in nature. This means that the value and effect of a particular experience is determined by the person experiencing it and not by the *intent* of the person providing the experience. Therefore, the nature of specific selfobject experiences cannot accurately be known by another person through objective measures, but only by means of empathic understanding.

In order to develop the unique and innate self that resides within each of us, and to further develop and maintain that self throughout our lives, we require *continuing* selfobject experiences. Early in our lives, those who care for us most basically provide these experiences, and they require someone's physical presence. As we mature and develop, these experiences can be provided by significant aspects of our wider environment, such as family members, friends, our work, important hobbies, music and art, literature, objects of symbolic value to us, and our homes.

Although the form these experiences take and that which mediates them changes as our development continues over the course of our lives, our need for them never ceases (Wolf 1988, 53–54). Despite cultural values that applaud self-sufficiency, the self remains vulnerable throughout life to absent, insufficient, and inappropriate selfobject experiences, and this vulnerability is heightened at major developmental thresholds (Wolf 1988, 65). As Wolf (1988) unapologetically states, "The self cannot exist as a cohesive structure—that is, cannot generate an experience of well-being—apart from the contextual surround of appropriate selfobject experiences" (14). Using somewhat different language, John McDargh (1986) states, "The human person is born with *a primary and irreducible need for the confirmation and affirmation of relationship*" (255).

The *selfobject needs* required for the maintenance of a strong sense of self throughout our lives include the following: (1) the need to feel affirmed, recognized, accepted, and appreciated by others, especially when we reveal, expose, or share ourselves in some way [mirroring needs]; (2) the need to experience ourselves as part of someone or something that is admired, respected, powerful, wise, protective, and nonanxious [idealizing needs]; (3) the need to experience ourselves as "like" others in significant ways [alter ego needs]; (4) the need to experience being in opposition with someone who encourages and supports our active opposition without threatening to withdraw support and responsiveness, thereby affirming our autonomy [adversarial needs]; (5) the need to feel totally one with that which affirms us and/or that which we idealize and hold in respect and admiration [merger needs]; and (6) the need to experience ourselves as capable of affecting others and our environment in a manner that evokes from them the selfobject experiences we need [efficacy needs] (Wolf 1988, 55).

When these experiences are available to us in ways that allow us to internalize them, they promote the development of a vital and cohesive self. When they are absent or insufficient, especially at key developmental periods, a lack of vigor and emptiness pervades whatever sense of self has developed to that point. In extreme cases of deprivation, neglect, and outright assault on the self, the self can fragment. The subjective experience of one's self fragmenting is so frighteningly distressing that the natural response is to do whatever is possible to stop it, including the extreme measures of dissociating from the self, drugging and numbing the self, and even harming or killing oneself or someone else (Wolf 1988, 49).

For a secure symbiotic relationship between infant and caretaker to evolve, the caretaker must be nonthreatening, nurturing, and tuned into the infant enough as to intuitively learn to recognize and eventually know that *particular* infant's needs. As a caretaker is responsive to the gestures and cues offered by an infant and responds by satisfying the underlying need, the baby becomes aware of important things, such as bodily sensations often reflect underlying needs, one need can be distinguished from another, needs can be communicated, and the satisfaction of needs by others is possible. This type of attachment is also crucial for the development of a trusting attitude toward others and life in general. It even provides the foundation for developing the capacity to use symbolic communication so important in the acquisition of language skills.

In closing this chapter, it is important to underscore that the holding environment created by a child's caretakers forms a container within which necessary selfobject functions are fulfilled *and* protection and soothing is available. These traits of protection, nurture, sustenance, and soothing are key dimensions in any restorative holding environment. The ability to tell someone who will listen to us talk about the hurts we inevitably experience in life becomes crucial to healing and the restoration of self-development. In the words of Joan Borysenko (1996), "To speak, to be heard, and to be held are basic to healing" (131). When caretakers do not perform these functions, a child feels adrift. As one woman stated, "I did not grow up in the holding arms of caring family. I was left adrift in a sea of strangers." The impact of the lack of, and destruction of, such sustaining and restorative holding environments is the focus of the next chapter.

4

Trauma and the Self

SELF AND OTHER are constantly engaged in an interpersonal dance of co-creation as they mutually call one another into being through the interactions they have with one another. Some of these interactions facilitate the growth and development of the self. Other interactions become blocks to the healthy development of the self. Still other interactions can be outright destructive of persons. The most severe of these are called "traumatic."

Trauma Defined

The word *trauma* comes from a Greek word meaning wound (Figley 1985). A trauma wound can occur at any and all levels of a person's being—physical, emotional, psychological, relational, and spiritual. Because these dimensions of persons are intricately connected and interact with one another, severe trauma affects all aspects of a person's life. Although the effects of abuse, violence, and neglect are often chronic in nature, that which is more commonly considered traumatic is something sudden, violent, brutal, or catastrophic, and it touches a person's life in some intimate way.

Trauma is most commonly defined as a state of being overwhelmed—physically and psychologically. While the traumatization of persons often involves bodily injury and always produces systemically important physiological reactions, it is the psychological, emotional, and spiritual impact of trauma with which we are most interested here.

65

From a psychological perspective, one is overwhelmed (or trauma-tized) when there is excessive stimulation of one's affect systems (Lee and Martin 1991, 278). These systems are involved in managing and making meaning of that which we experience in some way (see van der Kolk 1987 and Borysenko 1996, 129–31). A given experience, therefore, can be overwhelming because the severity and amount of stimulation produced by it is unmanageable and/or because the experience does not fit into a context of meaning that allows the person affected to "make sense" of the event.

While stimulation can originate inside or outside a person and can take many forms, the most basic forms are pain and pleasure; something feels good or it feels bad. A person naturally has a particular amount of stimulation that is manageable and tolerable. Stimulation that is equal to or lower than this threshold level is manageable, but stimulation that exceeds this level is not. These threshold levels exist in all areas of our lives. Examples of these levels include such things as the degree of pain and discomfort one can tolerate, the degree of physical and emotional closeness and distance one is comfortable with in relation to others, the amount of hostility and intrusion from others one can manage, the amount of noise one can tolerate, and the amount of social interaction or time alone one can manage.

While overwhelming in its effect, trauma can also be viewed as part of normal human life experience. Life as we know it through our expe-rience will naturally and periodically confront us with events and cir-cumstances that are overwhelming to us. This perspective is discussed by Giovacchini (1979) when he states, "Trauma is viewed as an inevitable consequence of ordinary development, beginning with the trauma of birth" (333).

While this perspective may initially seem to trivialize trauma, it in fact calls attention to a key ingredient regarding the impact a particular trauma can have on us at any point in time. That ingredient is whether or not those persons around us respond to our hurt, and the nature of their response. The extent to which such a response is timely and appro-priately soothing will in large part determine whether or not there will be a traumatically lingering influence and ripple effect throughout the rest of a victim's life.

Examples of trauma occurring naturally in the course of development abound in stories parents tell about mischief and accidents involving their children. Falling off a bike while learning to ride it, requiring stitches from cutting one's head on the corner of a coffee table while still in the clumsy stage of learning to walk, and crashing through a barbed-wire fence while sledding down a snow-covered hill are but a few examples. We can also think of the trauma experienced by a child being left in a church nursery for the first time with strangers and being overcome with the fear and rage associated with normal separation anxiety.

Engaging life and living it fully exposes us to the potential of trauma every day. None of us escapes its scars. Reminding ourselves that trauma is an "inevitable consequence" of our life journey keeps us realistically aware of two important points: we cannot expect to live life fully without being traumatized, *and* we depend on one another for the healing of our trauma wounds.

The extent to which any given event or situation is overwhelming to a *particular* individual is generally determined by a number of important variables. These include (1) the nature and severity of the event itself, (2) the frequency and duration of the trauma, (3) one's genetic vulnerability to overwhelming experience, (4) the developmental level a person has achieved at the time a trauma occurs, (5) the strength and flexibility of one's psychological defenses, (6) the strength and clarity of one's sense of self prior to the event occurring, (7) the extent to which there has been a history of trauma in one's life, and (8) the degree of external protection, nurturing, soothing, and social support available to a person after the event is over.

While recognizing individual differences in responses to trauma, including their intensity and duration, there are a number of customary responses to severe trauma worth noting. Quoting from the early work of Kardiner (1941) in his study of combat veterans, van der Kolk (1987) lists these responses as "(1) a persistence of startle response and irritability, (2) proclivity to explosive outbursts of aggression, (3) fixation on the trauma, (4) constriction of the general level of personality functioning, and (5) atypical dream life" (2). Referring to the work of Lindemann (1944) and Horowitz (1976), van der Kolk (1987) notes that normal human responses to psychological trauma have been characterized as involving a "phasic reliving and denial" of the traumatic event "with alternating intrusive and numbing responses" (3).

Traumatic events shatter those internal psychological structures that provide a sense of meaning and purpose and support the illusion of invincibility that allows many of us to live each day relatively free of the dread of impending extinction and death (Becker 1973). Lee and Martin refer to Janoff-Bulman's (1985, see also 1989) three basic assumptions that if shattered constitute trauma. These are "(1) the belief in personal invulnerability, (2) the perception of the world as meaningful and comprehensible, and (3) the view of oneself in a positive light" (cited in Lee and Martin 1991, 282–83).

When a child develops in an environment that does not support the development of these basic assumptions or shatters them, the child has no protection. The result can be chronic terror, despair, and/or demoralization. The shattering of these assumptions, and the shield of invincibility they help erect, takes with it all the defenses, fantasies, and illusions we create in order to feel safe. As a result, our sense of self becomes exposed, vulnerable, and threatened. This happens not only in a psychological and existential sense, but also in a social and meaning sense.

The farm crisis of the 1980s was traumatic. Farmers and their families lost not only their financial security, but family legacies, social standing, and the dreams and wishes entrusted to them by the generations that preceded them and the generations that hoped to follow them. In essence, they lost all that had previously defined and sustained them. As a result, domestic violence, drug abuse, homicides, and suicides claimed the lives of persons previously considered examples of strength in their communities. Likewise, the government's decision to replace, rather than rehire, striking air traffic controllers in the early 1980s had a similar effect on a different population of people. Persons who had never dreamed, desired, or planned on doing anything else as a career suddenly suffered a loss of self-identity, purpose, and meaning along with the loss of financial livelihood.

Experiences such as these crystallize and make irrefutably real van der Kolk's (1987) description of the essence of psychological trauma as "the loss of faith that there is order and continuity of life" (31). He goes on to say:

> Trauma occurs when one loses the sense of having a safe place to retreat within or outside oneself to deal with frightening emotions and experiences. This results in a state of helplessness, a feeling that

one's actions have no bearing on the outcome of one's life. Since human life seems to be incompatible with a sense of meaninglessness and lack of control, people will avoid this experience at just about any price, from abject dependency to psychosis. Much of human endeavor, in religion, art, and science, is centrally concerned with exactly these grand questions of meaning and control over one's destiny." (31)

In a similar vein, Peter VanKatwyk (1997) refers to trauma as "those hurts that overwhelm and disrupt human possibilities to adjust and go on with life" (284–85). He continues, "Trauma represents suffering in escalating intensity which increasingly cripples and disrupts the person's orientation and functioning in life. Trauma is the wound that multiplies itself through the persistence of intrusive thoughts, dreams, images, and flashbacks" (287). The overwhelming nature of a traumatic event is so profound it "seems infinite, all-powerful, and wholly other" (Mogenson 1989, 2). In its attention-demanding qualities, trauma becomes God-like and "creates and organizes life after its own image" (VanKatwyk 1997, 287).

Trauma's Impact on the Developing Self

At the beginning of the section entitled "The Developmental Process" in chapter three, it was noted that the meeting between an infant and her caretaker(s) can be one of welcoming warmth or one of coldness and even hate. If this latter type of environment is present, the developmental process of the infant takes a tragic detour from that outlined (see Johnson 1985). In such a case, the infant's natural desire to attach to her caretaker(s) diminishes as her focus shifts from relationship building and mental development to the satisfaction of the more primitive needs of psychic and physical survival. The infant also personalizes and incorporates the hostile environmental response, resulting in an extreme sense of terror and rage and a sense of self-loathing and affective deadness.

In such cases, the infant turns against itself and "stops living in order to preserve its life" (Johnson 1985, 57). This move is not only driven by an innate desire to survive, but also results from the introjection of the rejecting caretaker, which then "suppresses the life force" of the infant from within (Johnson 1985, 57). These psychic maneuvers have a tremendous impact on the life direction of a child trapped in this tragic dilemma. Two decisions are made that begin to govern how the child goes on to think of herself in the world. These decisions are "There is something wrong with me" and "I have no right to exist" (Johnson 1985, 57).

When an infant internalizes its experience of a noxious caretaker, that internalized object can be so toxic that it remains unintegrated much like an indigestible piece of food in one's stomach. Not surprisingly, Johnson (1985) refers to the powerful combination of this hate-filled and rejecting unassimilated introject and the child's natural reactive rage as a "destructive, demonic force" that is experienced as alien and beyond one's control (67). As in the case of persecutory alters in cases of dissociative identity disorder, these unassimilated introjects are sometimes behind-the-scenes participants in acts of self-harm. They play a role in keeping internal messages of self-loathing and self-depreciation active and constantly present, and they can also be responsible for a good deal of the resistance encountered in a therapeutic process.

All the while, these same introjects can paradoxically serve a survival function by working against acts of self-assertion which in the past would have triggered the wrath of a dangerous abuser (see Goodman and Peters 1995). In cases of severe privation and abuse, the environment can be hostile enough as to limit or even prohibit the formation of a symbiotic relationship between infant and caretaker. In such cases, even the development of such basic abilities as the recognition and communication of needs is severely affected.

Balint underscored the important role selfobjects play in an understanding of trauma, and coined the term "traumatogenic object" (cited in Lee and Martin 1991, 278). From this perspective, a parent can become a traumatogenic object if the following necessary conditions are met: (1) the child has a dependent and trusting relationship with the parent, (2) the parent does something that is experienced as painful, frightening, or exciting to the child, and (3) when approached, the parent unexpectedly rejects the child's desire to continue the excitement or to receive comfort and understanding for being misunderstood or ignored (Lee and Martin 1991, 284).

Such material further complements an understanding of the vital role played by the primary caretaker(s) in a child's development. Building upon the work of Winnicott and Modell (1981) has observed, "to have a childhood requires the presence of a holding environment" (491). Part of the work in providing this holding environment is providing what is referred to as a "parental shield" (Modell 1981, 496–97). Such a shield not only performs a protective function from outside threats, but also from the threat of overwhelming affect from *within* the child. The absence of such a "parental shield . . . induces the formation of a precocious and premature sense of self, a sense of self that retains its fragility and must be supported by omnipotent, grandiose fantasies" (Modell 1981, 496–97).

The seemingly endless search for ways to create such self-sustaining fantasies (in the absence of actual self-sustaining selfobject experiences) is often a "behind the scenes factor" in the types of violence discussed by the emergency-room physician in chapter two. This process can also be a contributing force in driving a desire to destroy others in the vain attempt to avoid one's own immortality as noted by Ernest Becker (1975) in chapter one and in one's need to protect and maintain whatever sense of self one already has (Becker 1968, 124, 328).

The Self's Response to Trauma

Because it depends upon an interpersonal environment in which to grow and develop, the self is generally conceived as being social in origin. The self is in large part a synthesis of what our experience suggests we mean to others. The self is built up slowly over time through interactions with people important to us and becomes structured around the attitudes and impressions gleaned from our interactions with those persons. As those significant to us selectively affirm or discourage the innate traits and talents we freely express, we *integrate* into our sense of self those dimensions that are responded to positively and valued, and we *split-off* and keep unintegrated those traits left unaffirmed, or responded to with displeasure. We keep these split-off parts of ourselves separated from the rest of ourselves, and they often remain undeveloped. If they do develop, that development often occurs behind a protective wall of detachment from others who, because of hurtful past experience, are perceived as threats to be warded off. While this detachment creates some psychic safety, it eliminates the types of social interactions so critical to the development of important psychic structures and mental capacities. The result can be deficiencies in such fundamental matters as one's level of self-cohesion, reality relatedness, and object relatedness (Horner 1984, 42). When the environment and the people in it are traumatogenic, these same results become manifested in more severe forms.

Disengaging from Self and Others

Whenever the interpersonal environment is perceived as threatening to the survival of the self, a person may choose to retreat behind a protective wall of emotional and psychic detachment in order to protect whatever sense of self is already present. While this defensive move may be crucial to the protection of the self, it carries with it a loss of interpersonal connectedness and the forfeiting of important dimensions of the self that remain unexpressed. As the following example demonstrates, one of these dimensions can even be something so profoundly personal and integral to the sense of self as one's dreams.

A young man in pastoral psychotherapy told the following story, which he entitled, "The Saddest Story about My Mother." After a long period of ambivalence about whether to return to school to complete her education, this man's mother mustered up enough courage to enroll in a transitional program for mothers going back to school. During the second class period, the teacher took the class to the college library to familiarize them with the resources there and how to access them. As his mother was exploring the stacks, she overheard a conversation several stacks away between her teacher and another teacher. She heard the woman ask her teacher what she was doing at the library that day. Her teacher responded, "I'm here with the old housewives class." This response was so humiliating to his mother's fragile and already depreciated sense of self that she retreated back within herself and never returned to school after that.

This woman's need to protect her self was so important that it took precedence over the pursuit of her dreams. This effective, but self-disabling, solution to a perceived threat to the self clearly demonstrates how important it is to keep the self safe, and how easily an already fragile self can become threatened. This example also demonstrates how casual and callous we can become in categorizing people into derogatory groups rather than celebrating and rejoicing over their persistence and courage to keep moving on.

As a result of disengaging from others to protect one's self, particular attributes of a person can develop in highly refined and sophisticated ways, while their interpersonal skills and sense of self remain undeveloped and quite fragile. Horner (1984) talks of such development as occurring outside the realm of object relatedness (41–72; 209–23). This process can be seen in the case of a highly functioning nurse in psychotherapy. This woman was reared in a home with rigid, impulsively hurtful, emotionally unaffirming, and abusive parents. They were so overwhelmingly intrusive that as a little girl of age six she sat in a shed contemplating eating rat poison. This woman's childhood home was devoid of anything comfortable or soothing. Even the stuffed furniture in the home was kept covered with plastic, and children were prohibited from sitting on it.

Graduation from high school and admission to nursing school on a scholarship provided a welcomed and well-planned escape from the home. Despite this childhood environment, and due largely to the development of a successful characterological defense behind which she emotionally withdrew and cut-off from people, she was able to go on and develop extremely sensitive and technically advanced nursing skills, which she empathetically and effectively applied in her care of patients. While able to open herself empathetically to patients dependent on her care, she remained defensively closed-off to anyone with actual or perceived authority over her. This self defense also contributed to her difficulty in setting realistic work expectations for herself and communicating those to her superiors. She consequently worked fifteen-hour days and accumulated weeks of vacation and sick leave, which she was reluctant to use in ways that could have been helpful to her.

Defensive detachment from others to save one's self can create incredibly complex dilemmas for those who adopt this position. In the example just shared, this woman's learned ways of protecting her self created a state of chronic fatigue and dreadfully fearful interpersonal dilemmas. Furthermore, it created significant religious and spiritual questions for her. These were first manifested when seemingly out of the blue she surprised her therapist one day by saying, "I've been reflecting lately and have begun to raise the question with myself about just how much I would be willing to risk in order to begin to let people into my life." She then posed the related faith question that perplexed her: "Do you think the fact that I've done this [locked people out of her life] is a sin?"

It is often clear to neutral and outside observers, such as caregivers and friends, that persons in abusive environments have had to cut-off from others in order to protect themselves. For the observers, the initial problem (or sin) is seen to arise from the broken and distorted family relationships that produced the terror and the need for such a desperate form of self-protection. But persons who have lived in these environments and detached from their selfs at very young ages do not see things in the same way. From their perspective, abuse is "normal." In addition, they see themselves as the cause of all their pain. As one woman put it, "People who have not been abused do not understand. When you are chronically abused, your sense of reality becomes based upon what you have experienced. That experience, no matter how awful, becomes reality for you. That which others consider 'abnormal' is very 'normal' for you."

There is a different form of protection for the self that also results in a person's disengagement from her own self. This is the creation of what is called a "false self" (Winnicott 1965, 145). This is a self structure that evolves in reaction to the intrusive and impinging imposition of requirements and expectations by others that ignore the innate and spontaneously expressed characteristics of the developing child. This "false self" is juxtaposed to a "true self" that develops in an atmosphere of parental attunement with the natural needs, characteristics, and spontaneous self expressions of a particular child (Winnicott 1965, 145). Together, the "true self" and "false self" comprise the "central self" as understood by Winnicott.

In this self-defensive posture, the false self is the self that actively functions in the world and becomes known to most people. It is the self through which one lives life. At the same time, however, the false self functions as a defensive shield behind which any existing true self can remain safe as it keeps a watchful eye out for nonthreatening opportunities to reveal itself. (In cases of dissociative identity disorder, alter personalities function much as false selfs. Each handles those tasks and interactions with which it is most familiar and skilled, while also protecting the more fragile and wounded true self or core personality.)

Disengaging from Basic Needs

Not only do we engage and disengage from others, integrate or split-off certain aspects of our selves depending on the response significant others have to us, but our basic needs are subjected to a similar fate. As Sands (1994) so eloquently reminds us, not only is "bad stuff" dissociated, but "good stuff" is as well. This includes basic attachment needs and the basic selfobject needs discussed in chapter three.

As in the case of other personal expressions of our selves, our needs are either responded to in a receptive fashion and affirmed, thereby facilitating their integration within our concept of self, or they are ignored or rejected, in which case they are kept split-off from our sense of self or are firmly rejected in their own right. In the latter case, they are not only left unintegrated, but they are rejected, repressed, and left unacknowledged and unmet. In the case of the nurse above, despite the pain and fear of her emotional isolation, she steadfastly denied any need for people, as well as her basic needs for soothing, affection, and care.

This repression, splitting-off, and dissociation of basic human needs are often responsible for the inability of survivors of severe and early trauma to recognize what their needs are. These same processes are also responsible for the inability of some survivors to communicate their needs to others. These inabilities can be readily overlooked by caregivers who are unfamiliar with these processes and by those who narrowly focus on content, affect, and recollection of traumatic memory. This confounding aftermath of human-induced trauma is responsible, however, for a number of pitfalls that trip up many caregivers in their attempts to be helpful.

It is these basic needs, for example, that are responsible for the vicissitudes of tremendous fear and dependency that become confusingly troublesome to therapists and survivors as their particular caregiving relationships intensify (Horner 1984, 218). As a working alliance becomes stronger, and there is an awakening awareness of previously split-off needs, the hope of unmet needs becoming fulfilled is naturally kindled and builds in intensity. As these previously unmet and dissociated needs become mobilized, they become quite strong and can easily confound an already complex therapeutic endeavor.

Therapists are not the only caregivers affected by this aftermath of trauma as they seek to be helpful to survivors. Similar levels of intensity and complexity can occur between survivors and anyone with whom they have begun to relate on an ongoing basis. This includes friends, co-workers, pastors, mental health personnel, and even family members.

Persons who suffered early life trauma and disengaged from or split off their basic needs have no experience dealing with these needs and the strong affective states generated by them. They may not be able to verbalize them, identify them, or even manage them. Some of these mobilized needs may also stir up life experiences of pain from earlier times when needs *were* expressed but were met with rejection or punishment or were even used as justification for continued abuse. Reactions such as these make the mobilization of unmet, repressed, split-off, and dissociated needs frightening to survivors. Their mobilization can also lead to massively confusing and ambivalent feelings about therapists, other caregivers, and even the helping process itself.

The inability of trauma survivors to recognize their basic needs and to label the affective states associated with them can also produce frustration and anger in caregivers, who see their role as helping persons "get in touch with their feelings," but who may be unaware of this particular aftermath of trauma. In such cases, the anger and frustration of caregivers can actually be retraumatizing, since survivors feel increasingly compelled to do something they are presently incapable of doing and that they intuitively know they cannot effectively and safely manage.

The Problematic and Confounding Nature of Self Defenses

In preceding sections of this chapter, we have outlined just a few of the profound ways a person's self can be stunted in its development and weakened in its structure by traumatizing interpersonal interactions. It is clear from this material that the protection of the self is so utterly crucial that persons will go to any and all extremes at their disposal to insure the survival of the self. The extremes we have discussed include detaching from self and others and disengaging from basic needs to the point that we are unaware of their existence. The results of such maneuvers leave persons isolated from others, disengaged from their selfs, and radically weakened and broken inside. Further consequences for persons who have needed to defend their selfs in these ways include a limited ability to communicate clearly with others about themselves and difficulty maintaining stable and loving relationships with others.

Consequently, the mechanisms used to defend the self often result in behaviors and actions that are ultimately problematic and destructive for the survivor herself. More specifically, these self defenses can block and frustrate the creation of helpful relationships with others that she so desperately needs. The chief characteristics that make self defenses so problematic include the fact that their use (1) is defensive, unconscious, and automatic, (2) costs a great deal in the areas of self-awareness, life satisfaction, personal integrity and wholeness, and interpersonal relationships, and (3) remains unaffected by reason, or even threatened punishment.

It is important to recognize that the use of these effective, yet tragically damaging, self defenses is commonly one result of abuse and neglect. It is equally important to realize, however, that the continuing reliance upon these same self defenses often plays a significant role in one's becoming a perpetrator of further abuse and neglect. For these reasons, it is critical that we understand the confounding nature of these defenses.

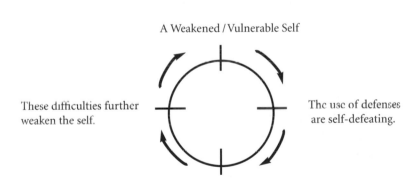

A Weakened / Vulnerable Self

These difficulties further weaken the self.

The use of defenses are self-defeating.

These defenses cause difficulty and get in the way of evoking the positive responses from others that are needed and desired.

Figure 4: The Confounding Results of a Weakened Self and the Problematic Nature of Self Defenses (Top View)

The manner in which the use of self defenses can contribute to increasingly problematic interactions with others, and to the further weakening of an already fragile self, is depicted in figures 4 and 5. Figure 4 is a cross-section view looking down at the top of figure 5. Figure 4 is designed to provide a perspective on the circular nature of the interaction patterns created between a person using self defenses and those persons most apt to become reactively engaged with her. Figure 5 depicts the increasingly restrictive, self-focused, and entrenched nature of this confusing and tragic process.

An increasing
loss of control
over one's life

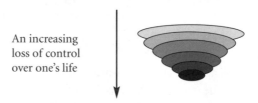

An increasing use of problematic self defenses leads to an increasingly weakened self; an increasingly restrictive and narrowed perceptual field; increased desperation, reactivity, and irrationality; the imposition of more extreme measures of external control; and more extreme attempts to protect the self.

Figure 5: The Confounding Results of a Weakened Self and the
Problematic Nature of Self Defenses (Side View)

An illustration of this process can be seen in the case of Terry, a sixteen-year-old high school student. Terry was an attractive young woman who was a good student, involved in extra-curricular activities, and responsible in working at her part-time job. She lived at home with her younger brother and her natural parents.

Over a period of three weeks, Terry had increasingly isolated herself from the family, refused to carry on conversations of any length with her parents (something unusual for her), lost interest in her girlfriends and school, and obliquely talked of being depressed and suicidal. In this process, she succeeded in scaring her generally attentive parents enough that they called for family counseling.

As the precipitating events leading up to this crisis were explored, the following series of confounding and intensifying events unfolded. Terry reported that four years previously there had been a number of occasions when she had come home excited about something she was involved in at school, and her mother failed to respond in as affirming a manner as Terry wanted. In addition to these experiences, she reported that on a family trip to relatives for the holidays, she was talking freely and spontaneously in her customary manner as the family drove down the highway. At some point, her brother interrupted her. Terry accused him of interrupting her. Her parents responded by telling her to "be quiet" and to let "your brother talk!" This sudden and sharper-than-ordinary response, on top of her previous experience of not being adequately affirmed by her mother, assaulted Terry's sense of fairness and her sense of self was wounded. She reported disengaging from her parents and going deep within herself at this point. While she had continued to interact with her parents over the ensuing years, she was always selective in what she said to them and generally less revealing of her true thoughts and feelings. The false self she developed did this so well, in fact, that her parents had not even noticed her disengagement from them. This inward journey of disengagement was so deep, however, and Terry closed off so much, that over time she became unable to express herself spontaneously to others.

Terry lived within this protective shell until she met her boyfriend, Bobbie, who was three years older and out of high school. This relationship was initially difficult and tumultuous for Terry. Bobbie was a self-confident, outspoken, and somewhat egocentric young man who wanted to engage Terry in reciprocal conversation. Whenever he tried, he would get frustrated at Terry's inability to express her self in an equally confident and assertive fashion. His frustration would get so great at times that his verbalizations took on an abusive tone. If they were out together at a football game during one of these times, he might storm off into the crowd leaving her unclear as to his whereabouts and whether she would have a ride home. On some of these occasions her brother had been present, and as younger siblings often do, he reported these events to his parents. Consequently, Terry's mother and father developed a negative impression of Bobbie as someone who failed to treat their daughter with the respect they felt she deserved, and they became genuinely concerned for her safety.

At some level within herself, Terry began to realize that her relationship with Bobby was an opportunity to get back in touch with her true self. As she struggled within herself to find the words to fit how she felt and then struggled even more to express them, she reported that she experienced an actual physical pain in her gut as she seemingly wrenched open the protective doors around her self she had shut so tightly years ago. As she successfully began to come alive again, she naturally began spending more and more time with Bobbie—even to the point of losing track of her curfew. Since her parents already had a negative impression of Bobbie anyway, and since Terry's uncharacteristic lateness increased their anxiety, the logical consequence seemed to be to forbid her from seeing Bobbie. This they did.

The resulting crisis erupted in more grand proportions than Terry's parents anticipated, and it caught them totally by surprise. Because of the previous history of being wounded by them (something her parents were unaware of at the time) and because of the tremendous satisfaction Terry was getting from coming out of her shell of detachment and reconnecting to her self, her parents' action seemed like a "death sentence" to Terry. She could not hide her hurt and anger as effectively as she had done four years ago, and she did not want to. She was also not yet strong enough to talk to her parents directly about how she felt. The response left to her was to go into a depression and make the veiled threats that brought her and her parents into counseling.

Because of the existence of basically strong bonds of respect and love these family members shared for one another, this particular case had a positive outcome. Mother and father expressed regret about their earlier wounding of Terry, and she expressed regret about cutting them out of her life. As Terry's self-assertion and self-respect increased, and as their confidence in Terry's ability to "handle herself with Bobbie" grew, mother and father were able to disentangle themselves from their feelings about him. Terry responsibly took her consequences and then began a successful endeavor to negotiate increased levels of freedom, including the right to see Bobbie again. The family terminated therapy will all parties more firmly differentiated and new levels of respect for one another in place. By way of closing, it is important to note that this is a "tame" example of the processes being discussed. When basic love and respect for one another is lacking in a family, cases similar to this can have disastrous results as all parties increasingly react, dig their heels in further, and become more and more belligerent with one another.

An understanding of the reactively destructive process exemplified in the case just presented and in figures 4 and 5, can be helpful in two ways. First, it can help us resist being co-opted into instinctively reacting to the self-defensive actions of threatened persons in ways that make matters worse. Second, an understanding of these dynamics can help us at a cultural level. An appreciation for the complexity of these dynamics, for example, can help policymakers understand why the "threat" of lengthy prison terms does not stem the tide of crimes that are more basically the result of people's desperate attempts to protect their already fragile selfs.

Trauma's Threat to Attachment Bonds

As humans, we live, develop, learn, and get our sense of self, meaning, and purpose through the attachments we form. We have seen how these attachments—with our children, spouses, friends, animals, homes, material possessions of symbolic importance like photographs, musical instruments, and works of art, and even our belief systems—contribute to and support a sense of self. This means that our concept of self includes not only our physical, emotional, and spiritual selves, but extends out from us to also include our significant relationships and relational networks.

As a result, the important shield of invincibility that protects our selfs can also be cracked, threatened, or destroyed when someone with whom we have had an emotional bond (or something to which we have been attached) is threatened, harmed, taken away, or lost in some fashion. Any rupture of such attachments is consequently experienced as a tremendous loss. Nel Noddings (1989) discusses this in terms of the pain, separation, and helplessness experienced at such times (90–121). The more significant the relationship, the more it has become a major part of our lives, and the more it has been a key element around which we have come to define ourselves and think of ourselves, the greater the loss, distress, grief, and trauma when that relationship is severed. Jim Ashbrook (1994) likens this to the basic "cry of separation" common in mammals and notes that this distress response occurs whenever there is an experienced gap between a person and some significant aspect of her necessary environment (15; see also Horner 1984, 48–51).

While ruptures in the attachment bonds adults have with significant objects can be extremely destabilizing, the rupture of attachment bonds a young child has with significant objects can be even more devastating to their developing, and much needed, sense of security. When these ruptures are caused by significant adults upon whom they depend, the impact is more severe and long lasting still. The most disturbing examples of this we have seen are in cases where parents harmed something of importance to their child as a means of getting control, compliance, or silence. We have seen cases in which a "macho" father forced his three-year-old son to throw his security blanket into the home fireplace because "he was a big boy now, didn't need it, and didn't want to be a sissy." In an even more disturbing case, a father terrorized his little girl into silence about his sexual abuse of her by forcing her to watch as he took an electric drill and drilled a large hole through the shell of her pet turtle, killing it in the process. He then proceeded to tell her he would do the same to her if she ever told anyone what he did to her.

Summary

The purpose of this chapter has been to call attention to the marvelously complex processes human beings use to protect our selves from traumatic events and interactions that threaten our psychological well-being and sometimes our very lives. No matter how adept we are at these defensive maneuvers, others can be equally adept at attacking and damaging us.

The various interactions between particular selves and other persons can be considered to fall along the three continua presented in chapter one. Interpersonally traumatic interactions can be perpetrated by persons who have varying levels of awareness about themselves, what they are doing, what the actual consequences of their actions are for people, and just how profound and long lasting these consequences can be. Traumatic interactions can be perpetrated in an active fashion or can result from passivity and neglect. Traumatic interactions can be intentionally perpetrated or can be the unintended result of something a person has or has not done.

Concepts such as these are helpful in formulating a cognitive understanding of the complexity underlying the interpersonal interactions that routinely damage persons. They also impress upon us how susceptible each of us is to perpetrating harm on another. At the same time, human beings are capable of doing horrifically devastating things to one another that are not so neatly conceptualized and contained within our minds. Every fabric of our beings wrenches with pain and agony for the young woman who lost her "voice" and for her parents whose conscious intent was to protect their daughter from a "disrespectful" boyfriend; for the little boy whose father's narrow sense of maleness deprived him of an important transitional object that he used to soothe himself; and for the thirty-five-year-old woman who was radically split and divided within herself as the result of years of childhood abuse and terror-filled encounters with a father who tore down her budding shields of invincibility as easily as he drilled through the shell of her pet turtle when she was but a child.

While these interactions and millions of others like them fall within the category of "traumatic life experience," we intuitively feel that some of them go far beyond what is normally considered "traumatic." Those traumatic interactions that tear into the very selves and souls of persons are better described by the term "evil." This distinction is the focus of the next chapter.

5

Evil's Attack on the Self and Soul

THERE IS A NATURAL CONNECTION in the minds of most people between trauma and evil. Hurt is generally the most obvious effect that evil has on people, and the most severe forms of hurt are usually considered traumatic. In fact, human-induced trauma is the most devastating form of trauma, especially when it is perpetrated by a significant person in the victim's life upon whom she depends in some way.

While trauma and evil often go hand-in-hand, it is not helpful to label all trauma as evil nor to reduce evil to that which is traumatic. In fact, differentiating them one from the other is more helpful because such a distinction can help us better understand how evil and trauma become woven together into the complex Gordian knot that so devastates people's lives. While this distinction can make our work with victims and perpetrators of abuse more effective, this distinction can also disturb us as it makes us more aware of how prevalent and close by evil really is. The focus of this chapter is making this distinction between trauma and evil and defining evil in a way that makes it understandable and useful to caregivers and survivors alike.

The Distinction between Trauma and Evil

In the previous chapter, we described how, from a physiological and psychological standpoint, trauma is a profoundly *subjective* experience. Whether an event is considered traumatic or not is generally determined by the effect it has on the internal physiological and psychological systems of each *particular* individual. Constitutional and developmental variables play a major role in whether or not the term "trauma" or "traumatized" can be used in describing the impact of a specific event upon a particular person. Whether a particular trauma is viewed as caused by a natural calamity, some accident, or the action of a person or group, the focus of attention generally comes to rest on two issues: (1) whether or not a particular experience would likely be overwhelming to *most* people, and (2) the subjective experience of the victim and her own particular strengths and vulnerabilities.

While this way of thinking may be technically and scientifically accurate, it nevertheless shifts the focus of attention away from what has been *done* to the victim by a perpetrator and *onto* the victim herself. This shift provides the necessary rationale for people to feel justified in judging a particular victim. A further outgrowth of this shift is that a victim's vulnerability to a traumatic event can more easily become a weapon used against her by others. Examples of this include questions as to whether or not she exercised sufficient precaution to maintain personal safety, whether she could have been stronger and resisted more forcefully, and in some cases even questions about whether she may have in fact provoked an attack.

A major consequence of this way of thinking is that it divides victims within themselves and separates them from one another. This is accomplished by calling attention to the natural differences among persons— for example, some people are fragile, while others are more resilient; some are sensitive and easily wounded, while others are better defended and less affected by whatever happens to them. What one person finds traumatic another may not. This subjective quality of overwhelming experience also makes it an easily accessible weapon for survivors to use against themselves. It is common for a survivor to endlessly compare herself to others and judge herself harshly as a result. This takes the form of comments, such as, "Others have experienced worse and they seem to manage!" or "My sister grew up in the same home I did, and she came out all right! What's wrong with me that I was affected so much?"

Whether the focus of attention comes to rest on the variable severity of traumatic events or on the variable ability to defend themselves in a traumatic situation, the result is the same—victims are evaluated, rather than the event or perpetrator of the event, and the actual helplessness of victims is denied. While these responses are in some measure a reflection of cultural denial in the service of maintaining the illusion of personal invulnerability (i.e., "we should all be capable of protecting ourselves"), they are also a reflection of the limited perspective a purely psychological and physiological study of trauma offers.

Having said this, it is important to note that the serious scientific study of trauma (and its close relative, stress) within the last two decades has been tremendously helpful in numerous ways. One of the most far-reaching results of this study is a rekindling of an awareness of the significant role actual trauma plays in the etiology of a wide range of "mental health problems" that are more accurately viewed as "normal reactions to abnormal situations." This study of trauma has also led to significant discoveries contributing to our understanding of the neurobiological and psychological processes that are associated with traumatic experience, and that play a pivotal role in the difficulty persons have recovering from traumatic events. These contributions have in turn spawned innovative and effective interventions to help persons heal from trauma. The competent use of clinical hypnosis, as well as Eye Movement Desensitization and Reprocessing [EMDR] (Shapiro 1995) are but two examples.

A trauma theory perspective has also offered a more accurate and helpful understanding of the dynamics operating in some highly reactive and troublesome patients. This understanding is slowly changing attitudes that led to previous tendencies to summarily dismiss such "difficult" patients as "borderline personalities" who required too much in the way of resources and too little in the way of hope for recovery to make working with them "worth" a provider's time.

The psychological study of trauma has also offered some relief from the institutionalization of behaviorally focused treatment programs emphasizing rigid limit setting and boundary reinforcement with troubled youth and adults. Such interventions are indeed helpful for effective treatment of behaviors driven by borderline dynamics. These same interventions, however, can contribute to needless and reactive acting-out behavior on the part of persons whose dynamics are primarily trauma driven. In such cases, these interventions are often ineffective and, to the extent they replicate earlier experiences of privation, depravation, disrespect, exercise of power, and abuse, they can be hurtful (Earl 1991). Such interventions can also further erode any hope that may remain in someone who wants and needs help.

On the other hand, this same physiological and psychological approach to trauma has not addressed the issue of evil, and how evil confounds the already complex effects trauma has on persons. Major researchers in the field of trauma are cognizant of the limitations of science in this arena, however, and of the vital role evil plays in human misery. In the closing section of a thorough review of the effects of traumatic stress on persons, van der Kolk and McFarlane (1996) state the following: "There are aspects of the experience of trauma that cannot be captured in medical and scientific models, but that go to the core of what it is like to be human. . . . Scientific, empirical frameworks. . . leave little room for the vital human dimensions affected by trauma: . . . Attitudes toward trauma and victimization must . . . reflect people's basic beliefs about what it means to be human, and people's positions about the eternal questions of good and evil" (573). Similarly, Judith Herman (1992) says that "to study psychological trauma is to come face-to-face both with human vulnerability in the natural world and with the capacity for evil in human nature" (7).

Evil is illusory and mysterious and at the same time blatantly obvious and concrete. It is a term often used for emphasis but with little understanding of how it really works behind the scenes to destroy life. We can objectively talk of persons being overwhelmed, but this is a far cry from evil. Evil refers to something so overwhelmingly confusing and self-disintegrating that people are torn apart emotionally and spiritually. Such things rarely occur "naturally," but are instead most often the result of human action.

When the focus is only on the effects *trauma* produces in the lives of people, and the *evil* dimensions underlying and embedded within the traumatization of persons are ignored, a key opportunity for understanding the fuller impact human-induced trauma has on persons is missed. Survivors have also told us that an understanding of evil, as distinct from trauma, provides a powerful perspective that can aid in helping them heal from tremendously hurtful and confusing actions on the part of others for which they blame themselves.

Trauma is an event; evil is a process. It is evil, not trauma, that destroys the selfs and souls of persons. The more trauma is created and directed at hurting a person or group, or manifests a disregard for the sacred selfhood of others, the more we are dealing with evil rather than trauma. The main criterion separating trauma from evil is whether the damage to the self-structure of a person and the symptoms suffered by her, like feeling hopeless, helpless, bad, insecure, ashamed, abandoned, and fearful, are natural outgrowths of having survived an overwhelming experience (trauma), or whether they have been produced, heightened, or used by a perpetrator against her in a way that frustrates healing and leads to further destruction of the self (evil).

Trauma is generally more impersonal than evil, which, in its most radical forms, is extremely personal. Elizabeth Johnson, in her book *She Who Is,* refers to the work of Robin Morgan and a "litany of remembrance of the holocaust of women" (1992, 262). Johnson notes some of these chronicled atrocities—carried out under the auspices of the church—against women and children accused of being witches, and refers to these atrocities as the "Inquisition murders." While the methods of execution are certainly cruel in their own right, the nature of these acts takes on a personal quality that makes them even more ominous and hideous. For example, thirteen-year-old Veronica Zerritsch was reportedly made to "dance in the warm ashes of her executed mother" before being burned alive herself in 1754. While her young son was forced to watch, Agnes Wobster drowned in 1567. Emerzianne Pichler was first tortured and then burned alive with her two children in 1679. Frau Dumler, who was pregnant, was "boiled to death in hot oil" in 1630 (Johnson 1992, 262).

Regardless of the worldview operative at the historical time and place in which these atrocities took place, it is impossible to read these accounts without being struck by the intentional and sensitively attuned cruelty with which they were implemented. These were more than the "justified execution of persons deemed dangerous to society." Rather, they reflect a hideously cruel and personal attack on the selfhood of the persons executed *and* all who were held dear to them. It is also important to realize with Kathleen Norris (1998) that "Inquisition is not something people used to do. . . . Inquisition begins . . . in the human heart. And it is what has occurred in the twentieth century, not the fifteenth, that should most concern us" (217).

The Destruction of the Self and Soul of a Person

We have described how the self develops within a context of interpersonal exchanges with others, and how the self depends on others to summon into being the unique and inherent potentials that lie within the self. We have also discussed how sensitively attuned, nurturing, and restorative interactions can lead to the evolution of a true self, while insensitive and hurtful interactions can precipitate disengagement from self, the creation of a defensive false self, or even the fragmentation and destruction of the self. But what about soul?

The more we reflect upon and study the nature of self, the more we are moved to conclude that there is an intimate connection between the self and soul of a person. One way of viewing this connection is to think of the self as the social expression and reflection of the soul, or as the main medium through which the soul of one person can become known to another person. The most common means we have of experiencing the soul of another person is through our experience of interacting with the self of that person. In the language of Winnicott (1965), we could say that the various expressions of a true self are among the most direct reflections of the soul we are capable of experiencing. This suggests that the formative interpersonal environments responsible for the development of the selfs of persons play an equally key role in nurturing the souls of persons and helping their souls find expression in the world.

In a reinterpretation of what is involved in the "care of souls," Jim Ashbrook (1996) discusses how *minding the soul,* or remembering and attending to who we are, is a fundamental task of pastoral care and counseling (34). Ashbrook (1996) reports that at the urging of Rollo May, he undertook a study of the "functional meaning of soul" and determined that "the idea of soul identifies our uniqueness—our capacity for centered decisions, our capacity for taking initiative, in short, the primacy of the whole over the parts" (175–76). Continuing, Ashbrook indicates that "*soul is that which each of us can call our own. It is our unique essence, that which distinguishes us from everything else in the universe*" (178). This essence is integrally dependent upon the matrix of relationships one has with all levels of life, and it is formed in relationship with them and in reaction to them (Pfafflin 1995, 396).

Ashbrook (1996) calls us to consider soul as the integral and insepa-rable "core" of who we are, or our characteristic ways of experiencing and expressing reality (169). Depending upon memory as a reservoir upon which to draw (170), soul involves remembering and making meaning of the life experience unique to each of us (167). Ashbrook sees this meaning-making process as "the equivalent of integrating our expe-rience" (179). As we shall go on to explore in chapters six, seven, and eight, evil attacks the personal resources and integrating functions so crucial for remembering and meaning-making. This is one of the most profound ways in which evil can be viewed as not only involving an attack on a victim's self, but also as a direct attack upon her soul.

The calling out and into being of the true selves and souls of persons is facilitated and nurtured, or alternately frustrated and starved, by others with whom those persons are in relationship. If those interpersonal envi-ronments are traumatic and neglectful enough at the early stages of a person's life, or are incessantly traumatic, destructive, and abrasive throughout one's life, a profoundly disturbing question arises: "To what extent can the central self and soul of a person wither up and decompose from within or be ground up and ultimately destroyed from without?" We still cringe in horror when we recall the first patient who said, "All that was inherently me has been destroyed. I feel like I have been cored!"

When those elements necessary for evoking and sustaining the self are taken away or attacked, and coping mechanisms naturally used to defend the self—such as numbing, dissociation, and splitting—are rein-forced to the point they become a way of being and functioning in the world, the threshold has been crossed from trauma into the realm of evil. This is the case whether these defensive maneuvers are brought about by intentional cruelty, as in the case of torture, or unintentional cruelty, as in the case of some infants being reared within neglectful, impinging, or even hate-filled homes. It is the reinforcement of the naturally occurring defensive responses to an attack on the selfs and souls of persons that belies the presence of evil. In this sense, it is evil, not trauma, that changes these normal and adaptive responses to hurt into charactero-logical patterns that are so intransigent and difficult to change. Chroni-cally severe and repetitive trauma is so destructive of people because it crosses this boundary from trauma into the realm of evil.

A disturbingly blatant example of evil that clearly portrays the distinction between trauma and evil that we are presenting, and also demonstrates evil's directed attack on the self and soul of a person, concerns the case of a twenty-three-year-old, single female in outpatient pastoral psychotherapy. This woman had been repeatedly sexually abused, starting at the age of six, by an older male cousin. This abuse continued on a periodic yet unpredictable schedule at the time she presented herself for assistance. As a child, she had told her parents about this abuse. They did not believe her, refused to offer any protection, and stated that if "anything did happen" between her and her cousin, it must have been her fault. Over years of being repeatedly raped by this man, this woman had developed an almost automatic and reflexive ability to quickly dissociate in order to protect her self and escape the horrendous levels of physical and emotional pain she experienced. As she moved into early adolescence, she also developed the habit of cutting herself after these sexual attacks. She described this cutting as something that brought her relief and as something she did to appease the voices inside her head that shouted out to her that she was bad and ought to die. Cutting was also something she was so ashamed of that she actively hid it from others by wearing clothing that covered her entire body and even by avoiding medical exams that would require her to disrobe in any way.

This man was not only intimidating, but because of the family's denial and her own functional helplessness, he had free access to her at any time. Her dissociation had become such an automatic response that it now contributed to putting her in greater danger. This was manifested in the fact that, even as an adult woman, she would become helplessly compliant whenever he would come around and impose himself on her. Consequently, when she was twenty-three he was still raping her at will. At one point, he even forced her to house him in her apartment for a period of time. Because he was so intimately familiar with her and her dissociative tendencies and cutting rituals, he consciously took advantage of these processes to gain access to her and further humiliate, demean, and subjugate her. After raping her one night in her own apartment, he yelled out to her, "Why don't you go get your blades now and cut yourself. You haven't gone deep enough yet." Using this woman's naturally developed defenses, and habitual cutting behaviors, against her in such a profoundly destructive way can only be described as evil.

Evil Defined

As a way of more clearly conceptualizing how evil and trauma can be distinguished and how evil confounds and intensifies the impact of trauma on persons, the following definition is offered: Evil creates and builds upon brokenness in the world by threatening, attacking, destroying, and desecrating the integrity of the relational nature of life. Furthering and exploiting the naturally occurring divisions within and between persons, evil leads to increased fragmentation, alienation, and polarization as it turns people against themselves, others, their natural environments, and their God. Evil works against reconciliation and healing and is the chief obstacle and threat to the wholeness and interconnectedness of God's creation.

It is clear from this definition that evil can work at multiple levels within human systems (e.g., families, social institutions, and cultures) as well as within individual persons and the various dyadic relationships that comprise their interpersonal lives. These different planes of relationship are intimately connected and often interact in a reverberating manner with one another. What happens outside an individual has an effect on the internal world of that person and can produce effects that control and dominate a person's entire life, as well as the lives of all with whom she comes in contact. This means that evil affects all of us no matter where it makes itself known, and it means that evil must be addressed at each and every level of life. While the viewpoints and concepts presented in this book are an outgrowth of our work with the effects of evil on individuals, we believe they can also be interpreted and applied at higher systemic levels.

We saw in the review of how the self develops that we depend on the social networks in which we live to care for the souls with which we have been created and to evoke and sustain the selfs that become the expressions of our souls. Through our mutual interactions, we call one another into being and create one another. These interactions can further the naturally occurring divisions within our selfs and between us and others, or they can foster healing and reconciliation. One path leads to greater exclusion and violation of other people and parts of ourselves and is an expression of evil; the other leads to mutual respect, connection, integration, and wholeness and is an expression of mercy, grace, forgiveness, and love.

The definition of evil we are offering emphasizes its divisive and splitting nature. This suggests that any effective approach to reducing evil's influence must address these processes. For this reason, we will continue to discuss in succeeding chapters how persons can become defensively disengaged from their selfs and others, how split-off and dissociated parts within the self can develop a life of their own, and how the resulting disconnectedness increases the potential for evil. The more divisions within the self are kept defensively in place, the more they have the potential for influencing our lives in ways that leave us out of control and with no way of taking responsibility for what we do.

When more than one person in a relationship is engaged in an internal struggle of managing split-off parts of their selfs, the potential arises for the mutual projection of unacceptable parts of self onto and into the other through a projective identification process. The result of such a process is that each person begins to feel and act like she is not herself: the boundaries between self and other become blurred, emotional intensity builds as each person reacts to the unacceptable and disavowed parts of her self now lodged within the other, and cognitive confusion and behavioral lack of control rule the day. It is this type of process, exacerbated by stress-induced emotional reactivity, that often forms the ground out of which incidents of domestic abuse and violence erupt.

This type of process does not just occur within and between individuals, but can also occur within and between groups of people (e.g., religious groups, races, and nations). Within our own country for example, some of our most vehemently espoused negative responses to persons suffering from drug and alcohol addiction, homelessness, or other perceived "weaknesses" are actually expressions of our rage and dislike for the weakest and most disavowed parts of ourselves. In order to deal effectively with these processes, we need to develop courageous, creative, and inviting ways to work with the cut-off, disengaged, disenfranchised, and unacceptable parts of ourselves, others, and groups within our communities and world. The rigid, isolating, and self-righteous imposition of external power and control in dealing with these split-off parts or groups strengthens evil's influence rather than weakens it.

If evil is to be effectively dealt with, ways must be developed to heal and integrate disavowed parts of ourselves and our culture rather than respond to them in ways that threaten or alienate them and further divide us within and among ourselves. Some responses and approaches to this conundrum will be offered in later chapters.

Before moving on, it is important to state briefly what we mean by the term "integration." This term has already been used a good deal and will play a central role in the discussions to follow. By "integration" we mean the achievement of the internal capacity for appropriate, collaborative, and cooperative interchanges among the various distinct and differentiated aspects of one's internal world. Working together, these integrated dimensions comprise a person's self, and her integration contributes to self-cohesion and self-continuity across situations. When integration is lacking, one's capacity for self-continuity, intentional action, critical self-reflection, modulation of affect, responsibility-taking, and appropriately determined and morally guided behavior is greatly reduced.

Finally, the distinction we are offering between evil and trauma is no small matter. It is in fact critically important for a number of reasons. While understanding and working with *trauma* is clearly within the purview of science (e.g., psychology and physiology), addressing issues of *evil* also requires a willingness to embark upon a journey into the moral, ethical, and spiritual dimensions of life. This is not to suggest a separation between science and these other perspectives on life of the type we have witnessed in the debilitating separation of the physical, psychological, and spiritual dimensions of human life within Western culture. Rather, it is to recognize that healing from abuse, violence, and neglect requires a dialectic involving the physical, emotional, ethical, and spiritual dimensions of life. The more evil has been a dimension of a specific traumatic experience, the more important it will be to include in the healing process an appreciation for the moral, ethical, and spiritual dimensions of human life.

This means that caregivers working with cases of human-induced trauma—a category that comprises a large segment of persons suffering from a wide range of mental health disorders—must be willing and able to incorporate these dimensions into treatment processes, especially with persons who have strong faith and spiritual commitments. These dimensions will become a more intentional focus of the following chapters as they inform an approach to healing the divisions evil creates.

Part III

Healing the Self and Soul

6

A Call to Pastoral Care: Walking through the Valley of the Shadow of Death

IN HER REFLECTIONS of the wrenching experience of caring for parents who lost children in the bombing of the Murrah Federal Building in Oklahoma City, which occurred on April 19, 1995, at 9:02 A.M., Dianna Moore (1995) writes:

> As I sat with a number of parents who were waiting for the bodies of their children to be recovered, I was invited into a kind of loss, pain, and crisis of meaning that I had never experienced. Words could not touch its depths or its breadth. . . . But most of us strug- gled to be on this holy ground, this inexplicable messy ground with a loving and humble silence. We struggled to be with those who had to walk through this darkness rather then trying to somehow move them from pain/despair to healing.
>
> We found ourselves walking with the victims on the fragile ground where the secular, the sacred, the personal, and the political converge to make life so complex, rich, and often overwhelming. And in a new way I experienced this place where life and death intermingle and where no part of us is left untouched or unchanged. On this fragile ground, devastated victim and coun- selor struggle together with profound sadness, despair, rage, and intense longing for meaning. (5, 23)

This moving statement confronts us with the multidimensional havoc evil wreaks in people's lives and how it leaves no corner of one's life unaffected. It also aptly describes the disturbing and personal reac- tions touched off within caregivers when we "look evil in the face" and work with the powerful and frightening aspects of ourselves and others that set the stage for such tragedies. This experience is captured by the psalmist in the phrase "walk(ing) through the valley of the shadow of death" (Psalm 23, parenthesis added).

The Book of Psalms captures the pain of those devastatingly hurt by evil and left struggling for a sense of meaning and purpose. Setting this experience before us in lyrics and verses of poetry that reach into the otherwise often silent depths of our own experience, the Psalms help us find voice for the human struggles and hurts that afflict us all to one extent or another.

Paradoxically, the Psalms also capture the anguish and turmoil of those wrestling with overwhelming desires to strike out at others in revenge and retaliation for being hurt (e.g., Psalms 79 and 137). These passages put us in touch with dimensions within all persons that can lead to hurtful acts perpetrated against others. They also give expression to the strong and potentially destructive reactions and urges for vengeance we have in response to felt fear, pain, despair, and loss, especially when these intense emotions are triggered by those we consider to be our enemies (Brueggemann 1997, 630).

Revisiting the Definition of Evil: Some Background

The definition of evil presented in chapter five grows out of listening to the stories and messages people have brought to us about their experiences with destructive and hurtful human interactions. As a prelude to an in-depth examination of these interactions and how to intervene to reduce their destructive potential, as well as to heal and transform them, it is helpful to review what we have said about how evil works: "Evil creates and builds upon brokenness in the world by threatening, attacking, destroying, and desecrating the integrity of the relational nature of life. Furthering and exploiting the naturally occurring divisions within and between persons, evil leads to increased fragmentation, alienation, and polarization and turns people against themselves, others, their natural environments, and their God. Evil works against reconciliation and healing and is the chief obstacle and threat to the wholeness and interconnectedness of God's creation."

By design, this definition focuses attention on the forces within and between persons that destroy persons and relationships. These forces lead to behavioral expressions of abuse and violence toward self and others and support and exacerbate the already fractured lives of victims. Paradoxically, through the pain and despair they create, these forces also call out for healing.

We originally searched for a way to define evil that would be true to our experience of evil as it was making itself known in and through the lives of those with whom we were working and in the cultural milieu that formed the larger context for our work. This naturally drew us to those processes our counseling work suggested caused the most difficulty in the individual and relational lives of people. Primarily two types of counseling cases caught our attention in this regard. The first was our work with survivors of childhood sexual abuse and trauma. The second was our work with couples caught in abusive marital and family dynamics who often presented as having "just a few communication problems." Both types of cases were most often chronic in nature. In addition, behind the presenting symptoms and problems were persons with fragmented lives and relationships who were divided and at war within themselves.

As we studied these cases, we were struck by the chaotic and repetitious nature of these persons' lives and with the apparent lack of understanding and awareness they had about the actual roots of their difficulties. This reminded us of the reality and power of mental processes that occur outside of conscious awareness. These aspects of human mental life are not talked about much in present-day mental health circles. Consequently, they are easily overlooked, except when it becomes overtly clear that many times persons have no idea what their real problem is and what can help. Sometimes they think they know, but they are actually misinformed or deluded by mental and cultural processes that misguide them. Most of the time, there is a mixture of the known and unknown as we all "see through a glass darkly." At other times, of course, people are *clearly* aware and are the best judges of what their own difficulties are and what they most need. Learning to recognize which of these situations exists at any point in time is part of the *art* of effective caregiving, since each requires a different type of response.

Our attention was drawn, therefore, to those dynamics people use

defensively, unconsciously, and automatically to protect their developing selfs, but which also result in the greatest cost to their self-
awareness, general life satisfaction, sense of integrity and wholeness,
and interpersonal relationships. This brought us back to those internal mechanisms discussed in chapter three that enable persons to
split and divide themselves within, and wall off, and attempt to get
rid of, elements of themselves and their life experience that are
problematic to them in some major way. It became increasingly clear
to us that the entrenched use of those same mechanisms was not
only exacerbated by experiences of devastating abuse and neglect,
but that those mechanisms also played a major role in producing
conditions conducive to the perpetration of abuse and neglect.

Focusing on the Divisions within Persons

In chapter four, we described how people go about protecting themselves in various ways in response to impinging and hurtful environments. Chief among these are the ability to disengage defensively from
that which is hurtful and the ability to split-off, segregate, and/or get rid
of, various aspects of one's self and life experience so as not to be overcome or continuously disturbed and frightened by them. This segregation and "getting rid of" process takes a multitude of forms but includes
the splitting-off of experience, the splitting-off of affect, the splitting-off
of basic needs, and/or the splitting-off of other dimensions of one's self
and experience deemed unacceptable, disturbing, or in some way dangerous to one's self or significant others.

The ability to disengage self and segregate various dimensions of
experience within the self are a manifestation of two main ego defense
mechanisms—dissociation and splitting. These are supported by the
additional mental processes of projection and projective identification
that are designed to protect the self from some disturbing elements
within it by getting rid of that which is defensively split-off.

The active use of these mechanisms, and the presence of symptoms
resulting from their use, is more common in caregiving settings than is
often recognized. Examples of presenting complaints pointing to the
possible presence of these phenomena include the following: (1) a feeling of not being integrated within one's self; (2) acute and chronic affec-

tive volatility that makes interpersonal relationships chaotic; (3) dreadful existential anxiety or panic resulting from powerful affects and needs being mobilized, pushing for recognition, or being spontaneously and mysteriously triggered by life events and interpersonal encounters; (4) alcohol/drug abuse reflecting desperate attempts to numb oneself from the pain and grief created by overwhelming and unintegrated life experience, or to gain access to important split-off dimensions of self that are otherwise defensively sealed-off outside of awareness; (5) a sense of life being unreal due to living out of a detached stance or a protective false-self; and (6) lives traumatically shattered into parts and fragments, some of which vie for literal control of one's body and life, that leave persons with a tragic absence of personal continuity and identity. The deleterious effects of projection and projective identification are most clearly seen in chaotic and abusive relationships that present for marital/relationship counseling, in family cases involving an acting-out child or adolescent who has become the identified patient, and in persons who have a history of difficulty interacting in various institutional/work settings.

In our experience, these types of symptoms are common in many persons who present for counseling and psychotherapy, and include persons labeled by caregivers as "difficult people," and persons who act out in ways that bring them into conflict with other people and the law. These are also symptoms found in a wide spectrum of persons irrespective of socioeconomic level. This is not surprising since the traumatically wounding life experiences that lay the psychological groundwork for these symptoms do not respect socioeconomic boundaries. The self disorder and/or trauma history often underlying symptoms such as these are not generally recognized, understood, or addressed from illness and symptom-based models of assessment and treatment represented by the *DSM-IV*.

It is our belief that therapeutic approaches designed to work effectively with these split-off dimensions of self that exist within individuals will go a long way in promoting healing in two areas: (1) helping victims heal from abuse and violence that have torn their lives apart and often lead to acts of self-harm, such as beating oneself, cutting oneself, and even killing oneself, and (2) healing those divisions within persons that lead to abuse and violence directed at others.

The sections that follow seek to expand further on these internal mechanisms and provide insight into issues that must be addressed if the processes described in our definition of evil are to be changed and transformed.

Learning from Severely Hurt and Traumatized Persons

Before moving into the more technical dimensions of working with mental processes that result from and lead to the expression of evil in human interactions, we want to share some "non-clinical" lessons gleaned from the many patients who have courageously and patiently taught us. Perhaps most importantly, we have learned that in those persons who seek help, there is a persistent and seemingly unquenchable drive for connection with another human being who will care and is willing and able to help.

Many of the more severely abused persons seen by various caregivers have experienced repetitive failed attempts at getting help. These seem to be the result of numerous variations on two major themes: (1) symptomatically, rather than dynamically, based assessment approaches that pay little attention to the types of mental processes discussed here and fail to provide caregivers with an adequate understanding of a patient's internal dilemmas, and (2) unsuccessfully managed interpersonal dynamics between the caregiver and the survivor leading to a failure in the working alliance and ultimately to termination of the helping relationship. This termination can be precipitous in appearance or the result of a gradual process of caregiver and survivor wearing down.

While numerous factors contribute to the frequent playing out of these themes, there are two predominant factors that consistently reappear. The first factor is a general lack of "adequate enough" knowledge within the helping professions about the marvelous and mysterious complexity and capability of human mental process. The second factor concerns caregivers untrained and unskilled in the knowledge and techniques available in working with these processes and the powerful dynamics they stir up in the caregiving encounter. Despite these overwhelming lacunae and the pitfalls we stumble into as a result of their presence, desperate persons continually search for help, and we cannot help but marvel at the seemingly unquenchable drive for healing and relatedness that exists within the human spirit.

An equally important lesson we have learned is that caregivers cannot do this work without being willing to listen and be instructed by those who seek help from them. We are as much learners as helpers. Jon Allen and others are productively pursuing this view at the Menninger Clinic in his psychoeducational research and writing project. This project has lent credibility to the creative conceptualization and discovery of knowledge that is possible when patient and caregiver work together in a consultative and mutually respectful relationship of equals who both have areas of expertise (Allen, 1995).

Most unsettling of all, we have learned that caregivers cannot do this work without being willing to embark upon a lonely, tumultuous, and sometimes terror-filled journey of their own. This journey will take caregivers into split-off aspects of themselves they did not know existed. It will lift one to heights of joy and hope and plunge one into the depths of grief and despair; it will cause one to rejoice in the marvelous diversity and resiliency of human personality and simultaneously cause one to react with revulsion at the utter ugliness and cruelty humans are capable of perpetrating on one another. This journey will elicit a gratefulness for the ability of people to share sacred moments with one another, and it will elicit a profound sense of helplessness and incompetence that makes caregivers question their competence and ability to help anyone.

The following sections pertain to a more in-depth discussion of mental processes that enable the human psyche to separate and compartmentalize aspects of self, other, and experience. It is the entrenched and highly active (and reactive) nature of these psychological processes, operating outside of awareness, that is a result and potential cause of evil as we are defining it.

Splitting

As described in chapter three, the main function of splitting in early development is to keep "contradictory primitive affect states separated from each other" (Kernberg 1966, 238). In his discussion of splitting, James Grotstein (1985) refers to the work of Gazzaniga and LeDoux (1978), which suggests that the two cerebral hemispheres of the brain do not fully communicate with one another until adolescence. This provides a physiological basis for the inborn ability of the infant to keep information from the bicameral mind separated so the full dimensional impact of life experience remains, in a sense, deadened until the person is more developmentally capable of handling it (Grotstein 1985, 7).

Grotstein (1985) defines splitting as "the activity by which the ego discerns differences within itself and its objects, or between itself and objects" (3). He goes on to state: "In the perceptual or cognitive sense, an act of discriminative separation is involved, while in the defensive sense splitting implies an unconscious phantasy by which the ego can split itself off from the perception of an unwanted aspect of itself, or can split an object into two or more objects in order to locate polarized, immiscible qualities separately" (3).

Consequently, splitting is both a mental mechanism and a means of experiencing, or *not* experiencing, one's world. This process can be active, that is consciously or unconsciously driven, or passive as in the case of it just "happening" in the face of some overwhelming experience (Grotstein 1985, 4). Splitting can therefore be viewed from a cognitive, phenomenological, or defensive perspective, and it has a wide range of influence over other key psychological processes.

Continuing his focus on the influence splitting has on perception, Grotstein (1985) indicates that "splitting . . . alters the perception of the object by inappropriate divisions, by splintering and fragmentation" (9). This splitting of one's "perception of an object is also associated with a splitting of the self, divided along lines comparable to a cleavage in the object" (9–10). Normal development brings with it the development of repression, which leads to the continuation of splitting outside one's awareness of it (18).

With regard to the defensive use of splitting, Grotstein (1985) offers the following: "The significance of defensive splitting lies in the experience of confronting alienated aspects of oneself. 'Split-off' really means that a part of one's being has undergone alienation, mystification, mythification, and re-personification—in effect, has become someone else, an alien presence within. . . . Defensive splitting is an act of the imagination which bequeaths to the split-off portions of the personality a life-support system with the will to live, which then repersonifies this creation in a way that it might as well be thought of as someone else—were it not that some unconscious, mysterious connection, much like déjà vu, persists to cause the splitter the agony of being haunted by a split which he can neither remember or forget!" (11).

Although a normal process of human mental life, splitting can function in an abnormal fashion by attacking cognitive and "perceptual linkages," and by causing "abnormal cleavages between objects and their relationships to the self" (Grotstein 1985, 211). Grotstein then goes on to say, "The term 'splits' denotes separate subpersonality organizations within the psyche, which operate overtly, covertly, simultaneously, sequentially, or alternately. Clinically, we are less aware of their independent existence because of the organizing, integrating, and rectifying capacity of the ego. Generally, we observe them compositely as a montage" (212).

In this regard, the continuing and "alternate activation of contradictory ego states" to which Kernberg (1966) refers not only points to the presence of splitting as an active mental process, but is also the chief quality of splitting that causes such severe internal and interpersonal instability and conflict (238).

Changes of State and State-Dependent Learning

Although comprising only a small portion of our counseling work, our work with persons suffering from dissociative identity disorder has been particularly challenging and informative. Persons divided within themselves in this way represent one of the most traumatized, suffering, and fragmented segments of the nonpsychotic mental health population. While these patients are not considered psychotic, there are frequently psychotic dimensions to this disorder that add to its complexity and contribute to premature and misleading diagnostic errors. In our experience, for example, some alters who suffered and now hold particularly violent and neglectful experiences beginning at preverbal stages of development can be blatantly psychotic. More commonly within a system of alters, there are particular delusional beliefs such as each alter has a separate physical body. Patients with this disorder also frequently experience various types of hallucinations. Because of the severely abusive and violent nature of the experiences suffered by these persons, our work with them propelled us into the trauma literature in a search for helpful and practical advice (for a classic in this regard, see Chu 1988).

The more we learned, the more we recognized this particular group of patients was teaching us a great deal about working with other patients as well. This was especially the case in our work with those patients suffering from symptoms that included self-fragmentation and lack of self-cohesion, splits in self and object representations, rapidly shifting ego states, split-off and conflicted affective states, and severe childhood abuse and trauma. As time went on, we became aware of ways that this complex and difficult work helped us in *all* our therapeutic work. One of the most important lessons we learned was to look for and recognize changes of state that will often occur within a therapy session.

Learning to recognize the presence of different alter personalities (alters) within an individual and when a person was switching from one of these part-selves (parts) to another was particularly helpful in this regard. These parts develop internally behind barriers of varying degrees of dissociation and amnesia and exert varying degrees of control over a person's daily living. While different in some key conceptual dimensions, we were struck by how similar in function these parts seemed to more commonly described psychological entities, such as "internal children" (Price 1996), "ego states" (Putnam 1988), and the "true-selves" and "false-selves" discussed earlier.

Learning to recognize the presence of different alters also helped us learn to look for indications a person was switching, or moving, from one alter to another, one ego state to another, one state of consciousness to another, and even from a false-self to a true-self, and vice versa. The more we paid attention to this switching, or state-changing, phenomenon, the more we recognized elements of it in many of our patients.

Walter Young (1988) defines an ego state as a "specific and consistent mental organization that is dominated by a particular affect that links a particular self representation with a particular object representation" (35). He goes on to say, "A given ego state may vary within limits according to its affective variance, but is relatively stable in its self and object representations" (35). In summary, he says: "The term ego state is obviously an oversimplified rendering of a highly complex mental organization that includes multiple contributions from instinctual urges, character traits, defensive constellations, somato-sensory processing, ego ideals, and moral pressures that reflect not only states of the ego, but many processes normally understood as functions originating from id and superego components as well" (35).

The process of changing states of consciousness in an appropriate and smooth manner, as well as the capacity to recover from disruptions of state, is something that a child learns with the help of caretakers who initially facilitate these processes for the child (Putnam 1988). When this process has not been facilitated by caretakers, when different states exist without much co-consciousness, and when mental and physiological regulatory processes are undeveloped, changes of state can be quite disruptive and unpredictable.

Learning to be aware of changes of state in those we work with is crucial, since when switching occurs rapidly, learning does not occur (Putnam 1988, 27). The extent to which therapy is a learning process that requires some self-continuity of presence and attention, unconscious, spontaneous, and uncontrolled switching during the therapy hour can greatly limit its effectiveness. While some patients have the ability to switch states without drawing attention to themselves in any obvious way, many switches can be noticed by caregivers who are attuned to their possible presence. Signs of such switching noted by Putnam (1988) include changes in personal dimensions, such as affect, cognitive and perceptual style, speech, facial expressions, and interpersonal relatedness (26). Sudden changes in countertransference reactions within the caregiver can also be an indication there has been a significant shift in state within a particular patient. One of the more common tip-offs we have noticed in clearly dissociative patients is a quick glance at a clock in the office in an attempt to reorient themselves and figure out how much time has gone by since their last awareness of the time remaining in a given session.

In the process of learning about state-changes, we also learned about state-dependent learning. This concept describes how learning occurs when a person is in a particular state of consciousness, and that recall of what was learned while in a particular state is best recalled when one returns to a similar state. Particular states of consciousness can be induced by the contexts we are in at any particular time. Thus, a context that replicates the one in which a person originally had a given experience or learned something, will reactivate access to memories of the experience and what was originally learned at that time. This process helps explain some of the seemingly spontaneous abreactions troublesome to survivors.

A nontraumatic example of this process can be seen in reference to some complex activity such as skiing. A person somewhat adept at skiing who is standing in a living room in stocking feet on a summer day will have some difficulty verbalizing and demonstrating to a friend the different moves involved in skiing down a mountain. If both persons are on a ski slope with snow on the ground, the information needed to ski and teach skiing more easily returns. Likewise, the moves required to hop off a lift and ski down a slope may be totally outside our awareness until that moment when we slip off the lift and our skis hit the snow. At that point, what we have learned over many years of skiing suddenly returns—we hope!

The changes in states of consciousness being discussed here can occur as instantaneously and without warning as do the mental and behavioral processes involved in the common sequence of driving down a neighborhood street, suddenly seeing a squirrel running out in front of the car, and slamming on the brakes and swerving to miss it. These events take on the quality of instinctual responses that occur outside of conscious intent, are ego-syntonic, and have great survival value. In persons well practiced at switching from years of abuse, and in those who use switching as a habitual response to stressors, these same characteristics make such switching processes difficult to change. On the other hand, learning how to get control over these processes is crucial for effecting positive changes in one's sense of self-integrity and self-continuity, in one's life circumstances and in one's taking responsibility for her life.

Dissociation

In chapter two, dissociation was discussed as one of the processes operative at a cultural level that is responsible for keeping evil hidden from us. We want to focus here on dissociation as a mental process.

In a helpful manner, Walter Young (1988) has discussed the difference between the defense mechanism of splitting most often associated with borderline personality disorder and the splitting of the self into dissociated alter personalities and ego states that occurs in severe dissociative processes. He does this by calling attention to "certain assumptions about psychic structure" that the defense mechanism of splitting requires but dissociation does not. These include the activity of underlying contradictory ego states "organized around polarized affects and introjects," the existence of a "primitive personality organization," and an "underlying structural defect" that takes the form of a lack of integration (33). The distinction between splitting and dissociation is important for diagnostic and treatment purposes, since it is not uncommon for patients with dissociative identity disorder to be mistreated as if their principal diagnosis is borderline personality disorder. In terms of our discussion, we can perhaps best think of dissociation as a state of disconnectedness existing within a person that can vary according to degree of severity.

By learning to recognize dissociative processes, we began to be more sensitive to the subtle shifts made by many survivors as they periodically "space out" at points in a therapy session. A helpful way to think about this process is to think of it in terms of moving into an ever deepening trance-like state of consciousness in which one sensually disconnects from the immediate surroundings. These episodes of drifting into a dissociated state in which attention to the outside world is radically narrowed and eventually suspended indicate the person is no longer present and tracking with the caregiver. This process of drifting into a dissociated state of "mindlessness" (Allen 1998) is so prevalent that caregivers would be well advised to look for it in their work with all survivors of early and/or chronic abuse.

This characteristic of dissociation makes it an obviously effective defense mechanism in cases of severe and chronic abuse from which physical escape is impossible. In the majority of life situations, however, the implementation of this defense actually *increases* the potential for suffering further harm. There are a number of reasons why this is the case and why it is important for a caregiver to recognize this drifting process as it is occurring—which allows some intervention to help patients learn to gain control of it.

First, if a person is to be helped, she and the caregiver must be in the same place at the same time and as fully present to themselves and one another as possible. Dissociation moves a person mentally to another place, a place that is usually isolated and separated from where the caregiver and patient actually are. Second, as one moves increasingly to a deeper level of dissociation, awareness of one's external surroundings narrows and the synthetic functions of the ego necessary for information processing and learning to occur are suspended. Third, as awareness of one's external world narrows, awareness of one's fantasy- and memory-filled internal world can widen (Allen 1995, 75–76). To the extent this world is filled with split-off and unintegrated aspects of hurtful and terrifying experience and/or with rich and vivid fantasies and delusions, moving into such a dissociated state can actually *increase* the potential for being retraumatized from within.

The traumatization brought on by this self-induced process of dissociative drifting is much akin to the retraumatization that can occur in the precipitous and unplanned use of clinical hypnosis with persons who have severe, chronic, and unintegrated abuse histories. In such cases, a patient who already has a learned ability to rapidly dissociate can quickly lose her bearings in reality and suspend her ego functioning. While moving into trance, she can be suddenly confronted with the chaos and terror of split-off pockets of overwhelming experience and unneutralized affect. In such cases, a startled caregiver can be suddenly confronted with a decompensated, ungrounded, and terrorized person.

It is crucial, therefore, that caregivers learn techniques of grounding to help patients remain present and reverse this dissociative drifting when it begins (Allen 1995, 87–88). Techniques of distracting, as well as self-soothing and calming, are also important, as are learned methods of containment and of accessing and discharging affect in a graduated and controlled fashion. It is also important to teach these techniques to patients for use outside the caregiving relationship.

Many survivors of severe and chronic early childhood abuse have repeatedly used dissociation to the point where it has become an immediate and ego-syntonic response to any stressor. In fact, this process can be spontaneously and automatically initiated with no apparent internal or external trigger. In such cases, the learned and habitual use of dissociation becomes a chief obstacle to learning from experience, as well as to working through the normal stresses and strains of psychotherapy, other caregiving relationships, and the normal stresses and strains of life itself.

While it is important to be sympathetic toward the historical causes that have made this defense such an active part of a survivor's life, it is all the more crucial to her present and future welfare to point out the many ways its ongoing use sets her up for continued abuse and interferes with effecting change in her current life situation. This requires education and persistence, since a survivor can easily feel as though the caregiver is asking her to give up the only effective means she knows of numbing herself enough to stay alive amid the overwhelming pain in her life. This is one of those places where the caregiver and patient can both begin to feel caught between what seems like equally impossible, unappealing, and potentially dangerous alternatives.

Listening to Stories and Perspectives from Within

Another aspect of working with those suffering from dissociative identity disorder that was helpful and applicable to work with other types of patients was learning to attune ourselves to the life stories of numerous alters. These included the recognition that each could be a different age and take a different form (Hendrickson et al., 1990]) and that each alter has its own unique life history and perspective.

The developmental levels and histories of each alter are important to know in order to determine how to talk and work with particular parts so as to piece together a picture of the life history of the person. This seems analogous to a quilting process in which different pieces sewn together by different persons become sewn together into a coordinated whole. In this illustration, each quilting piece contains one part's perception of all it has experienced in life by itself, or in conjunction with other alters, and that part's unique view of the characteristics, motivations, and lives of all other alters known to it. Together with the host personality's perspective, these stories comprise a relatively complete autobiography of the person's life. After reflecting on the wealth of useful information and insightful perspectives shared by different parts of herself, one woman once said, "This is like listening to the stories of my lost and found selves."

This experience has attuned us to the various perspectives all people have on their lives at different points in time along their continuing developmental journey, and how some of these perspectives can become frozen in time and left unaffected by alternative points of view and subsequent experience, development, and/or maturation. It seems this may also be the case with "inner children" and even true- and false-selves (personal conversation with Susan Pierce, October 1997).

Therapeutic Mediation

Learning to negotiate and therapeutically mediate amid all the mixed loyalties and amnesiacally influenced patterns of complex relationships existing among alters and the various levels and subsystems into which they are often organized was something else we learned that could be generalized to our work with other patients. This process is quite similar to working with an identified patient's family system. In this particular case, however, the "family" is composed of various internal dimensions of a person's self. The importance of this mediation approach to alliance building and therapeutic intervention is particularly clear with "persecutory alters" (Watkins and Watkins 1988; Goodman and Peters 1995). These particular alters often manifest a paradoxical mixture of roles involving internal persecution (and self-harm) and protection from the major perpetrators of the original abuse.

In our experience, a persecutory alter is often an internalization of the abuser that at one time served a survival function but in the present becomes a continuing source of fear, self-loathing, potential self-harm, and, in rare instances usually involving the experience of being cornered, potential harm to others. Quite often, one function of such an alter has been to terrorize the person from within so as to prevent her from lapsing into behavior that would put her at risk of further harm from the actual perpetrator. Examples of this would include her telling someone about the abuse, saying "No!" or not otherwise doing what she was told, or breaking some rule that would set off the abuser and result in severe punishment.

Gaining the trust and respect of these alters, empathizing with their difficult yet important function over the years, and gradually teaching them new, safer, and more gracious ways of fulfilling their protecting functions greatly facilitates healing and stabilization. Not establishing such an alliance or doing something that threatens the self-image or power position of such an alter can likewise increase the potential for harmful acting-out against self or others and can result in tremendous conflictual battles within the person herself. Learning to work with these alters is much akin to learning to respect, court, and analyze resistances in traditional psychotherapy (Reich 1972, chapters 3 and 4) or negotiating with powerful figures in a dysfunctional family system. Just as it has also been our experience that a successful alliance with a transformed persecutory alter can be one of the strongest and most helpful alliances a caregiver will have in terms of bringing about positive change in the larger mental system, so it is with alliances with patients' resistances and/or family members.

As a result of all that these patients have taught us, we have become mindful of how learning to work with the internal processes and systems of persons is helpful in working with the *interpersonal* systems in the outside world where people routinely interact with one another with varying degrees of direct knowledge and trust. In short, whether we study life from a macro- or micro-level perspective, we end up working with similar processes.

Working with Persons in Chaotic and Abusive Relationships

Along with our individual work with survivors of childhood abuse and neglect, we have also worked a great deal with chaotic and abusive couples. One or both of the persons comprising these couples tend to manifest one or more of the following patterns: one person's self feels threatened and/or unsupported by the other; one person's chief method of protecting and defending the self is itself a threat to the self and selfobject needs of the other; there is an attempt to place blame and responsibility outside of self and onto the other; there is an inability or reluctance to look within self for the roots of one's difficulties with the other; there is little respect and empathy shown for the other; there is a sense of being caught up in interactions over which each feels little control and about which each has little understanding; and at least one person feels "unlike" her/himself during times the couple experiences the greatest distress and turmoil.

Increasingly we have viewed these persons as attempting to live and relate to one another in the midst of powerful and complex personal dynamics of which they are unaware, but which control much of their personal and interpersonal lives. These dynamics often escalate and drive incidents of domestic abuse and violence and seem primarily related to one or both of the following dynamic processes: (1) the experience of one's self being threatened and overwhelmed by the other—i.e., one becoming a traumatogenic object to the other; and (2) the activity of split-off parts within one's self and/or partner that, while outside of awareness, nevertheless determine and control the confusing and terrifying interactional patterns in which each feels caught. Because of their importance and prevalence, we would now like to discuss each of these in some detail.

A Threat to the Other's Self

In this first cluster of cases, there is often the lack of a cohesive self in one or both partners. Despite outward appearances and a strong self-presentation, the self can be quite fragile and ill-defended. This in turn contributes to the creation of an internal state of constant alert so the self will not be threatened or overwhelmed by the other in some unexpected way. This takes on more complexity in those cases where both individuals lack cohesive selves and where the very things one needs to feel safe and secure are the very things that most threaten the other. This is often the underlying dynamic, for example, in those relationships in which one partner distances and the other pursues, or in which one partner fears engulfment and the other fears abandonment. Another example occurs in relationships in which one partner needs to receive affection in a certain way that is unfamiliar and uncomfortable for the other to give. It is not uncommon in these types of situations for one or both partners to feel as if the other is an "enemy" who may say, "I love you," but interacts in a fashion that feels like, "I want to destroy you!"

In such cases, we have found the following four-step *conjoint* process to be helpful in disentangling the destructive web that has been woven. Each step will often take more than one therapy session, and, in severe cases, these steps may need to be repeated until enough internal and systemic shifting has occurred as to bring more stability to the relationship.

The first step is to allow the couple's intense interactional process to unfold in a conjoint context but in a fashion in which the therapist actively intervenes at points to stop destructive interactions and to keep the intensity manageable for all parties present. This can sometimes be done in a more disengaged and controlled fashion by asking each partner to describe *to the therapist* a recent encounter that represents his or her characteristic pattern. It is also crucial early on to establish signals each can use with the other to call "time out" if interactions at home begin to escalate, and to obtain a commitment from each person to honor those signals and do whatever is necessary for safety to be re-established between each partner. A basic message that needs to be delivered to the couple here is that they have done enough damage to one another and their relationship already, and that any further damage will destroy any likelihood that the relationship can be salvaged and healed. By actively intervening to manage the interactions between partners and reduce the tension within those interactions, the therapist models the importance of control. Risks of premature termination at this point include continuing high levels of distress and hurt, the inability to recover from the large amount of previous damage to the couple's individual selves and their relationship, and a fear of impending loss of power and control if things do change.

The second step is to work with each person to identify how she or he feels during the encounter and what each most basically wants and needs from the other at these times. The important element here is to focus on feeling and need states rather than thinking and to keep each person focused on self rather than other. This is the most difficult part of the work since it involves disentangling them from one another psychologically and emotionally by facilitating some increased degree of differentiation. To be successful here, the therapist must work to keep each person focused on self while remaining overtly sensitive to the hurts each will report suffering at the hands of the other, the subsequent anger experienced toward the other, and the normal desire to protect self by defending self and retaliating. This is another place where the couple can be reminded that their characteristic ways of interacting have been hurtful and destructive of one another and the relationship, and they cannot afford any additional hurt. Significant risks to premature termination at this stage include an increased sense of personal vulnerability, a discomfort with the increased focus on self, and the fear of losing the symbiotic or enmeshed attachment perceived to be crucial to one's psychic and emotional survival.

The third step in the process is to help each person see and understand at a *cognitive* level how the interactions between what each wants and needs from the other in order to feel safe and secure is perceived as threatening to the wants, needs, and self of the partner. This is the place where there is an opportunity to help each partner build empathy for one another. Empathy is often possible at this point because each is more sensitized to his/her own and the other's needs, as well as to the sense of threat each experiences. By this time the threat has lessened, a relative sense of safety has been established, and the view of the other as "the enemy" has been changed to a view more along the lines of "mutually wounded and concerned friend." Premature termination can occur at this point due to one or both partners becoming overwhelmed by grief, hurt, and/or a sense of accountability.

The fourth and last step is to decide the best therapeutic context in which to do the major share of the reparative work usually necessary with each person. This is most often based on an assessment of the nature and extent of the work to be done and an evaluation of the pros and cons, for each individual and the relationship, of doing that work within an individual or conjoint framework. The most common pitfall at this juncture is a desire on the part of one or both partners to terminate therapy, since at this point the acute stress that precipitated their crisis has been substantially reduced.

Projecting Split-off Parts of the Self

In this second type of case, the fragmented internal world of one or both of the individuals involved contributes to the lack of a cohesive and consistent self with which to relate to the other. This, of course, also creates an unstable internal world for the person(s) involved, leaving her/him in a constant state of anxiety about possible self-fragmentation. In this situation, a couple's interactions with each another are most commonly driven by unintegrated and polarized affective states and/or by unmet yet mobilized selfobject needs, which are periodically activated and contribute to the great intensity and hostility with which the partners typically interact with each another.

In addition, these couples often engage in attempts to manage their own internal worlds by externalizing disturbing parts of them, thereby creating confusion and hostility in those around them. The chief defense mechanism used for this purpose is projective identification. Through this process, a person projects parts of her/himself onto and/or into another person and then attempts to manage and control those parts by managing and controlling that other person. This can obviously lead to intense, bewildering, manipulative, and quite dangerous interchanges.

Grotstein (1985) offers one of the most helpful and thorough treatments of projective identification (also see Malin and Grotstein 1966; Adler and Rhine 1988; Scharff and Scharff 1991, esp. chapter 3; and Slipp 1984, esp. chapter 4). Depending on the mental process of splitting to provide the unwanted and split-off aspects of the self that will be projected, Grotstein indicates that projective identification is "a mental mechanism whereby the self experiences the unconscious phantasy of translocating itself or aspects of itself into an object for exploratory or defensive purposes" (123). The many functions of projective identification include (1) being a primitive and preverbal form of communication between mother and infant, (2) being a way of ridding the self of some unwanted or feared aspect, (3) being a way of attempting to control or disappear into the object, and (4) being a way of having someone else "hold for safe-keeping" an aspect of self one is not yet capable of handling on her/his own, thereby creating a needed sense of safety and security that is otherwise unachievable.

Used defensively, this process is a form of "disidentification" since the self is attempting to rid itself of some unwanted aspect by placing it into another. As Grotstein (1985) states: "If projective identification is defensive, the self may believe that through translocation it can rid itself of unwanted, split-off aspects; but it may also have the phantasy that it can enter the object so as to (actively) control it, or disappear into it (passively) in order to evade feelings of helplessness" (123).

The defensive use of this process within the context of intimate interpersonal relationships can be devastating. In this regard, Grotstein (1985) states that projective identification is "implicated in states of confusion, disorientation, autistic detachment, claustrophobia and agoraphobia, and phantasies of controlling and being controlled. Object relations under the influence of projective identification are characterized by coercion, manipulation, ensorcelment, seduction, intimidation, ridicule by imitative caricature, and martyrdom" (123–24).

William Goldstein (1991) offers the following framework in which to understand the projective identification process within a *therapeutic* context. This framework is illustrated in figure 6. The first step (see figure 6, point 1) occurs when a part of the self is projected into the object. This loss of part of one's self and the lodging of it within another person produces a number of possible reactions within the projector. These include a blurring of boundaries between the projector and the recipient; the projector feeling a sense of loss and emptiness as a result of giving up a part of self, and/or feeling at one with, estranged from, or even threatened by the recipient; and the recipient feeling related to the projector by virtue of the fact she/he now contains part of the other.

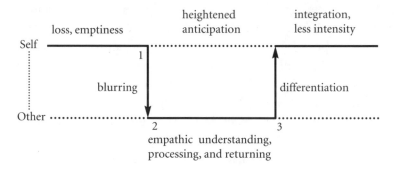

Figure 6: Projective Identification (Therapeutic)

The second step (see figure 6, point 2) occurs when the recipient begins to be controlled from within by that which has been projected and when the interpersonal interaction between the projector and the recipient takes the form of the recipient feeling actively pressured into thinking, feeling, and acting in accordance with the projection. The recipient of the projection most often feels at this point as if she/he is being compelled to act out of character and can feel ashamed and guilty as a result of this loss of integrity. A person who has experienced this process may even comment, "I don't know what got into me! I usually don't act like that."

The third step (see figure 6, point 3) involves the reinternalization of the projection after it has been psychologically processed by the recipient. The goal here is to reunite the person with that part of the self that needed to be projected in the first place. To be therapeutic, however, this must occur in a fashion that provides the projector a new and less threatening way of relating to this split-off and disturbing aspect of self. This may simply take the form of the recipient holding the projection and not reacting to it, expelling it, or being consumed or destroyed by it. As the person who made the projection watches intently to see how the recipient responds and relates to that disturbing part of her/himself that was projected, she/he can begin to formulate new ways of relating to it.

What most often occurs in the course of *nontherapeutic* and regular social interactions, or in the more intense interactions between intimate partners, is quite different and is more often destructive than constructive (see figure 7).

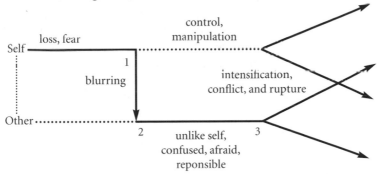

Figure 7: Projective Identification (Nontherapeutic)

This is the case because the interactions between partners are almost entirely composed of this projective identification process. The result is that neither party understands what is happening, no one has control over this process, and it ignites almost spontaneously. Each person is involved in the complex process of projecting a part (or parts) of her/himself, receiving the part projected by the partner, feeling controlled from within by the projection received, reacting to the projection in ways that threaten the projector, and feeling compelled to act behaviorally in accordance with the projection received. This obviously becomes a very complex, intense, and confusing process, which few people can sort out on their own or extricate themselves from in a controlled fashion. These are the very characteristics that make it so potentially dangerous and violent.

In working with the projective identification process therapeutically in couple work, a therapist can follow an outline similar to the one offered for working with persons who threaten each other's self as was discussed in the previous section. In this type of case, however, the therapist uses her/his own countertransference reactions to each partner and the partners' responses to one another to understand the nature of what each partner splits-off and projects outward. Work is also done with each partner to develop the strength and resources necessary to *not* initially respond to the projection from the other and not to accept or hold onto the projection forced upon oneself, but rather to accept responsibility for those parts of oneself each projects and to do the work needed to heal the divisions within oneself that lead to one's own need to project.

As a result of these interventions, the intensity within each person and the relationship initially increases since each partner is increasingly *unable* to make use of this effective defense (projective identification). The therapist's primary role in all of this is to provide a "good enough" therapeutic framework (or container) in which the projections that occur can be held and slowly processed, and to constantly look for avenues in which the projections that occur can be returned in a nonthreatening way to the person from whom they came. If this is successful, the interactions within the couple will gradually become less intense, and each partner will feel increasingly secure since his/her respective projections are now being received and treated with more care and respect than previously experienced. In essence, the lesson being taught is that it is appropriate to use a therapist as a container for split-off parts of one's self, but it is not appropriate to use others for this purpose, especially when it is destructive.

This projective identification process can play an active role in all interactions between caregivers and survivors irrespective of the context and format of their working relationship (i.e., even outside formal therapeutic settings). It plays a major role in provoking the countertransference reactions within caregivers that result in the types of premature terminations referred to earlier. This process is also vital in creating the wide range of reactions caregivers have to the material that survivors share with them, including the creation of feelings of confusion, fear, and profound helplessness.

In closing this section, it is important to note that caregivers who work with victims of abuse and violence will often feel a need to provide answers to the existentially disturbing life situations and questions that are ever present in survivors. When this happens, a caregiver can feel compelled to do something or say something to "make a difference." This can be understood as a form of the projective identification process in the sense that the survivor transfers to the caregiver the existential questions she has that beg for answers and also transfers the intolerable feelings of anxiety and fear associated with having no control and not knowing what to do. While this can help the caregiver existentially know more directly what a survivor's dilemma is, the caregiver can hinder the process by offering premature solutions and making interventions that cause the survivor to feel in even less control of her situation. In these cases, in order to relieve his/her own anxiety, the caregiver becomes an "answer bearer" and becomes caught in the same dilemma the victim is in—feeling the burden of responsibility for something he/she did not create and cannot fix but must learn to hold.

At the same time, this process provides the informed and skilled caregiver with an existential and intimately empathic understanding of the survivor's felt dilemma. The projective identification process can be beneficial in the healing process to the extent that caregivers can hold, rather than impulsively react to, that which is projected into them, and use that experience to inform their intervention strategies. This approach, however, requires a willingness on the part of a skilled caregiver to be used as a temporary container of aspects of another person that may be weak and fragile or strong and potentially dangerous. This not only requires a high level of psychological and emotional development within the caregiver, but also is best done within a wider context of supportive and available resources, which undergird the caregiver and can be accessed as needed. Such a context provides a larger and communally grounded holding environment for that which the patient and caregiver may not be able to contain on their own.

Turning One against Herself

If all of what we have been describing were not complex and devastating enough, it is common in the more virulent forms of abuse for a perpetrator to take advantage of the processes just described to further intimidate the victim and obtain a greater level of compliance to his demands. These more severe cases often involve victims in traumatized states of being who are already highly sensitized and spontaneously reactive. On top of this, their previously unmet basic needs and the naturally occurring defensive processes used to protect the self from annihilation are mobilized and used to do more damage to the victim. Because of its tremendously deleterious and fracturing effect on persons, it became clear to us that this aspect of abuse and violence had to be recognized within any definition of evil we would propose.

In a disturbing yet clear example of turning one against herself, a twenty-six-year-old woman reported that her abusive husband knew her very well and kept meticulous records on each of her alters. Using this information, he would periodically call out particular parts for his own entertainment, as if he were directing a play with members of a cast. After divorcing him, she befriended an abusive and drug-addicted male who mobilized the unmet needs in this woman for someone to care, pay attention to her, and comfort her in her felt isolation and lack of purpose. For example, referring to his willingness to provide needed transportation she lacked on her own, she said, "He is the first person in my life that has been willing to wait for me." All the while he was meeting some of these basic needs, he was also taking advantage of scared and compliant early adolescent alters within her to get access to safety and drug money. In the first instance, the maneuvers on the part of the husband were consciously and intentionally planned. In the second instance, the maneuvers of this empathically attuned but sociopathic "friend" appeared to be driven by more spontaneous, intuitive, and unconscious processes. Nevertheless, over time he literally robbed this woman of anything of material and symbolic value and importance to her. This included her family heirlooms, gifts from her children, all the music she used to comfort herself, her integrity, and her self-respect.

This profound example demonstrates how a person's naturally learned and reinforced techniques of survival, e.g., splitting-off one's basic needs for love, affection, and attention, can actually leave her in a more vulnerable position and can be used against her. If these needs are mobilized, they can be used consciously or unconsciously by a perpetrator to do unfathomable harm. At a deeply profound level, such a set of circumstances humiliates the victim and creates a vast amount of shame, guilt, and distrust of herself. This has the effect of turning her increasingly against herself by providing a wealth of evidence that leads her to believe she is her own worst enemy. Similar dynamics are involved in cases where a needy, and perhaps elderly, person begins a correspondence with a prison inmate. If, in the course of this correspondence, previously unmet needs are mobilized, the now vulnerable person can readily become an easy target for victimization.

Split but Not Traumatized

It is important to clarify that persons need not be terribly traumatized for their internal world and psychic structure to be split and/or divided in some profound ways. Normal life experiences of pain, loss, and disappointment can create such divisions and partitions within persons when they live within nonresponsive and neglectful environments where support and nurture are lacking, and/or within environments that actively discourage integration and wholeness. Significant others, institutions, and the culture itself can reinforce naturally occurring tendencies to split and divide experience and persons and can encourage the viewing of self and others in terms of part-selves, rather than whole-selves. In short, the mental processes being described here can be created and sustained within persons not only by violence and abuse perpetrated by other persons, but also by forces and attitudes within a culture, which push in the direction of increased divisiveness and lack of acceptance and are supported and encouraged by the influence of significant and powerful persons, alliances, or subgroups within that culture (see Tannen 1998, and Ross 1989, esp. 178–79). These cultural forces are also encompassed in our view of evil.

The Importance of How Hurt Is Processed

Most caregivers do not work with criminals sentenced to serving time within the prisons of the criminal justice system. At the same time, most of the violence and abuse in our culture is not initially perpetrated by that population of people. Rather, most of the violence and abuse we encounter is perpetrated within our own families and the institutions of which we are a part, by neighbors and persons we know and by those to whom we entrust the welfare of our children. In short, most of the abuse perpetrated within our culture is by people more like us than unlike us.

Most of the persons to whom most caregivers provide care fall into this group. At the same time, many of the persons we work with in our various settings suffer symptoms that reflect the presence and activity of split-off dimensions within themselves. We see this in persons who *suffer* hurt and in those who *cause* it. The extent to which we will make a major contribution to transforming the processes that lead to the propagation of evil and to reducing the prevalence of abuse and violence will depend on the extent to which we can do two things: (1) effectively identify dimensions within ourselves and others that are defensively split-off but nevertheless control how we perceive life and interact with others, and (2) work effectively toward transforming and integrating those split-off dimensions.

As discussed in chapters four and five, traditional perspectives on trauma have centered on the victim in ways that have been both helpful and unhelpful. These perspectives presume no direct connection between the healing work necessary with victims and the work required to transform the forces within the internal worlds of persons that contribute to them hurting others. Clinical experience suggests, however, that the massive fragmentation of selves that abuse, violence, and neglect creates within persons, a person's internal responses to that hurt, and the degree of subsequent reparative work one has done with the mental structures and processes resulting from it, all play a major role in determining one's own potential for becoming a perpetrator of abuse.

Several factors directly influence one's internal responses to hurt and can set the stage for the expression of evil. These factors include such things as the degree of ego development one has obtained; the extent to which a person predominantly uses the more developmentally primitive ego defenses; the extent to which one has achieved firm self-cohesion; the extent to which one has integrated hurtful experience with the rest of life experience or keeps it split-off and isolated; the meanings one attaches to hurtful experiences; and the conclusions she/he draws from hurtful experiences about self, others, and the world-at-large.

The critical role played by others in the amelioration or exacerbation of processes that create the potential for the manifestation of evil cannot be underscored enough. In this regard, a number of factors play a key role in ameliorating the processes and attitudes that can otherwise contribute to the continued propagation of evil. These include the availability of responsive and supportive others who are willing and able to (1) help one heal from hurts received, (2) protect one from future hurts as much as possible, (3) lend their own ego processes to attempts to place hurtful life events in some context of meaning and understanding, and (4) teach attitudes and skills supportive of integration and cooperation rather than separation and alienation.

A Case Illustration: Sam and Louise

The following case presents many of the concepts just discussed and is an example of how these concepts play an active role in "more normal-looking" life situations free of blatant abuse and neglect.

A middle-aged couple, Sam and Louise, entered marital counseling when Sam's affair with a neighbor came to light. The couple had been married for twenty years and had two daughters, ages twelve and eight. Sam traveled during the week, and Louise was an energetic homemaker who worked part-time outside the home on weekends.

Over a period of months, this couple became attached to a younger couple, Sally and Jim, who were similarly new to the neighborhood. This couple had toddlers for whom Sam and Louise's older daughter, Myra, baby-sat. Through her baby-sitting, Myra became increasingly attached to these toddlers. The two mothers occasionally watched each other's children, and seeming alike in their mothering roles, they shared parenting insights and frustrations with one another. Sally seemed to admire Louise's experience, which fed Louise's sense of self, and Louise admired Sally's youth and liveliness, traits she saw lacking in herself.

Rather quickly, Sally began intruding into the lives of Sam and Louise, becoming more and more like an impinging object. She would be out for a walk and "just drop in to say, 'Hello.'" Once inside, Sally would presumptuously roam around their home, as if part of the family, checking out their artwork, jewelry, and bedrooms, and commenting on Louise's "fine taste in decorating." While on a Sunday afternoon stroll through the neighborhood, Sally and Jim would catch the eye of Sam or Louise, who would then feel obligated to invite them to join the family in the dinner they were just putting on the table on their outside deck. Louise increasingly felt she had no time to herself with Sam and the girls, and inwardly she began to resent Sally and herself for not maintaining more boundaries and a more differentiated stance.

Sally actively showed interest in Myra, whom she would take shopping at the mall or out to lunch to show her appreciation for the fine baby-sitting she did. On some occasions, she would buy Myra and her sister items that Louise had ruled out, thereby representing herself to Louise's daughters as a more gratifying caretaker than their mother. Sally stepped up her bonding with Louise by empathizing with her about how difficult it must be for her to be separated from Sam during the week with his travel schedule as it was.

Increasingly Sally wedged herself in between Sam and Louise by using the natural tensions she sensitively garnered from being around them, thereby further weakening the loosening bond between them. She increased her intrusion by sharing with Sam that she knew he must get lonely on the road and need a lot of loving when he got home, and by sharing with Louise that she must get frustrated doing the lion's share of parenting herself since Sam was inevitably out of town when a crisis hit. On weekends, Sally would volunteer to "stand in" with Sam for Louise at her older daughter's soccer games since Louise's weekend work made it difficult to attend. Sally increasingly devalued Louise in the eyes of Sam and their children, presenting herself as a warm and nurturing object, in sharp contrast to the more rational and somewhat cool personality Louise naturally exuded.

Over the course of time, Sam became infatuated with Sally. When the two couples were out together, their open and mutual flirting, while disturbing to their respective spouses, was dismissed as the mere expression of affection between two friends. Sally's attuned intrusion escalated as she began calling Sam when Louise was out of the house. One night she suggested they get together, and Sam agreed. Their clandestine rendezvous continued and were occasionally threatened as Sam's "I'll be back in a minute" trips to get gas turned into hours, and Louise and the girls began to wonder where he was.

Eventually the relationship between Sally and Sam became sexual. All the while, Sally kept up her characteristic interactions with Louise, Myra continued to baby-sit for her children, and the couples continued to socialize together. As tension within Sam and Louise's marriage rose, Sally even suggested Louise consider counseling since she seemed increasingly "unhappy," and she knew Louise wanted to "save their ideal marriage." In Louise's presence, Sally began to admire Sam more boldly, frequently telling Louise what a wonderful guy he was and that she really needed to appreciate him more.

One night the affair unraveled and came to light. Louise was devastated and enraged, feeling betrayed by Sam and violated by Sally. Reactively, Louise forced Sam to tell their children what he and Sally had done, and the children in turn became enraged at their father and angry with Sally, who had become like an older sister to them. The girls began to openly disrespect their father at home and began to procrastinate and stonewall around simple chores like brushing teeth, bedtime, eating dinner, and taking out the garbage. Their common line became "I don't have to listen to you anymore!"

Within a few days after initiating counseling, while still enraged herself, Louise encouraged the girls to begin sharing their anger at their father verbally and directly, rather than passive-aggressively or by acting it out on one family member and then another. Sometimes she even facilitated those discussions and served as a mediator. Reacting to her betrayal by Sally, Myra told her mother she wanted to return a gift Sally had given her saying, "I want to give back the beanie baby Sally gave me! I don't want it anymore!" While recognizing her daughter's desire to get rid of the gift, Louise also reassured her daughter it was all right if she wanted to keep the gift. "But if you choose to give it back," Louise said, "we can get another one that you and I will buy together."

The girls also expressed displeasure about having to walk past Sally's house on the way to the school bus stop, saying, "Why do they have to live here anyway! They should move!" Their mother responded by saying,

"They have a right to live here just as we do. We'll find a way to cope with this together. I'll walk you down to the bus stop this morning and meet you there this afternoon."

In this illustration, Louise exemplifies the critical role key caregivers (in this case parents) play in ameliorating or exacerbating attitudes and actions that can lead to the continued propagation of evil. Louise had every "right" to lash out at a neighbor who systematically, manipulatively, and intentionally worked her way into the primary relationships that sustained her and did unfathomable damage to those relationships and the people she most cared about. Without relying on a splitting defense, which would have made her daughters and herself "good people" and her husband and the neighbor "bad people," Louise was able to support her daughters as they struggled to make sense of their conflicted feelings about two people they loved but now also hated.

It also would have been tempting to dissociate herself from or deny the devastation of this experience for herself and her girls, to reinforce the felt rage and hate that urged them to impulsively cut-off from Sam and their neighbors, or to search for a way to "expel" the offenders from their immediate surroundings. While remaining sensitive to these urgings and fully connected to her own powerful affect, Louise gradually became able to offer a fairly nonreactive presence that facilitated the expression and integration of conflicted affect within herself and her girls. In this endeavor, Louise exhibited a mature internal strength, as well as the type of personal courage and resolve it takes if the cycle of abuse is to be stopped.

7

Wrestling with the Angel until Blessed

As we have seen, the healing process confronts us with a basic human dilemma—we are hurt by other people, and we depend on others for healing. Carroll Wise made this point a number of years ago in a sermon entitled "To Preach . . . To Heal" in the chapel at what is now Garrett-Evangelical Theological Seminary. In that sermon, Wise said the following: "The crucial fact of life is this: we are hurt by other persons, we are made sick through our relationships with other persons. We are also cured through other persons. The healing process is a process of relationships" (Means 1988, 211).

When a member of the human community is hurt, it is the responsibility of other members to offer shelter, care, and assistance. To stem the tide of evil, we must continue to search for effective ways to respond to the hurts of others and to heal the divisions evil creates and magnifies within persons and within systems, rather than use those divisions to further divisiveness, antagonism, and retaliation.

Stemming the tide of evil and facilitating a healing process requires a particular attitude on the part of caregivers that was pointed to by the question Wise posed in his sermon: "To what extent are we healing persons?" Specifically, Wise asks us to consider the extent to which our relationships with others reduce anxiety and increase faith, lessen isolation and foster a sense of belonging, offer unconditional acceptance to those who see themselves as unacceptable, and encourage people to be who they are before God (Means 1988, 211).

Even with these qualities in place, the journey of healing is arduous and fraught with difficulty. The sections that follow address two areas critical for healing from the effects of abuse, violence, and neglect. The first has to do with helping a survivor deal with guilt, shame, and self-blame. The second involves meaning-making. These endeavors can make a significant contribution to reducing the deleterious after-effects of life experiences that otherwise can lead a survivor into cyclical patterns of thought and action that are potentially hurtful to self and others. These are extremely complex endeavors in which survivor and caregiver intimately wrestle with themselves, one another, and the issues involved until some acceptable resolution is achieved, knowing all too well that it will be reworked and reshaped again and again, and that both will leave the encounter different from when they began.

Working with Guilt, Shame, and Self-Blame

In working with guilt, there is a need to be cautious so as not to move quickly and prematurely. Guilt is a complex and sacred thing. It takes sensitivity and skill to explore and ferret out the many idiosyncrasies of each person's particular guilt and the many ways it metastasizes to multiple areas of one's life. The danger in dealing with guilt, as with issues of meaning, is that we will assume too quickly we understand, or that we will move too quickly to close the process down due to our own discomfort. Resolving guilt is a process that occurs over time.

An important part of the task in working effectively with guilt is to discriminate between legitimate guilt and irrational guilt. Legitimate guilt refers to that guilt that is appropriately experienced by a person as the result of something she/he did that produced pain and distress in another person. This is usually the result of some transgression against a moral system, which may be within or external to the person who transgressed. Gail Price (1990) defines guilt as "the subjective awareness of having violated a moral system through having committed a fault or engaged in a wrongful act, and carries with it the anticipation of chastisement" (160). She goes on to describe how someone can "earn" guilt through engaging in "wrongful behavior" or guilt can be "imposed from an external source" (160).

Referring to the work of Harris, Archer, and Waltke (1980), Price (1990) states that there are four levels of guilt that comprise any moral system. These are "(1) the theocentric level issuing from a deity; (2) the forensic level evolving from laws created within a society; (3) the ethical level developed in response to society's sense of responsibility for its members; and (4) the personal level" (164; also see 160–61). Any particular expression of guilt "is structured into four basic components," which she labels the "behavioral, cognitive, affective, and spiritual" (161). In cases of legitimate guilt, all these components are present at a conscious level within the person who violates a moral system.

As Price (1990) indicates, these components are not generally present in perpetrators, though they may experience distress over the "fear of loss of the object that provides the offender with a sense of self-cohesion" (161). In such a case, the distress expressed by an offender who breaks a moral code is not necessarily an indication of guilt. Although he may say he "feels badly" about the incident, that distress is more often than not an indication of the vital stabilizing function the victim has played in his mental world, and which is now threatened. This dynamic is common in cases of domestic abuse and violence and is indicative of a developmental failure within the perpetrator to achieve self-cohesion, object constancy, and mutually responsive object relations. These developmental failures leave persons in a position from which they are only able to use others to preserve their own sense of self, rather than being able to relate to others out of a capacity for genuine love and concern for them.

Price goes on to suggest that the "presence of apathy, loss of vitality and creativity may signal unacknowledged guilt in perpetrators" (Price 1990, 162). While this is often the case, it is wise to be cautious at this point since these symptoms may also be a manifestation of an offender's dissociated stance with regard to his hurtful actions. In a massive attempt to maintain his sense of self in the midst of external evidence and the overwhelming self-awareness that he has harmed someone, an offender may detach and move to a defensive and dissociated state of numbness and lack of care. When in this state, the subjective experience of guilt is not possible nor is learning from one's mistakes.

Those approaches designed to "force" an offender to experience his guilt, often at the potential cost of annihilating whatever sense of self he has been able to achieve, run headlong into the primary need each of us has to protect our selfs. Such attempts will either fail or will precipitate a fragmentation process within the person. Neither of these outcomes is beneficial. Such a bind can be produced in perpetrators by treatment strategies that view him as "in denial" and do not give adequate consideration to the underlying dynamics behind such a resistant stance. Referring to someone as "manipulative" who is merely working creatively to protect a fragile self can produce similar binds. An offender's coming to a true awareness and subjective experience of his guilt will generally take time and is best facilitated within an environment composed of a mixture of affirmation and confrontation. If successful, this leads to what Jory (1998) has called the "anguish of accountability." The presence of such anguish marks a major step in the direction of an offender's true transformation.

Another pattern generally seen in abusive relationships is that in which the offending party quickly "apologizes" and then pushes in a premature and intrusive manner for resolution, forgiveness, or moving on. This is quite often an attempt to return things to the previous status quo as soon as possible so as to regain the sense of internal mental stability and interpersonal security so necessary for a sense of well-being. This is a dynamic often seen in marital therapy where one spouse has been caught in an extramarital affair. The guilty party goes through a process of repentance, acknowledges he/she was in the wrong, and even willingly does penance for some period of time. In such cases, however, the offending spouse exerts a constantly present pressure on the partner to move on so he/she can feel better, and he/she quite often lacks a sense of genuine remorse.

At these times, there is often an undercurrent of annoyance directed at the hurt spouse that takes the form: "Why can't you just put this behind you so we can move on?" This attitude reflects a lack of true awareness about just how much the actions have hurt the partner and can be another variation on the same old manipulative theme, "If you loved me, you would do this for me." In such cases, the person hurt is revictimized by making him/her "responsible" for whether the couple moves on or not. Forgiveness and moving on cannot be demanded of another any more than an awareness and acceptance of guilt can be demanded of someone.

A lot of survivors suffer from a deep sense of shame, self-blame, and culpability that must be distinguished from guilt and can also be uncomfortable for caregivers. As caregivers, the risk is that we will try to take these uncomfortable feelings away, minimize, or even ignore them because of our assessment that they are "irrational" or because of own discomfort with them. It is important to respect the fact that these responses to victimization represent normal responses to being traumatized and initially represent a victim's best effort at making sense out of what has happened. These responses are initial attempts to develop a cognitive framework out of which to understand the traumatic event and cope with the overwhelming nature of it. Therefore, working with these attempts in a sensitive fashion toward a gradually more realistic perspective that lodges responsibility in the appropriate place is very important.

Returning again to Price, she indicates that shame is a "common experience of all victimization," involves a "profound sense of self-loathing," and may involve "wishes to disappear or die" that are "accompanied by a sense of helplessness" (1990, 162). She then states, "The resolution of shame depends on the restoration of loving attachments, while the resolution of guilt involves changed behavior and reparation" (162). It is this shame dimension that leads people we are working with to say, "I'm afraid if I say what happened out loud, you will think a great deal less of me and not want to see me again."

Self-blame is also common on the part of a survivor following some traumatic event and "involves post hoc explanations of how choices made led to the victimization experience" (Price 1990, 162). In traumatic situations, one way a victim can make sense of what happened is to take on the burden of responsibility for why things developed the way they did.

Those who experience someone else being traumatized can also take on the burden of responsibility, as if they were the cause of it. This is not an uncommon occurrence in children. Billy was a twelve-year-old boy living with his mother, who was divorced from Billy's physically abusive father. Billy had seen his mother beaten by his father, had seen his mother's strength and determination to build a new life for him and her, and had seen the look of disappointment in her face every time she failed to get a job. Miraculously, one day she was offered an office job. She seemed to be enjoying it, and Billy was happy that she was so happy.

Then one day Billy got sick. Wanting to care for her child, Billy's mother stayed home with him. The next day her employment was terminated, and Billy saw the look of disappointment return to his mother's face. That evening Billy took an overdose of his mother's medication. While in the hospital, he declared he had taken the pills because he wanted to "stay asleep" because he felt responsible and guilty for his mother losing her job.

It is natural for the child who is abused, or even the adult woman who is raped, to assume she did something to cause the abuse or violence someone else perpetrated. This normal response serves several important psychic functions in the immediate aftermath of a traumatic experience. By shifting the responsibility or "locus of control" from the perpetrator to one's self, the victim moves herself mentally to a place of increased control over what occurred (Ross 1997). This is an emotionally better place than having to face the reality she had no control whatsoever of the situation in which she was hurt. Blaming oneself is also a way to maintain whatever positive views and attachments the victim may have with a perpetrator, as in the case, for example, of an incestuous relationship with a father from whom the survivor gained some occasional care and nonsexualized attention. In terms of working with self-blame, Price states, "The resolution of self-blame involves strengthening the individual sufficiently to bear the pain of the helplessness and terror (of) victimization" (Price 1990, 162, parenthesis added). This is a further reminder that strengthening and resourcing are key intervention strategies to help a person move from one way of thinking to another. Confrontation and cognitive reframing are not sufficient in themselves.

As in the case of the responsibility for an incidence of abuse, the *guilt* of a perpetrator can also be shifted to the victim through a process of attribution and/or terror (Price 1990, 162). In the case of attribution, the perpetrator directly places blame for his behavior onto the victim. This can be an especially insidious process that serves to further alienate the victim from herself. It occurs when a perpetrator (and even particular intervention procedures and cultural attitudes) exacerbates the natural tendency of a victim to blame herself by calling attention to reasons she herself may consider as possible causes for the victimization, and/or by taking some actual element of the abusive event out of context and using it to substantiate the claim that it is her fault. Examples would include the following statements: "You know you shouldn't be out this late by yourself," or "I noticed the seductive way you looked at me across the bar," or "I know you like this because I can see and feel your body responding to what I'm doing to you." This is one more example of how a perpetrator can reinforce, strengthen, and further ingrain within a victim naturally occurring defensive maneuvers, and in the process further alienate her from herself, further unload onto her the responsibility and accountability for the hurt she suffers, and make the healing process more difficult and lengthy. In our view, it is this type of process that is the ultimate expression of evil as we are defining it.

In terror-filled situations, the guilt rightfully belonging to the perpetrator, including his behavior and worldview, can be internalized by the hypervigilant victim through a phenomenon called the "Stockholm Syndrome" (Price 1990, 162). This process occurs rapidly and serves the survival function of helping victims adapt to the perspective of the abuser, as well as protecting them from the overwhelming realization they have no control and could die.

The major contribution Price makes to our understanding of these complex processes is her observation that "Guilt imposed on the victim by the perpetrator is taken in at the level of the perpetrator's offense" (Price 1990, 164). This means that the violation of each particular level of guilt carries with it a particular requirement as expiation. Violations at the theocentric level require death or radical self transformation; violation at the forensic level requires some penalty; violations at the ethical level require some form of reparation; and violation at the personal level "requires some form of self alteration which restores self-regulation and benevolent intent" (Price 1990, 161).

An example of this phenomenon is seen in the tendency of victims of incest to take on the perpetrator's theocentric guilt and feel a need to die (as in severe suicidal ideation), or a need to become a radically transformed person through a religious conversion experience or the cleansing and rebirthing process symbolized in baptism. This process of a victim "taking in" a perpetrator's guilt appears to have characteristics in common with a projective identification process in the sense that an unacceptable part of one's self (the perpetrator's real guilt) is placed within another person (the victim) who receives that projection and then reacts as if that disavowed aspect of her abuser is really hers to carry.

The Detour of Forced Meaning-Making

A basic dilemma of those traumatized by evil is how to make meaning out of what has happened to them. This is understandable since meaning-making is central and crucial to human nature. At the same time, abusive and violent manifestations of evil fall outside our consensual contexts of meaning, thereby defying attempts to locate them in some recognizable context of meaning. This creates a dilemma that is irresolvable. On the one hand, there is an urgent need to find meaning in what has happened, and on the other hand, there is no readily apparent meaning other than someone did something that had a harmful effect.

In the trauma literature, references to this dilemma occur in discussions about how trauma leads to states of cognitive confusion and double binds. These terms describe emotional and mental Gordian knots produced by traumatic experience. As an example, a woman once confronted her therapist with the cold hard fact that there was no way therapy and future life experience would ever "make up" for the constant and abusive alcohol-induced stupors and rages her father inflicted on the family. Throughout her childhood, these fits deprived her of the experience of a father's loving presence. In utter frustration she shouted, "Don't you understand that enough will never be enough!"

In the same session, this woman later related her fear and trepidation about the certainty of seeing her father in a couple of months at a sister's wedding. This of course put her in a tremendous bind. On the one hand, she did not want to see her father because she was enraged with him and deeply hurt. She was also not yet secure in her ability to see him and engage him in even superficial conversation without getting emotionally hurt by him again, or flying into her own rage at him. Both of these possibilities were likely, since she knew everyone in her family would be drinking, and their mutual drunkenness would make it more likely the original family traumas would be replayed once again. On the other hand, she could not fathom not going to the wedding, because it was important for her to support her sister. In frustration she blurted out, "I have so much to say to him, and yet I have nothing to say to him!"

As caregivers who work with hurt and suffering persons, these dichotomous thoughts drive us and them to distraction. It's like those we seek to help are caught in a continuous production of unsolvable doublethinks that have a circular logic to them from which they cannot get extricated. These ways of thinking make absolutely no sense, and they make perfect sense. In fact, a person will say after one of these mental onslaughts, "None of this makes any sense, does it?" The only appropriate response to such an existentially intense inquiry is, "It makes perfect sense!"

These suffering people are telling us that the structures of meaning currently available to them, or offered by us in a premature attempt to be helpful, are not sufficient containers for their experience. In such cases, there is no reason for us to respond defensively as if these meaning structures are sufficient, because they are not. At such times, we may even struggle inside ourselves uncomfortably and eventually blurt out all sorts of "But what about . . . ?" statements trying in vain to help them "correct their logic" and "create some meaning." But if we listen to what they are saying, the only sense or meaning that can be made out of what happened to them is that it makes no sense, it has no meaning—at least for now.

Acknowledging this truth immediately plunges us into the same despair and confusion they are in, and we want to resist that with all our might. At such moments of sheer ambiguity, we will try anything to make sense out of the nonsensible. But this is a detour that leads into a cul-de-sac that traps us in prematurely conjured-up forced meanings that become obstacles, rather than stepping stones, to the healing process.

In this context, the mysterious silence of Jesus before Pilate that has always been so profoundly disturbing takes on some clarity. Jesus' experience reminds us that sometimes silence is the only thoughtful response. By refusing to participate in the proceedings against him, Jesus refuses to submit himself to the shallow dichotomy of guilt and innocence being arbitrarily thrust upon him by Pilate and the mob (Hessert 1993). Jesus' silence also kept the focus off himself and squarely on his accusers.

Paul Hessert (1993), in his thought-provoking book *Christ and the End of Meaning,* discusses the culturally derived structures of meaning that provide us with a sense of security and purpose, but which also hinder us and bind us up. Hessert notes that the crucifixion and passion of Christ shatter our basic underlying structures of meaning. In discussing the silence of Jesus before Pilate, Hessert says, "In regard to the Passion, meaning would make him either guilty or innocent. . . . His silence is his refusal to claim the support that meaning could offer him" (95).

In ways such as this, Hessert calls attention to the almost driving tendency we each have to rely on our ability to make sense and meaning of what happens in the world in order to feel secure. The result, however, is that meaning usurps the central place of faith in our lives. The dynamics of power and control and the mutually exclusive categories of guilt and innocence dominate the culture, dichotomize life, and harm persons. Blame gets fixed on an unfortunate few who are caught, and a communal sense of shared responsibility is ignored. When meaning and meaning-making usurp the place of faith, *unfaith* becomes more prevalent and the likelihood of becoming ensnared in evil increases.

Jesus moved through his passion and crucifixion experiences in a different way. Hessert says the following:

> In place of meaning, just as in place of power, he has faith—not a belief that somehow there is meaning or will be meaning or will be a show of power, but a trust in God who is enough. . . .
>
> Christ's Passion is his deliberate undergoing all that is entailed in his rejection of the refuges of meaning and power.
>
> Passion has to do with Jesus rejecting the customary ways people have of blunting the reality of suffering through comforting thoughts such as, "Everything will work out in the long run." . . . Passion is refusing to take refuge in the make believe. (1993, 95–96)

Hessert's thoughts lift up faith as a resource for avoiding the seduction of prematurely forced meaning-making, and they remind us that faith can be sustaining even in the face of meaninglessness. Such an understanding of faith gives caregivers the resource needed to work patiently with persons whose life experiences currently defy meaning. It also helps caregivers avoid the trap of inventing forced and premature meaning in order to feel better themselves.

Hessert's work is also discomforting. He confronts all the intellectual, emotional, spiritual, theological, political, and legal contortions supported by culture that are used to avoid the reality that some experiences are outside current structures of meaning and cannot be contained without distorting, trivializing, or invalidating them. In the process of attempting to force such experiences as square pegs into round holes, the actual container of those experiences, the individual who had them, is once more overlooked, hurt, and violated. The person seeking help ends up getting hurt all over again because a caregiver forces meaning on a disturbingly complex and often arbitrary set of life experiences. This is most simply a variation on the old theme, "If you don't like the message, then kill the messenger."

A gift that people traumatized by evil offer us is the realization that meaning-making is a process that takes time and is constantly fluid. This is clearly represented in the case of the woman described in chapter two who grieved the loss of the clergyman who was the father of her daughter. As she continued in therapy to process her experience and memory of the early times they spent together when he was in seminary, she began talking with fondness, joy, and gratefulness for all they shared together. She reminisced about their many evenings by a fire shared with mutual friends discussing the events of the day from philosophical and religious perspectives. This intellectual stimulation and fellowship was invigorating and special to her.

As she recalled those times, she also began to talk about another dimension to her "not telling" about what had happened between them. She began to frame it in terms of "wanting to keep something that was so special and sacred from being misinterpreted and defiled by people who wouldn't understand." She began to wonder if perhaps she had kept the secret all those years as a way of holding it close to her heart for safekeeping. She was shocked and amazed by this new meaning she had come to in the process of her grief, since it was not expected and would not have come if she had felt a need to maintain her first interpretation of the situation. She never gave up the view that the sexual relationship they had shared was a violation of professional boundaries and trust, but she began to reclaim the positive side of their relationship. She rediscovered how important that community of friends was to her at that point in her life.

This example demonstrates that meaning-making is a process whose outcome cannot be prematurely forced to resolution, permanently set, or even foreseen. After sharing the insights and new ways of thinking that emerged from the profound wisdom and honesty she developed from years of reflection, this woman glanced upward to her equally surprised counselor and said, "You're actually going through this with me, aren't you?" This was her way of expressing surprised appreciation and gratitude for having a nonimpinging sojourner with whom to travel in the ever unfolding process of meaning-making.

8

Grieving:
A Bridge between Suffering
and Hope

GRIEF AND TRAUMA are like different sides of the same coin. They are different, yet they go together, and where you find one, you find the other. The felt loss that leads to bereavement and grief is a form of trauma. The work involved in healing from trauma is similar in ways to the work involved in complicated grief. As in the case of trauma, when loss occurs, we have no control or power to stop it. And as with trauma, while we are helpless to prevent loss and grief, healing from them requires us to be active (Neimeyer and Keesee 1998).

The losses that plunge us into grief are most traditionally thought of as a result of the rupturing of significant attachments we have with someone or something important to us. As we shall see, however, abuse and neglect produce myriad losses not often considered in our everyday thinking about grief. Because losses of any kind are often traumatic, many of the factors that play a role in determining the severity of a particular trauma also apply when thinking about loss (see Doka 1998, 2). For example, the earlier in one's life one has been traumatized, the more loss and grief one will likely experience. As with trauma, the grief brought on by a significant loss challenges our assumptive worldview and causes us to reevaluate what we think and believe (Janoff-Bulman 1989). Thus, as in the case of trauma, grief moves us into a profound, complex, and unsettling meaning-making process.

In this chapter, we want to look at the role grieving plays in healing from severe abuse and neglect. As we move into that subject, it is important to understand some of the losses behind the grief we will encounter.

Legitimate and "Illegitimate" Loss

When one's life has been ravished by the evil power of human-induced trauma and neglect, the resulting hurt, pain, and destruction are immense. So are the losses. For those of us who have not suffered in these ways, the breadth and depth of these losses seem utterly endless and unfathomable.

Some of the losses sustained as a result of trauma and neglect occur immediately. Many of these losses are readily apparent and tangible, as in the case of physical injuries sustained in a traumatic attack or the breakdown of body tissue resulting from gross neglect. On an equally tangible level, losing an income, the social network of co-workers, and a long sought after career position due to leaving an abusive work environment would also be losses easily recognized, "validated," and "sanctioned" by others.

In cases of human-induced trauma and neglect, however, the nature of the losses sustained is more often along the lines of those commonly associated with disenfranchised grief. By this we mean that *many of the losses survivors experience are generally not recognized by society-at-large as the losses they actually are.* This practice of invalidating the losses a survivor experiences as a result of a trauma, and failing to see these losses as "legitimate," creates yet another private hell for survivors. As Neimeyer and Keesee (1998) state, "However private our grief, it is necessarily linked with the responses of others, each constraining and enabling the other" (229).

When one's losses and grief are disenfranchised, then isolation, guilt, self-blame, and shame similar to that experienced as the result of abuse are rekindled. In this process, healing is hindered. The social isolation and exclusion brought on by the disenfranchisement process is similar to the mark of evil described in chapter two in the discussion dealing with the violation and desecration of community. An example of disenfranchised grief was shared in that section. An additional illustration of disenfranchised grief comes to mind.

A Case Illustration of "Illegitimate Losses"

In chapter six, we introduced the case of a woman whose husband had manipulated her system of alter personalities for his own selfish purposes. Within a few months of her separation from him, and after several hospitalizations, she began to associate with a sociopathic man who was a chronic drug addict. As previously described, her relationship with him had mobilized powerful unmet needs within her that dynamically took precedence over her physical welfare and other aspects of her recovery.

Several months into this relationship, the old family car she received in the divorce settlement required too many repairs for her to manage on her limited work income. She struck a deal with her "friend" to sell the car to him. She reasoned that he was mechanically inclined enough to keep it running, she could use the couple hundred dollars he offered her for it, and he promised he would drive her wherever she wanted to go. This seemed to work well for a while. The abusive nature of this relationship became increasingly clear to her, however, and after several altercations in which the authorities were involved and two hospitalizations precipitated in part by the stress of this relationship, she succeeded in breaking it off. This marked a major growth step for her, and she could recognize it and feel good about herself for it.

At the same time, this breakup resulted in her loss of transportation. This loss subsequently contributed to her sense of being "trapped" in an apartment she could not physically secure and that contained many traumatic memories concerning the abusive relationship she had just ended. She could not escape from the apartment except by means of rides scheduled well in advance with friends and volunteer organizations. While she appreciated these resources, her dependence upon them contributed to her feeling more helpless. Her lack of readily available and dependable transportation also hindered her ability to look for a different apartment, search for and maintain a job, and run the types of errands required for normal daily living.

In this particular case, the many losses resulting from the loss of her old automobile were invalidated by onlookers who dismissed them as secondary to her involvement with "a drug addict" and the result of "bad judgment" on her part. Her losses were not seen as "legitimate," and her grief was disenfranchised. While there was no doubt her involvement with this man was severely detrimental to her, he did fulfill some previously unmet basic needs. Paradoxically, her relationship with him also helped her maintain enough psychic equilibrium for her to buy the time she required to eventually become strong enough to sever her emotional ties with him.

Regardless of the *cause* of the losses she sustained, this woman's losses were nevertheless real. Her grief was deeply felt, and the various ramifications of her losses contributed further to her already deep sense of helplessness and hopelessness. The invalidation of her grief by others became an additional loss. Cases similar to this are not uncommon.

Unique and Invisible Losses

In chapter five, we devoted considerable attention to the idiosyncratic nature of trauma. The grief reactions that survivors experience also vary widely from one person to the next. The "contructivist approach" to understanding and working with grief recognizes this reality. This approach views each individual as "the constructor of a different phenomenological world and as occupying a different position in relation to broader discourses of culture, gender, and spirituality" (Neimeyer and Keesee 1998, 228). This approach to understanding grief suggests there is no simple "cookbook" approach to grief work. Consequently, helping persons grieve places demands upon the caregiver that are similar to those involved in meaning-making. In this regard, Neimeyer and Keesee, citing the work of Anderson and Goolishian (1992) as well as Nadeau (1997), state that the constructivist approach "challenges professional caregivers to approach bereaved individuals from a position of 'not knowing' . . . rather than presumed understanding" and with an emphasis on "each bereaved person's unique experience without the imposition of 'expert knowledge'" (Neimeyer and Keesee 1998, 228).

Not only are the losses suffered by survivors reflective of the uniqueness of each individual sufferer, but many of their losses are invisible. These losses are of the nature of what Mitchell and Anderson (1983) refer to as "intrapsychic loss" or the loss of something that "exists entirely within the self" (40). Such losses are often along the lines of privation, rather than deprivation, in the sense that they represent the loss of something that never has been, rather than the loss of something once possessed and later taken away. These losses usually remain unseen except by the most empathic and patient of listeners.

Many of these invisible losses are of experiences once held only briefly, or of experiences never realized and lost forever with the passage of time. A very nonexhaustive list of examples would include the following: the loss of a childhood; the loss of self-respect; the loss of persons to idealize; the loss of dreams and plans; the loss of simple pleasures of life, like a warm bath or a walk in a park in the fresh autumn breeze; the loss of the illusion of personal safety; the loss of love and warmth from the arms of a caring parent; the loss of peace of mind; the loss of basic trust; the loss of a sense of past, present, and future; the loss of knowing one is truly loved; the loss of a sense of personal efficacy; the loss of faith; and perhaps the most despairing of all, a loss of hope.

Finding Voice for What Lies Dormant and Goes Unrecognized

The major point we want to emphasize is that much of the grief buried deep within survivors—and perpetrators—is grief that goes unrecognized and unacknowledged. Some of this grief is manifested, respectively, in the "anguish of abuse" and the "anguish of accountability" (Jory 1998). One of the chief roles of caregivers is to help persons heal. This means finding effective ways to help survivors touch, move into, find voice for, and work through the anguish that lies silent and dormant within the split-off dimensions of themselves. A second and equally important role is to help them find ways for the appropriate expression of all that is associated with that anguish.

There are many reasons why the grief and anguish associated with abuse goes unrecognized. One of the main reasons for this is that this grief is disenfranchised as has just been described. A second reason this grief goes unrecognized is that grief involves, and is expressed through, a "bewildering cluster of ordinary human emotions" (Mitchell and Anderson 1983, 54). Depending upon the nature of the loss, these emotions can be confusingly varied and quite intense. This particular type of grief work, therefore, is potentially intimidating for all parties concerned, thereby making it something easily avoided by taking any detours readily available.

The emotions associated with grief can certainly be intense in and of themselves. Once mobilized, however, particular emotions can also tap into pockets of split-off affect that are similar to that being experienced at the time, but which have different origins. This phenomenon occurs because affect is stored according to *type* rather than *cause*. This characteristic of affect can be helpful in situations in which a caregiver desires to bridge from one feeling state in a survivor to a similar feeling state generated at some different point in her life.

This same associative linking of affect, however, also contributes to spontaneous abreactions that can suddenly overwhelm a person and the caregiver working with her. In these cases, split-off and dissociated pools of similar affect suddenly converge and condense, thereby producing an intensity that is too much for one to handle at once. An example of this was offered by an elderly man who was beginning to experience the "anguish of accountability" associated with years of lying and extramarital affairs, which devastated his wife. One day he said, "You have to face and accept these things one at a time. If you take on the whole elephant at once, it will kill you!" Whether one is struck by a singularly intense affective response directly related to a particular loss or is struck by a response that is "overdetermined" due to the consolidation of previously dissociated pools of similar affect associated with a variety of hurts and losses, the resulting reactions can be confusing and potentially traumatic in themselves.

For these reasons, the feeling states of those grieving can be ignored by caregivers who intuitively feel they are seeing just the "tip of the iceberg" and become uneasy with the perceived intensity of what lies beneath the surface. While it is definitely wise to respect the power and potential destructiveness of split-off affect, avoiding it because we caregivers are uncomfortable with it is ultimately unhelpful. In fact, such discomfort (and fear) can be unconsciously communicated to a survivor and exacerbate her own discomfort, since her perception of the caregiver's avoidance may be interpreted as "even the one I'm trusting is afraid."

The intensity of grief reactions, and the symptoms they spawn, can also mimic diagnosable mental health disorders such as acute and chronic depression, generalized anxiety, panic attacks, mania, and hallucinations. These symptoms can in turn precipitate impulsive interventions by caregivers that may include the use of psychotropic medications and even hospitalizations. A relatively frequent example of this is the person who has experienced the death of a family member and presents in counseling stating she has a "clinical depression." As she continues to tell her story, she reports that her doctor made this diagnosis and also prescribed an antidepressant medication. In such cases, grief not only goes unrecognized, but also becomes mislabeled as a "medical condition" that is "treatable" by medication.

Discovering Hope in the Midst of Suffering

Walter Brueggemann has spoken of grieving as a means of bringing private hurt to public expression. In his interpretation of the Exodus event, Brueggemann (1987) considers the loud and tumultuous expressions of grief by the Hebrews held in slavery within Egypt (Exodus 2:23-25) as a major catalyst that eventually empowered them to confront their powerful captors and escape (87). This perspective offered by Brueggemann provides a helpful alternative to viewing survivors as "difficult" and "hopeless" people (Means 1995, 302). Such a pessimistic and nonempathic view is easy to adopt because of the frequently persistent, loud, unpleasant, and demanding expressions of how these victims have been wronged and how hopeless they feel.

On the contrary, their wailing is perhaps more constructively viewed as public expressions of inconsolable grief. Such public grieving breaks the silence of years of intimidation and abuse and is a manifestation of survivors taking a stand on behalf of themselves. When it is finally heard by someone outside themselves, this expression has the potential of further empowering survivors. Such public expressions of grief may also get the attention of caregivers and the public who may otherwise remain defensively oblivious to the fact that someone in fact needs help!

Equally important, however, is the fact that it is only through such public expression that hope can be kindled. In the words of Brueggemann again, "Hope is not likely to come . . . among royal managers, among hired intellectuals, or among the muted oppressed. Who hopes? Those who enter their grief, suffering, and oppression, who bring it to speech, who publicly process it and move through it and beyond. They are the ones who are surprised to find, again and again, that hope and new social possibility come in the midst of such grief" (Brueggemann 1987, 86–87).

As survivors are listened to, the opportunity opens up for them to grieve as their many losses are re-membered in the telling of stories and memories long split-off in seeming oblivion. This process involves more than the recounting, recalling, or retelling that can occur repeatedly with no accompanying grief, because re-membering involves feeling the pain of suffering and loss (Means 1995, 302). This grieving, or the active experiencing of the breadth of those reactions touched off by re-membering, carries with it the potential to transform suffering into hope for reconnection and wholeness (Means, 1995, 303).

From this perspective, the actual work of grief begins as a survivor starts the process of re-membering. This involves the painful, frightening, and agonizing process of reconnecting with those aspects of her self that were defensively and/or traumatically split-off and kept separated within her. While this journey eventually leads to hope, it first takes one through suffering.

Christiaan Beker refers to hope that is "disengaged from suffering" as false hope. This type of false hope leads us to make what Beker (1993) calls "illusory responses" to persons in need, by which he means responses that have no basis in reality and are more along the lines of wishes, rather than authentic hope. By "authentic hope," we mean a hope that does not deny the destructive dimensions of life and the suffering those dimensions cause, but at the same time is grounded in the belief that change is desirable and possible, and that basic and realistic needs can be satisfied.

Grieving as a Turning Point in the Healing Process

A major turning point in healing is achieved by survivors when they are able to truly grieve. In some ways, it may be accurate to view a survivor's entire healing process as grief work. What we are referring to here, however, is the first time a survivor moves beyond the anger and rage associated with her violation and into the more vulnerable feelings associated with grief and loss. This time is commonly marked by the shedding of tears. It is also often the first time in the healing process she has been able to cry *with* herself and *about* herself. The willingness to allow oneself to connect with the vulnerable feelings associated with grief, especially in the presence of another person, in itself represents a major shift in the direction of increased internal strength and healing of the divisions within herself.

This movement into grief also represents an acknowledgment that something has happened that is important and has made a difference. This acknowledgment that "something matters" is an indication a survivor is moving away from the distancing and dissociative maneuvers with which she has numbed herself and toward a greater degree of connection with previously split-off dimensions of herself. Consequently, this may also be an indication that a survivor is becoming more internally capable of managing intense feeling states that would have previously overwhelmed her. Most importantly, however, this shift indicates a willingness to take the risks associated with reengaging life. These are also the types of risks she must be willing to take if new attachments are to be formed.

An ability to grieve also means that a person's concept of self is changing from that of a person with no worth and value, to one of a person who is beginning to see herself as worthy of life and the satisfaction of the basic needs all persons have. We do not weep for that which has no value to us. To grieve openly for oneself is an indication she is beginning to value and respect herself.

Grieving marks a beginning awareness that a survivor is not responsible or to blame for what happened to her at the hands of another. This is a major step in correcting the self-blame and guilt discussed in the previous chapter. Grieving marks the beginning of correcting the cognitive and emotional distortions resulting from "the locus of control shift" that a survivor makes in order to deal with the intense sense of helplessness at the time she was traumatized (Ross 1997). In addition, it is the beginning of a process in which a survivor no longer takes on the guilt, shame, and blame that her perpetrator succeeded in placing upon her and which she was previously willing to accept. In this sense, grieving is the start of a differentiation process that will eventually culminate in greater clarity about her being responsible for her healing but not being responsible for her abuse.

Last, the start of the grieving process marks a transition that takes one on a journey from being stuck in the hurt of the past, into the reality of the present, and eventually into the promise and hope for the future. Because of the overwhelming nature of human-induced trauma, we have seen how it is not easily contained, integrated, and put to rest within a person. Rather, it tends to continually break out in debilitating ways that affect all aspects of a survivor's life. Thus, in many respects, survivors are prisoners of a past that constantly taints the present in ways that make the possibility of a different future extremely remote. As the grieving process begins to bring about the many shifts just described, the present and future are slowly teased apart from the past and differentiated one from the other. This not only puts the past in a more circumscribed and realistic perspective, but also opens one for the first time to a tangible present in which she can engage herself in ways that will eventually move her into a different and more satisfying future.

Containment

Before concluding this chapter, we want to make a few comments about the subject of "containment." This is a term often used in trauma recovery literature but is a subject of some confusion. We have chosen to discuss this topic here because the idea of containment may seem to run contrary to the public expression of grief that has just been discussed.

The post-traumatic dimensions of trauma are most generally viewed as a "failure of containment." Quite often this refers to the inability of a survivor to modulate affect and keep from being overwhelmed and retraumatized by various forms of recall associated with the initial trauma. In this sense, a "failure of containment" refers to the absence or breakdown of sufficient protective mechanisms and methods of distress regulation, which subsequently leaves a survivor vulnerable to retraumatization by her post-traumatic symptoms. Such a "failure" also creates a potential for those close to the victim to be vicariously traumatized by that which unpredictably spills out and over them in the process of offering support and assistance.

The use of the term "containment" in working with victims of human-induced trauma and evil is unfortunate in many of its connotations. Its use does, however, confront us with some cultural assumptions that are problematic for effective caregiving and encourages us to evaluate them. First, the term itself runs contrary to everything we have said about the nature of trauma. Trauma, by definition, fractures one's self-structure, leaves no aspect of one's life unscathed, and threatens one's attachments to everything she holds dear. Evil greatly exacerbates these effects. To suggest that post-traumatic symptoms are a "failure" of containment is to make the ridiculous implication that traumatic and evil-inspired events should not have such a naturally devastating effect on people.

Second, the way the term "containment" is used carries with it an assumption that the model of good mental health is the person who can keep all that distresses her within herself so it will not bother someone else or even become known to others. Such a view takes "rugged individualism" to a new height of absurdity and ignores the communal nature of life and our shared responsibility for each other's welfare and healing from abuse.

Last, the idea that the symptomatic expressions of hurt suffered by persons who have been violated and injured severely and chronically by other people can be contained within themselves runs contrary to all we know about healing. Healing occurs most naturally and fully over time and in the context of restorative relationships, which offer comfort, support, and protection. As we have just discussed, healing *requires* that that which happened to someone *not* be contained and kept inside as if a secret, but rather be openly, even publicly, expressed and responded to in healing ways.

One of the reasons for the success and effectiveness of Twelve Step programs is that they provide a context in which the expression and sharing of self is encouraged. The framework provided by these settings allows previously uncontextualized life experience to be socially and interpersonally contextualized in a fashion that allows new meanings and stories to evolve from it. The end result is that the sharing of urges, wishes, longings, successes, and relapses that would ordinarily slowly shut one down with shame and guilt becomes instead a mechanism for integration, self-awareness, self-acceptance, and slow but persistent change.

The prototype for healthy containment, therefore, is not a strong and rugged individual, but rather secure and caring relationships offered to a survivor by caregivers who are in fact trustworthy. To fulfill this role, these same caregivers must be willing and capable of providing the persistent and nonanxious holding environment that forms the actual container for a survivor's revealed and shared experience of being devastatingly hurt. This is best done when caregivers are securely attached and embedded within a similarly supportive network of relationships that reinforces what they themselves are offering to the survivor. In this sense, the ability to "contain" disturbing life experience must first be provided *externally* before it can later be internalized and take root *within* an individual.

One of the marks of healthy mental functioning is the ability to set our concerns about one thing aside so we can focus on another matter that may be more pressing or require our attention in some way. This requires abilities such as (1) the ability to put boundaries around and "contain" some element of life experience, (2) the ability to set something aside, (3) the ability not to be unduly bothered or distracted by some aspect of experience, and (4) the ability to return to something of concern in an intentional manner at some later and more appropriate time.

When working with survivors who have suffered severe and chronic abuse at the hands of others, it is especially important to be sensitive to the extent to which a given person has, or does not have, these abilities. This allows us to assess what remedial work in this area is necessary and what abilities an individual already possesses that can be built upon and further developed. This type of assessment is crucial before any form of uncovering or abreactive work is done that entails reconnecting one to split-off feeling or need states.

As part of this assessment process, it becomes important for a caregiver to remain alert and sensitive to indicators of existing containment mechanisms within the person that can be strengthened and to avoid the inadvertent weakening or disregard of such mechanisms during a course of therapy. The following interchange between a therapist and a patient illustrates how this process can be overlooked even by skilled therapists who are not constantly sensitive to the critical importance of containment mechanisms and the metaphors that point to their existence. In this particular case, the patient is male and the therapist, Jamie, is female. The patient is describing his experience of the therapist's disregard for his internal structures of containment and his own ambivalent willingness to go along with her.

> Patient: "It's like I open the door and invite you into my house. As you enter, I say, 'Hello, Jamie. Let's go into the den.' As we proceed to the den, we pass another door with a sign that says, 'Do not disturb.' I'm afraid you will notice it and ask, 'What's in that room?' and you do. Behind that door is darkness. We enter it with flashlights. As we walk around in the black, we come upon some dusty old boxes."
>
> Therapist: "What's in the boxes?"
>
> Patient: (Silence) "There are some picture albums in the boxes."
>
> Therapist: "Tell me about some of the pictures."

In this illustration, the therapist did not pay attention to the many metaphorical structures this patient presented to her. In this brief interchange, there were references to doors, a house, rooms, signs, darkness, boxes, albums, and pictures. In each case, the therapist pushed beyond those structures of containment rather than respecting, working with, and/or affirming and strengthening the internal metaphorical structures this man apparently used with great effectiveness.

To summarize, matters of containment are crucial in terms of being indicators of the presence or lack of internal structures by which a person can compartmentalize experience in a manner that keeps her from being overwhelmed by too much at once. When these structures are present, even in rudimentary forms, it is important to affirm their usefulness and strengthen them. When they are not present, it is an indication of a lack of internal strength and structure resulting from a lack of early secure attachment, or the inability to internalize and integrate the comfort, support, and protection ordinarily provided by a nurturing and holding environment. In such cases, the establishment of a secure attachment with a caregiver, who is her/himself embedded within a supportive network of relationships, and the creation of a firm and communally supported holding environment that extends beyond the caregiver become early goals in the treatment and recovery process.

A Closing Word to Caregivers about Hope

Those of us who work with survivors are generally clear about the fact that remembering and telling are important because they give voice to that which has been stifled. We are also generally in agreement about the importance grieving plays in the types of healing processes in which survivors are engaged with us. What we are not as clear about is the bridge that grieving provides between suffering and hope. This is in part a result of the fact that many of the traditions in which we work are not conducive to hope. In this regard, Brueggemann (1987) has commented that "the dominant intellectual tradition of the West, that of Hellenistic philosophy out of which has come the ground of reasonableness for science, is not a tradition of hope. It is a tradition of *order* which seeks to discern, understand, decipher, know, and, if possible, master and control" (72).

For Brueggemann (1987), there are several "enemies of hope" that grow out of this "dominant intellectual tradition" (87). These "enemies of hope" infiltrate many of the worldviews and practices of us caregivers and get in the way of nurturing hope. The first of these are "silence, civility, and repression." These "enemies of hope" leave grief denied and keep suffering "isolated, unexpressed, and unprocessed in a community" (88). A second "enemy of hope" is what Brueggemann calls "fulfillment," which tempts us to believe that all that has been promised is already actualized (88). The third "enemy of hope" noted by Brueggemann is what he refers to as "technique," or the view that all problems can be analyzed, figured out, and solved (89).

The major point to underscore here is that there are powerful forces and worldviews within our culture and subsequently within the policies, theories, and methods of practice that guide the professions in which we work, that are obstacles to facilitating the development of authentic hope within those who suffer. The extent to which we buy into these worldviews will determine in large part the effectiveness with which we will be able to work to bring hope to those who are hopeless. As Brueggemann (1987) reminds us, dominant systems within our culture can become so seductively entrapping with their rewards and benefits that there is always the danger that those of us operating within them will become "consenting, docile, obedient adults" (81).

Hope is actually a revolutionary thing. This is because "Hope reminds us that the way things are . . . is precarious and in jeopardy. Hope reminds us not to absolutize the present, not to take it too seriously, not to treat it too honorably, because it will not last" (Brueggemann 1987, 80). This does not necessarily suggest that caregivers should become countercultural in their views. It does suggest, however, that we must develop and maintain a clearly differentiated stance with regard to the predominant and operative values that support and guide the systems in which we work. These systems and their values will at times interfere with what we and the survivors with whom we work deem is best for their particular situation.

While this type of differentiation is a necessary condition for action, it is in itself at times insufficient. There are times when, for the sake of hope, we must also remain open and willing to take on the role of a "prophetic advocate" and actively challenge the dominant values operative within the systems in which we practice. As in the case of those with whom we work, this will require a willingness to rely upon resources outside of ourselves for support and guidance. But most of all, it will require courage and faith.

Part IV

Responding to Evil with Courage in Faith

9

A Call to Prophetic Response: No Friend of Evil

YEARS AGO IN PSYCHOTHERAPY TRAINING, a supervisor told the following story: For years, a counselor worked with hurting people. She began to view herself as one who pulled drowning people out of a river and helped them build the strength and resources necessary to function effectively in the world. One day she had had too much. Her tolerance for hearing the pain and agony of those she worked with broke down and a flood of anger and frustration overwhelmed her. At that moment, she resolved to refocus her attention and look upstream to discover who and what was responsible for pushing people in the river in the first place and how to intervene to stop it!

Sooner or later, caregivers who work with victims of evil and trauma feel the same way. Wherever this story originated, it is a marvelous and powerful image with which to challenge ourselves to look beyond the immediate caregiving encounter to the larger cultural and social arenas that so concretely injure persons in ways that leave them mortally wounded and in need of emotional intensive care. We are called not only to care for persons, but also to speak out against all the forces in our culture that set the stage for violence and abuse.

The environmental sciences are increasingly confronting us with the unavoidable realization that human life is communal. It is also clear that we are all so interconnected that our individual singleness becomes overshadowed by our intimate connections with one another and the whole of life. While this includes an appreciation for the interconnectedness of life so marvelously portrayed by Margaret Wheatley (1994), we are most interested here in the inter*personal* attachments so crucial

to human life in particular. This web of human attachments and relationships moves us into the ethical realm since the "good enough"
attachments necessary for normal human development require us to
foster a "good enough" level of "right relationship" with one another.

Each discipline has different ways of talking about the different sets
of lenses through which the world can be viewed. These lenses not only
affect our worldview, but they also guide and direct us to the various
levels of life at which we will intervene. Within some social work circles,
for example, there is continuous debate about whether clinical social
work that focuses on psychotherapy with individuals, couples, and families is as valid an expression of social work as that aimed at the "macro"
or organizational and political levels of life. Historically within ministry,
pastoral care and counseling have focused on the side of care for the
individual, while the prophetic and Social Gospel traditions have been
viewed as more oriented toward intervention at the social and cultural
levels. More recently, liberation theology, feminist theology, and wom-
anist theology have also been helpful in addressing those forces operating within wider cultural arenas that contribute to the imbalances of
power and justice that subsequently nourish the potentials for abuse
and violence.

The Prophetic Tradition as Model

The prophetic tradition emphasizes the importance of communal
responsibility and ethical accountability for all persons at all levels of
the social structure. In so doing, this tradition provides a model for
effectively confronting evil and working for its transformation at the
individual and community levels. In their emphasis on communal
responsibility and ethical accountability, the prophets of the Old Testament focused on three dimensions: (1) they called their communities of
faith to shared responsibility to one another and their God, (2) they
reminded those communities about who they corporately and individually were (of their differentiated identity), and (3) they reminded
people of the resources God had reliably made available to them
throughout history and was continuing to make available. The importance of communal and ethical responsibility, clear and differentiated

identity (personal and professional), and a reliance on available resources are vital contributions this tradition offers as guideposts in the grueling task of working to transform the forces of evil.

The prophets also fulfilled their call in a fashion that clearly, firmly, passionately, and lovingly held people accountable for what they did and did not do at the individual and community (systemic) level. This meant that they directed people to look into themselves for what was in need of correction, rather than supporting and reinforcing the natural tendency to project blame *onto* others or project *into* others those aspects of themselves they considered most unacceptable and wished to be rid of. The prophets did this in a fashion that kept them intimately connected with the people to whom they were speaking. The prophets also called people to awareness of dimensions in their lives that created a nurturing ground for evil. These dimensions include such tendencies as reactively and defensively cutting themselves off from their God, harboring a sense of isolation and abandonment, maintaining a grandiose view of oneself based on position or social status, and living with a general fearfulness about life stemming from a sense of basic distrust and lack of faith.

A Lingering Resistance to Taking on the Prophetic Role

Psychotherapists and other caregivers who work with persons in well-circumscribed roles and contexts have often been uncomfortable with the role of prophet. At the same time, some have ventured to speak prophetically at times in their professional writing, e.g., Richard Chessick and Ernest Wolf. Even those of us in the field of pastoral care and counseling have exhibited remarkable resistance to taking up the prophetic part of our calling. When we have, we have tended to see it as an aside, rather than as an integral dimension of who we are and what we are about in our day-to-day work with persons.

In a review of the pastoral care literature, Frances McWilliams (1997) suggests it is a lack of confidence, skill, and resources of support, in conjunction with cultural biases, that is largely responsible for resistance within the field of pastoral care to the integration of worldviews that look beyond the individual to the social forces and structures that affect persons. McWilliams suggests this resistance stems from the power of unjust systems and the traumatizing and demoralizing affect their power can have on the personal lives of caregivers when they begin to confront these systems to bring about change. "When we consider these forces we confront the principalities and the powers and the over-whelming momentum of an unjust system. We look evil in the face and are subject to despair. It involves loss and pain for us, a surrender of our sense of efficacy, and at times a threat to our very livelihood. The skills we learned are inadequate for the task" (McWilliams 1997, 47).

As described in previous chapters, therapists and other caregivers who see the marks of evil in the powerful and dynamic internal worlds of individuals they work with day after day share a similar experience. We also confront the "principalities and powers" and the same "over-whelming momentum" of unjust systems. Our work also involves us in the same "despair . . . loss and pain" and also requires the "surrender of our sense of efficacy."

Whether we are working with persons whose lives are thrown into turmoil by dissociated parts of themselves periodically taking executive control of their bodies, with persons who vacillate from one split-off feeling state to another, with persons who chemically numb themselves to avoid the tremendous internal rushes of painful affect that threaten to overwhelm their still fragile selves, or with couples and families caught in the tragic dilemma of violent and abusive relationships, the power of entrenched dynamic patterns can seem too much at times for the meager skills and resources we have. At whatever level we "look evil in the face," we need resources and support to sustain us.

In McWilliams's view, resistance to change stems from a perceived lack of resources to confront and change that which has taken root in the form of established patterns and attitudes. Viewing resistance this way is a cre-ative and helpful conceptualization we can use at whatever level of life we might be working. Whether we are looking at the resistance in ourselves as caregivers to confront entrenched systems, or at the resistance to change in our patients or various organizational systems, this view is helpful. It suggests that an effective way to work with resistance is to empower and support a person (or system) that is caught up and stuck in patterns that might not even be in awareness but are nevertheless destructive.

Such a view of working with resistance is in sharp contrast to methods that exert increasing emotional pressure, or use persuasive maneuvers to "push through" whatever resistance is there, or even to views that consider resistance a problem rather than as a sign of strength. These latter approaches typically add to the burden of already beleaguered people, often strengthen the resistance already present, and can lead to a view of the person involved as "a problem patient who doesn't really want help." The conceptualization of resistance as reflective of a lack of resources redirects our focus from the resistance itself back to the person (or system) that is stuck and in need of assistance.

The Splitting of Prophetic Response and Pastoral Care

McWilliams's review also points to the tendency that has historically existed within ministry to separate (split) the pastoral care and prophetic roles, and pit one against the other. Even in the midst of talk about the need to integrate these two means of providing "critical caring" (DeMarinis 1993), they are often dichotomously split one from the other. While there is a trend in the direction of recognizing the wisdom of integrating these equally crucial expressions of care within our thinking and practice, there is an ever present inclination to emphasize one over the other. For the past decade, the climate seems to have favored the systemic view over and against the individual.

During the last decade, for example, seminary departments of pastoral care and counseling have searched for systemically and prophetically inclined faculty who will address the injustice and power imbalances within cultural and corporate life. At the same time, they have tended to avoid potential faculty originally trained in more individually oriented theories and forms of intervention. This shift in focus has offered a needed corrective and has resulted in an increasingly strong and prophetic chorus against social injustice. It has coincided, however, with a trend at the cultural level of losing an appreciation for the importance of understanding one individual and the particular dynamics of her/his unique internal world (Means 1997).

A number of other consequences have resulted from this trend. Within the church, one result has been less emphasis being placed on the care of souls, as clergy have been trained more to work with the systemic, organizational, and programmatic aspects of congregational life than with individuals. Within the field of psychotherapy, this trend, in conjunction with ineffective intervention and treatment strategies to address major cultural concerns such as domestic violence, has contributed to the gradual erosion of confidence in psychotherapy as an effective change agent, and to the subsequent erosion of its professional privileges as documented by Bollas and Sundelson (1995).

There is even some sentiment that the emphasis on intervention at the systemic, organizational, political, or macro levels has contributed to undermining individual accountability and responsibility-taking (Jory 1998). At the same time, the increased reliance on the criminal justice system (and programs associated with it) to solve our most severe and chronic problems has all too often left psychotherapists out of the intervention loop. For example, court-ordered batterers groups, which are often a part of these programs, are generally not led by experienced, psychodynamically informed psychotherapists, do not have transformation of perpetrators as a goal, and often produce graduates who proudly announce that the group has basically helped them to "do it [battering] better and wiser."

Recent trends suggest there is a returning appreciation for the importance of the internal worlds and belief systems of individuals. This is seen in the increasing awareness that educational approaches to social problems do not work on their own, as people continue to do things they "know" are not good for them or the ones they love. Most recently within the field of marriage and family therapy, Brian Jory's well-conceptualized and well-developed "intimate justice theory" and the intervention strategies stemming from it point to the efficacy of individual work with persons caught in the powerful and destructive dynamics of abusive relationships. This model also emphasizes the importance of gaining access to, and then working to change, the internal attitude and belief systems of perpetrators that support the rationalizations and internal dynamics necessary for their continued hurtful behavior toward others (Jory 1998).

Jory is staunchly supportive of the marriage and family therapy field in which he was trained. He is nevertheless critical of its rigid adherence to working only with systems (more than one person) and its underlying assumptions that victims of abuse, as participants in a system of abuse, have some level of control and responsibility for not only triggering abusive episodes, but for taking action to stop those episodes or protect themselves from getting injured. At a practice level, these are views shared by many therapists regardless of theoretical orientation. This suggests that we caregivers are more prone to being influenced by the types of powerful cultural attitudes discussed in chapter two than we may realize or be comfortable acknowledging.

We seem to be perpetually haunted by the tendency to freeze, at one end or the other, the natural pendulum swing represented in Tillich's (1967) basic ontological polarity of self (being as a part *from*) and world (being as a part *of*). Evidence for this can be found in those situations where the particular is separated from the larger context that supports it and of which it is an integral part, and in situations in which a contextual framework is focused on to the exclusion of the particular elements comprising it. This tendency is also evident when there is resistance, inability, and/or lack of commitment to facilitating a fluid movement back and forth between these poles, which, if present, could promote a more continuous process of integration. Perhaps this is in itself a manifestation of the ubiquitous role splitting plays in human thought and action, and how easy it is to move into dichotomous thinking styles.

The wisdom of integrating the prophetic and pastoral care roles was suggested by William Hulme (1969) when he stated, "Pastoral care is a function of the prophetic community. The prophetic concern is directed also to persons—in terms of their involvement in the structures of their culture. If they support structures that lead to injustice for others, they themselves are corrupted in the process. On the other hand, if they support structures that assist others, they are enhancing their own growth through their environment" (162). Hulme's emphasis on the role individuals play in the creation and support of social structures leading to injustice, or alternatively to the enhancement of persons, reflects the "extracultural nature" of human beings proposed by Francis Hsu (1977). This view suggests that the expression of cultural values and the ongoing reworking of those values occur in a feedback loop process as values flow from the culture through social institutions to the individual and back again.

At a clinical practice level, this process is demonstrated in the following not uncommon response of persons in the end phase of longer-term pastoral psychotherapy: "When I entered therapy, I thought it would make my life simpler and more comfortable. Instead, I find I am increasingly aware of the cruel insensitivity of individuals and social institutions, and I am distressed by it." In response to this awareness, these persons will often become actively prophetic in speaking out against social injustice and in taking leadership positions within organizations to which they belong.

The point is that it is time to move on! Whether we begin with an emphasis on the care of individual persons or a prophetic approach more directed at the communal level of life is not ultimately important. One is not primary to the other, nor are they mutually exclusive. Rather, one inevitably leads us to the other and then back again. The continuous interplay between the cultural, social, and individual levels of life can be summed up this way: unhealed persons lead to broken institutions that lead to a broken culture that spawns broken institutions that create broken persons in need of healing. As McWilliams (1997) states, "The times call for us to move beyond our separation of care for the individual from care for and by the community. We need healing from this split and liberation from the restrictive aspects of our tradition" (47).

Pastoral Counseling as Cultural Critique

As implied in the story at the beginning of this chapter, there is a seamless movement from counseling to prophetic response when we remain person-focused rather than merely symptom- and problem-focused. Over the course of working with persons in psychotherapy and other intense caregiving relationships, it becomes clear that people bring not just problems to be solved, but messages about the wider world in which we all live (Means 1995). As we listen to the "messenger" side of their stories, people will tell us about all the forces in life with which they have had to cope, which have subsequently shaped them and their problems and sometimes have drained them of their spirit. As they bring these forces to our attention, we inevitably begin to recognize recurring patterns and themes as one person and then the next tells us about similar experiences and struggles. They also tell us, more clearly than we often realize, what it is we can do to be of help.

Sooner or later in our work, we begin to wonder how the people we come to care about and work so many hours with will ever improve their lives while in the midst of destructive forces, patterns, and relationships that continue to wreak havoc. Some of them don't. On the other hand, one of the unrecognized and silent testimonies to the efficacy of individually oriented psychotherapy and the transcendent nature of the human spirit is that some persons *do* succeed in changing themselves and their lives while living in circumstances that would seem to mitigate against any such healing and transformation.

It is important to recognize and celebrate these victories as the major events they are. Like so many other things in life, they reflect the ultimate resourcefulness of life in all its natural diversity of character and circumstance. Yet it is important in our enthusiasm not to impose such breakthroughs on others as a generalized norm or expectation that then becomes yet another burden to already burdened people. It is also important not to minimize the tremendously overpowering and subtly divisive impact established patterns of injustice and destructiveness have on the continued propagation of evil.

Being in a position that graces us daily with the sacred life stories of countless people in pain, caregivers are constantly confronted with the destructive forces, policies, and realities that exist within their particular culture. They are also informed of more subtle pressures their culture exerts on persons. These forces, or "cultural wave-trends," slowly take their toll on the lives of persons as they repetitively break as waves upon a beach, and as they slowly saturate the very fabric of the culture (Means 1997).

Many of these "wave-trends" become so woven into the mainstream of cultural thought and expectation that they take on the power of "cultural truths and myths," which may not be recognized and challenged as the *untruths* they actually are. Examples of such untruths include the following: "It is not good to be emotionally dependent on other people," "If I don't love myself, it is my fault," "Over time, having sex with him will lead to my feeling loved," and "She can't be the easiest person to live with so she must have had it coming."

Other cultural wave-trends can become institutionalized in ways that preclude a realistic and balanced view of an organization. This was vividly demonstrated in the following case illustration shared in a pastoral care consultation group. A chaplain in an urban hospital with historic church connections found himself confronting forces he did not expect. As described in the preceding chapters, there is a natural tendency within individuals to split-off and deny unacceptable parts of one's self. Instead of searching for ways to integrate the unacceptable and put it to good use, forces, natural and/or imposed, can occur that reinforce this division of the self so as to at least maintain acceptability—or worse the delusion of perfection. The example shared by this chaplain demonstrates how a similar process can occur at an organizational level.

Over a number of years he had been active in a mission project designed to obtain medical supplies for missionary hospitals. As part of this commitment, he routinely visited various floors and departments of the hospital requesting discarded medical supplies that for one reason or another could not be used in the hospital but for all intents and purposes were still good. Over years of doing this, a cadre of medical personnel developed who kept their eyes open for these types of items. These supplies were gathered with the full knowledge of the hospital administration, were combined with those collected in a similar manner by others in different hospitals, and were packaged and shipped to missionary hospitals for their use.

The particular hospital in which he worked began a "quality management" program. One of the goals of this plan was the elimination of waste in the hospital. The chaplain reported that almost overnight the attitude on the floors and within the departments changed. Suddenly, "there was no waste" to collect for others to use. Since staff ratings now depended upon waste reduction, he attributed the sudden lack of waste not to increased effectiveness, but to people hiding and not acknowledging the continuing waste out of fear of losing their jobs. Thus, there was a denial of brokenness (how things actually were) in the service of protecting self by appearing to meet institutional goals and expectations.

Daily exposure to destructive forces and numerous culturally supported and internalized untruths, a deep appreciation for a developmental perspective on human growth, and an integrated faith perspective on the nature and purpose of humankind all come together to support the view of pastoral counseling as *cultural critique* (Means 1997). The ongoing work of psychotherapists within the confidential framework of their offices and pastoral care to persons in various institutions and churches offered by caregivers sensitively attuned to what people tell them about themselves and our world naturally call forth a prophetic response. Out of our healing work with individuals, we are called to be prophets within the various communities, personal and professional, in which we live and work.

In Good Company

While we may talk of waging a "battle" with evil, we have seen that evil cannot be fought on its own terms. Neither can evil be eliminated. It is important, however, to make a commitment to name evil wherever we encounter it and to commit ourselves to resist its pull and work for its transformation. The prophetic tradition, as exemplified in the Old Testament history of the Hebrews, incorporates this type of commitment. It recognizes the importance of confrontation and the importance of holding the community and individuals accountable for right behavior, justice, mercy, and shared responsibility for one's neighbors.

Resistance to prophetically speaking out to confront evil is not new. Those called by God in Old Testament times to speak out and confront people with their waywardness also resisted. In response to their call, they hurled all sorts of excuses and rationalizations at God about why they were not right for the job or how God's call came at the most inopportune time. Jeremiah sought excuses due to his young age (Jeremiah 1:4-10); Moses offered his lack of experience and authority as reasons behind his reluctance to take up God's call (Exodus 2:23—4:17); and Jonah ran as fast and as far as he could in the opposite direction (Jonah 1:1-3). Those of us in helping professions offer similar excuses. Silently offered, our excuses take the form of our retreating behind the closed doors of our offices (or sanctuaries) and operating as if we need not consider the world outside and its influence on the lives of those seeking help from us. Our excuses make themselves known when we resist revising the theories that guide our work, even when they do not take realistic account of the external forces impinging on people, and when our views of what people "should do" lead us to increase the burden already borne by those who are abused and oppressed by expecting them to do what they are *not yet able* to do.

We also offer excuses when we lack the faith and confidence to move into new and important territory with our patients as they struggle through their trauma, pain, and grief because we are afraid to be affected by all they have to share. This lack of faith and confidence can also be greatly exacerbated by compassion fatigue and vicarious traumatization. These occupational hazards, afflicting all those who work with victims of violence and abuse, are an additional reminder of how crucial it is to have resources to fall back upon that provide nurture and sustenance.

While it is important to be mindful of the multitude of excuses we can offer to avoid the prophetic task of confronting evil, Alan Keith-Lucas also reminds us of the importance of keeping in mind how difficult it is to resist evil's pull and transform those aspects of one's self most susceptible to that pull. In an address on "The Art and Science of Helping," he discussed elements that must be present for a person to seek and receive help from another person. He then offered this humbling reminder to caregivers: "One of the most dangerous type of helpers, or teachers, is the one who has solved a problem and has forgotten what it cost him to do it" (Keith-Lucas, unpublished address, n.d.). As it was for prophets of old, so it is with us—one of the most difficult tasks confronting us will be acknowledging our own fears and weaknesses. At the same time, keeping these at the forefront of our minds and hearts will go a long way toward making us the effective, humble, and compassionate caregivers and prophets we are called to be.

Liberation Theology

Liberation theology has made a tremendous contribution to our understanding of the multidimensional levels at which evil actively works to divide people from one another and themselves. As such, it is also a resource upon which to draw. "Liberation theology has taught us that when the church and its hierarchy, the political structures, and economic structures are all entwined to maintain an oppressive status quo, reform in one area necessarily involves reform in another" (Means 1995, 298). Jack Stotts has suggested that the church in North America has no sense of "corporate community of the oppressed or oppressors" and prefers to deal with issues of separateness and individuality rather than connectedness and structure (see Means 1995, 298). In response to this orientation, Stotts lifts up the Exodus Liberation model of theology as a resource that addresses three important levels: "(1) the isolated self that needs to find mutuality and equality, (2) structures of society that must be based on justice and equity, rather than might, and (3) the need to change images of self from that of object to subject" (Means 1995, 298). The material presented in preceding chapters suggests that persons suffering the aftermath of human-induced trauma also feel isolated and in need of mutuality and equality, have experienced oppression at the hands of powerful forces devoid of justice and equity, and need assistance in developing an image of themselves as subjects rather than objects.

Stotts suggests the Exodus Liberation Model offers three guiding and helpful principles: "(1) the realization that suffering is a locus of hope and transformation, (2) the solidarity of all humanity, and (3) an emphasis on practical theology, or 'What are we going to do with that which grabs us?'" (Means 1995, 298). As we have seen in the preceding chapters, these principles have a direct contribution to make to our work with victims of evil.

Faith Resources

In order to commit ourselves to naming evil and confronting it when and where we see it rather than shrinking from the weight of this responsibility, it is important to ground ourselves in the faith resources we have. In our own therapy work, especially that aspect of our work that involves working with forces of evil, we have found it crucial to look continually for resources. In addition to the support, affirmation, encouragement, and consultation we constantly receive from trusted colleagues, and availing ourselves of professional training events on a regular basis, the particular faith perspectives each of us brings to our work can also function as vital resources for us. These resources nurture us and remind us that we stand united with others in a long tradition of the care of souls.

Our own particular faith perspectives have evolved out of our lifelong involvement in the Christian faith traditions within the United States. Some readers will undoubtedly come from different faith traditions and perspectives. Based upon our own clinical experience in working with victims and perpetrators of evil, we believe it is critical to remain ever mindful of, connected to, and involved with, whatever faith perspective guides one's life and practice. By this we mean staying in existential contact with whatever it is that transcends yet sustains one's self in her/his work and that nurtures the courage and sensitivity required to care constantly and compassionately for persons, as Anton Boisen and Carroll Wise suggested, at "the point of their need."

The following review of resources is only representative of the vast supply available within the Christian faith tradition. The particular interpretations offered in this review reflect our own theologies and backgrounds. The reader is encouraged to look at them through her/his own particular faith lenses.

The Incarnation, Crucifixion, and Resurrection of Christ

Three events stand out as central to the Christian faith. Each of these in its own way serves as a resource in dealing with evil. The first of these events is the incarnation. This act of God is most basically about knowing and being known. God's willingness to enter fully into human experience by coming into the world in the form of an infant changed everything forever. No longer was God "out there," but rather God was "with us and among us." No longer was God all powerful, but God was also vulnerable and dependent upon human persons. God, in the form of Jesus the Christ, walked with us, talked with us, taught us, laughed with us, prayed with us, and suffered with us.

The incarnation is an act of profound love. By God taking on human form, we are shown how far God is willing to go to relate to us and to help us. This makes the incarnation the supreme model of empathy. God's willingness, in the form of Jesus Christ, to be affected by human life points to the importance of being willing to be affected and changed by those we seek to help.

The model of the incarnation invites us to change our view of one another, by asking us to look upon one another as "christs," who minister to one another and reveal God to one another in a panoply of ways. With this perspective, our view of the other changes by making it more difficult for us to think of one another as strangers or as potential enemies who are less than ourselves. As Elie Wiesel has pointed out, it is easier to hate others and do them harm when we see them as strangers or "other" than ourselves. Thus, the incarnation makes it more difficult for us to treat others with malice.

The second event central for the Christian is not an act of God, but an act of humans. It is the crucifixion. Through Christ crucified on the cross, we are jolted out of our complacency and are confronted with the reality that God knows firsthand the degree of suffering humans are capable of inflicting on other humans. Christ's journey to the cross, and his suffering and death on that cross, are stark reminders that God knows about human suffering brought about by powerful psychological, sociological, religious, and cultural forces, including the suffering resulting from individual and systemic complicity and denial. This also means that God is in solidarity with those who suffer. In the words of Dietrich Bonhoeffer (1997), "God lets himself be pushed out of the world on to the cross. . . . and that is precisely the way, the only way, in which he is with us and helps us. . . . The Bible directs man to God's powerlessness and suffering: only the suffering God can help" (360–61, date of original letter is 16 July 1944).

The crucifixion symbolizes the many layers of suffering and loss brought on by evil. It is a loss and pain suffered by both victim *and* perpetrator who, as we have already seen, suffer, respectively, the "anguish of abuse" and the "anguish of accountability" (Jory 1998). Upon reflection, the humiliation, pain, and ultimate death of Christ make us disturbingly aware of the impact of human cruelty. In a powerfully paradoxical fashion, the soul-wrenching violence of the cross offers an opportunity for victims and perpetrators, who accept their accountability, to come together in an empathic web of anguish that offers each of them the opportunity for life transformation and subsequent reconciliation within, and even between, themselves.

The crucifixion is a stark reminder of the cruelty, arbitrariness, and desecrating power of evil. Most disturbingly of all, the death of Christ on the cross is a reminder of the incredible and frightening power we humans have—the power to kill God. The Good Friday experience becomes a symbol of isolation and despair brought on by the loss of hope and meaning that evil creates through our own hands. Christ's death at human hands plunges us into the despair of "transitional space" where there are no "transitional objects" to comfort us. We are left with no recourse to anything of meaning to us and with no future possibility beyond the stabbing despair of the present.

The third event central to the Christian faith, the resurrection of Christ, is once again an act of God. The resurrection is our assurance that God is God and we are not! It is the ultimate manifestation of God's persistent and enduring strength and love in the midst of human cruelty. As such, it is a source of hope and possibility. In the miraculous surprise of the resurrection, we are reminded of life's power over death, love's triumph over hate, and God's triumph over evil. It is a gentle yet dramatic reminder of God's sovereignty. In the resurrection, hope is reestablished. The despair of a repetitive, never-ending past and present opens up to the possibility of a radically different future.

Ritual and Liturgy

Herbert Anderson and Edward Foley (1998) state that "human existence is structured in time and narrative. We comprehend our lives not as disconnected actions and isolated events but in terms of a narrative. We conceive of our lives as a web of stories" (4). As we have seen in the types of cases we have been describing, the lives of numerous persons go uncomprehended by themselves and others because their lives are experienced as a collection of "disconnected actions and isolated events" rather than as an integrated life narrative. Ritual and liturgy are powerful avenues the church has for facilitating the lifting up of split-off parts of persons for healing and reconciliation, for connecting persons to one another, and for creating and expressing meaning where it has not previously existed.

Rituals and liturgy help us maintain an intimate connection to our propensity for evil and our hope in faith. They are symbolic ways of keeping stories central to our faith alive and constantly before us so, as in the words of Anderson and Foley (1998), human and divine narratives can intersect (40). A story comes to mind shared by Lilian, who is a minister and the wife of a minister (Means 1995, 304). Her husband celebrated a communion service in his church one Sunday and, as is customary, he ritualistically broke the bread and poured the wine. Lilian and their three-year-old daughter were in the congregation. After the service, the family returned to the parsonage, and their daughter immediately sat down on the stairway crying. Lilian sat down next to her and asked her about her tears. Her daughter said, "I am very sad." When her mother inquired about what was making her sad, her daughter replied, "Jesus is broken!" "Yes, he was," said Lilian. To this her daughter quickly replied, "And my daddy broke him!"

This comment by a three-year-old girl is profound and disturbing as it evokes all sorts of emotional reactions within us. We quickly want to tell this child that she misunderstood what happened in the service. Her daddy broke only the bread, not Jesus. And yet we know that Jesus died because those around him either conspired to "break him" or remained silent as others "broke him." Those around him were not strong enough to confront and stand firm against evil in their midst, especially when it was coming from those in recognized establishments of power and influence.

This wisdom-filled comment by a child reminds us how celebrating the sacrament of the Eucharist is not only a means of grace for us, but also a constant reminder of our collusion in the persecution of Christ. People of faith know it is not just this little girl's father who has broken Jesus. It is not just the people of Jesus' day that conspired to break him. The Palm Sunday story of Jesus' triumphant entrance into Jerusalem, and the yearly walks on Good Friday to Golgotha, are constant reminders that the potential for good and evil exists within all of us.

To confront evil faithfully, each of us must be willing to ponder how our attitudes about ourselves and evil might change if we viewed the eucharistic celebration through the eyes of this small child. While in the end God used Jesus' death and brokenness for us and our salvation, Jesus was first broken by people like us. This perspective calls us to face how we ourselves conspire to "break Jesus" or remain silent as others break him.

Quoting from the work of John Dominic Crossan (1975), Anderson and Foley (1998) discuss the mythic and parabolic dimensions of stories (14). The mythic dimension serves the function of resolving contradictions and creating a belief in the possibility of reconciliation. The parabolic dimension concerns itself with contradictions. "Parables show the fault lines beneath the comfortable surfaces of the worlds we build for ourselves" (14). In the words of Anderson and Foley again,

"Mythic narratives comfort us and assure us that everything is going to be all right; parables challenge and dispute the reconciliation that our myths have created" (15). The liturgical rituals of the church graciously offer us this vital balance of comfort and challenge.

As a significant part of our liturgies, music touches our souls and emotions in ways that words and actions miss. The hymn "Were You There [When They Crucified My Lord]" is a reminder of our continued participation in the passion of Christ. Many of the most beloved and inspirational songs of faith grow out of the depth of commonly held and shared human experience. "Amazing Grace" is another such hymn.

The lyrics of a folk hymn, "Don't Wash Me," written by the Reverend David Butler for use during Lent reminds us of the uneasiness the disciples had with Christ being servant to them at the Last Supper. This folk hymn combines the mythic and parabolic dimensions of story in a most unsettling way. The lyrics touch and give voice to the struggle within us between our desperate yearning for reconciliation and healing and our fear that our entrenched habits and deep sense of felt unworthiness will sabotage or defile the grace offered through the sacrament.

> No, no, not this table, no;
> Not here and not now, Lord, don't wash me.
> I'm too weak, I'm too mean; I'm not good, I'm not clean,
> I don't know what you mean, please don't wash me.
> Yes I'm tired, I'm drained, I'm confused, lost and pained,
> I can't hear what you say, please don't wash me.
> Please don't ask me to pray, I'm too tired, I can't stay
> Awake one moment longer, don't wash me.
>
> Chorus: Take this bread, it is my body,
> Take this wine, it is my blood.
> Take this bread, it is my body,
> Take this wine, it is my blood.
>
> No, no, not this way, Lord no,
> With body and blood, Lord, don't feed me.
> I will lie, cheat, and steal when we finish this meal;
> I will run from your side, Lord, don't feed me.

I was never so good as your love thought I could be;
It's not worth your while, Lord, don't feed me.
Please don't leave me this way, I should die, you should stay,
Carry my sins away if you feed me.

Chorus

David Butler ©1997

This folk hymn's gift and power is that it calls forth the deep sense of unworthiness many persons feel, thereby making it available in worship for the healing grace offered in the sacrament of the Lord's Supper.

Confession/Reconciliation

Confession is a willingness to reveal to someone else our weakness and to let that person know us as we really are (Keith-Lucas, n.d.). While confession is a key element in any transformation process, it is not an easy thing to do. Some people prefer to avoid it altogether. But if we do avoid it, we rob ourselves of a potentially life-changing experience—we rob ourselves of a means of salvation and wholeness. This dis-ease with confession is exemplified in the following experience.

In a continuing education seminar composed of ordained and lay ministers representing a number of Protestant traditions, several pastors related the experience of groups within their local congregations vehemently requesting that the confessional part of the service be dropped from the liturgy. Their stated purpose was to make the service more "user-friendly" and more "comfortable" for people. Their concern seemed to center around a felt uneasiness in persons with acknowledging their own sinfulness.

The pastors, who reluctantly gave into this request under tremendous political pressure from powerful groups within their congregations, experienced an interesting phenomenon. After several months of worship services devoid of a Prayer of Confession and the Assurance of Pardon that follows, people began asking that the dropped elements of the worship service be reinstated. They indicated they missed the opportunity to confess their sins and experience forgiveness. They missed the cleansing nature of confession. Upon further reflection, they indicated these parts of the service had actually increased their sense of personal wholeness rather than lessening it. These parts of the liturgy provided a ritualistic and nonhumiliating way of acknowledging parts of themselves they were not proud of and could otherwise continue to avoid and deny.

Confession and reconciliation are important ways we have of remaining in contact with our histories as individuals and people of faith so the lessons of our sinfulness in the past and our continued potential for it will not be easily forgotten or overlooked. In *The Living Reminder*, Henri Nouwen (1981) recounts Elie Wiesel's reflections about how the people of the Hungarian town of Sighet, from which he and other Jews living there at the time had been deported to concentration camps in 1944, "erased the Jews from their memory" (17). Commenting on this phenomenon, Nouwen states, "This story suggests that to forget our sins may be an even greater sin than to commit them. Why? Because what is forgotten cannot be healed and that which cannot be healed easily becomes the cause of greater evil" (17).

Nouwen (1981) then goes on to say, "By cutting off our past we paralyze our future: forgetting the evil behind us we evoke the evil in front of us" (18). In chapter two, we discussed the importance of personal connections with the past, and how cutting ourselves off from history was one way we kept evil veiled. *Confession and reconciliation are not for purposes of shaming us, but are rather a ritualized way of keeping us in contact with the evil we have corporately and individually perpetrated and remain capable of perpetrating.* The likelihood of our reproducing the evil of the past increases exponentially when we purge our memories of our past sins. Within the church, the practices of confession and reconciliation help us remember the important lessons gleaned from our past sinfulness. It is in this sense that the profound liturgical, ritualistic, and sacramental nature of confession and reconciliation become a means of grace for us rather than a source of shame.

Three Dilemmas Facing the Church

In preceding chapters, we have outlined the profound ways evil creates and builds upon divisions within and among persons through experiences of abuse, neglect, and violence. In the preceding sections of this chapter, we have outlined some of the powerful roles faith resources can play in healing the divisions evil creates. This material suggests there are three critical dilemmas the church must intentionally address if it is to play an effective role in confronting evil in the world. (By way of reminder, the term "church" used here does not specify any particular Christian denomination.) These dilemmas are: (1) how to make better and more effective use of the shared life experiences of its members within the worship and life of the church, (2) how to encourage people to bring into the worship and life of the church those aspects of themselves and their life experience they are most ashamed of and split-off from, and (3) how to talk about sin in a way that takes it seriously but does not shame us or lead us to view ourselves and others dichotomously as "all good" or "all bad."

Finding effective ways of responding to these dilemmas is crucial for the church and will have a direct impact on important areas affecting its future. These areas include the following: (1) the vitality and life of the church, (2) the extent to which the church will be a place that offers care and support to those who have been hurt by violence and abuse, and (3) the extent to which the church will offer an environment of healing for those elements within people that set them up to interact with others in hurtful ways. In short, creative solutions to these three dilemmas within all dimensions of church life, including its preaching, worship and liturgy, educational programming, and pastoral care work, will determine to what extent the church will make a significant contribution to transforming the forces of evil that destroy people's lives and perpetuate the cycle of abuse and violence.

The three dilemmas mentioned above are exemplified in the following case. As a bright businessman in his late thirties, the man came to therapy seeking help with integrating a painful and shameful aspect of his past. For years he had remained terrified that part of his past he had kept hidden from all but a few people would spontaneously surface in some way and publicly humiliate him.

In his mid-teens, he had sexually assaulted a girl his own age after an episode of binge drinking. He was so drunk at the time, he suffered a blackout for the event and had no direct memory of his own for it. It was only over time, and with repeated exposure to descriptions of the event by law enforcement personnel and friends at the scene that he had come to an awareness of what he had actually done and the impact of his actions on the girl he had raped.

One day he reported how life-changing it had been for him years ago when he shared this aspect of his past with his first sponsor in his Alcoholics Anonymous (AA) recovery program. When he revealed this secret to this one other person, whom he trusted to hold it in confidence, he felt a new sense of relief. In response to this self-revelation, his sponsor revealed something from his own past that had been equally shaming for him. He decided, after this positive experience with his sponsor, to see a priest for the Sacrament of Reconciliation.

This experience was markedly disappointing to him, and he stated he came away from it with an empty sense that "nothing had happened." When asked why he thought this was, he passionately responded, "Because there was no shared life experience!" He then proceeded to say the reason he found church so unfulfilling was that people in the church, especially clergy, never share enough of their own life experience for him to feel they have anything he wants or needs for himself. When we in the church disconnect the divine narrative from our shared human experience, we rob it of some of its transforming power. John McDargh (1993) writes, "Our stories of God reflect, at their deepest levels, our most profound experiences of being met or overlooked, of being taken up and decoded or left unread" (239). When there is no shared life experience in the church, we feel as though we have been left "unread."

The importance of sharing our life experience (story) with others is underscored by Anderson and Foley (1998) when they state, "Telling our story honestly is a necessary component of reconciliation and wholeness in human communities" (167). Such honesty is crucial, they argue, since "secret keeping" is "deceptively mythic" and undercuts the parabolic function of ritual, which constantly challenges our complacency (17). It is the lack of shared life experience and our propensity for keeping our lives secret from one another, especially those experiences we are most ashamed of, that is one dilemma the church must address.

The second dilemma faced by the church is a corollary of the first. It revolves around the issue of how to encourage people to bring to church and into community and relationship with others those aspects of themselves they are most reluctant to acknowledge but are most in need of healing. In the words of Anderson and Foley (1998), "The future of faith communities depends on their capacity to foster an environment in which human and divine narratives regularly intersect" (40). This type of intersection does not occur when we keep our stories to ourselves. The type of healing and transforming environment that will make a difference in people's lives not only requires honesty of self-expression, but also must facilitate the lifting up of that which has been split-off and kept previously inaccessible. A female chaplain related the following story of how life-changing and freeing a new awareness and confession of a hidden part of a one's past could be.

While visiting in the hospital with a woman dying of cancer, the patient began sharing a desire to discontinue chemotherapy. The woman had been told the chemotherapy treatments would not cure her but might extend her life a few weeks or months. She wanted desperately to have her remaining time with her family as free of extraordinary medical procedures as possible, and she did not want the interference of scheduled chemotherapy sessions that might also leave her with unpleasant side effects.

Her question to the chaplain was this: "Is it all right to say, 'No more!'?" As the chaplain explored this further, the woman confessed she had been molested as a little girl by a friend of her family. This man had threatened if she ever told anyone, he would kill her parents. She had remained quiet about the abuse all these years, continuing to carry the burden of not feeling free to tell her story. As she related this experience to the chaplain, the woman became aware that her inability as a little girl to stop the abuse and her fear that her family would suffer if she did say something were still controlling her life through her inability to say, "No."

As her story unfolded, and as she discovered acceptance and affirmation in the chaplain's supportive assurance, she became able to muster the strength to say no to the doctor and the strength to maintain that position in the face of considerable pressure to get her to try new forms of chemotherapy. At that point, she regained control of her life, a control she had lost years ago at the time of her abuse. She could now free herself of the burden of passively enduring for someone else's sake.

This example demonstrates how the continued sealing off of unacceptable parts of our selves from ourselves, others, and God, leaves us prey to the hurts of the past and devoid of hope for the future. If those of us who attend worship services are hypocrites, it is not that we act differently outside of church than we do inside, but it is because we leave outside the church doors those very parts of ourselves most in need of hearing the gospel message. If people are going to bring into the worship and life of the church these dimensions of themselves, a way must be found to avoid repeating the all-too-familiar scenario of some persons making themselves naked and vulnerable and becoming sacrificial lambs for the community, while those standing around them all too willingly throw stones.

The third dilemma faced by the church has to do with helping persons find ways to reconcile and integrate split-off parts of themselves with the rest of themselves. When we become aware of the splits and divisions within ourselves, we come face-to-face with our sinfulness and our potential for perpetrating evil. The potential danger here is that shame and fear will lead us to condemn ourselves and keep ourselves split-off and out of touch with the grace available to us. The power of ritual and liturgy to surprise us and open up a healing process is portrayed in a vision a student shared with his professor upon their return from an overseas evangelism seminar (shared by Bob Tuttle, School of Ministry, Indianola, Iowa, 1997). The vision took place within one of the awe-inspiring cathedrals they visited while in Paris.

In this vision, the student saw himself walking down the center aisle of the cathedral approaching the chancel and the communion table. As he took the first step up to the altar, the chalice on the altar tipped and fell forward spilling the wine held inside. As the wine spilled out onto the table, the altar split open. The wine continued to pour out through the split in the table and onto the floor, which then also split open.

As the student visually followed the flowing wine down into the crevasse it was creating, a dreadful-looking leathery creature appeared out of the depths of the earth. It looked up at him with bright red eyes and a fiery mouth. In fear and trembling, but seeking to determine the nature of this beast, the student looked back at the creature and asked, "Do you know the Lord Jesus Christ?" The creature replied, "I am a part of you!" In the next scene, the student and the creature are at the communion rail kneeling next to one another and receiving the sacrament.

After sharing this vision, the student acknowledged that years ago he had split off a part of himself he was ashamed of and consigned it to hell. In this healing vision, the blood of Christ had graciously spilled from the chalice, descended into hell, and released that part of him he had long ago decided was evil and was destined to be condemned forever. This alienated part of himself could now be reconciled with the rest of him, and they became one once more as they received Holy Communion together.

10

God and the Devil:
The Ultimate Example of Splitting

NOT ALL RELIGIOUS BELIEFS and perspectives promote psychological health and healing. While there is little doubt that the diverse forms religious faith takes can provide comfort to many persons and promote remarkable healing, there is also little doubt that some faith perspectives and the religious practices supported by them can be hurtful to persons (Wipple 1987; Brock 1989).

An example of a religiously supported action that was unhelpful to a person is the situation involving the woman, described in chapter two, who received a letter from her pastor removing her from church membership. For several years, she continued to ponder the meaning of this action. When she learned years later the pastor took this action because he deemed her "a threat to the unity of the church" and "disobedient to her husband," her hurt and confusion were rekindled. The conclusion she could not let go of was that this action was confirmation she was "really bad," since "Even God rejected me and threw me away." This act on the part of the pastor served to reenforce her internal view of herself as innately bad and unworthy of life.

Scott Peck (1983) discusses reasons for psychology's lack of interest in the subject of evil and the subsequent lack of a "psychology of evil." He places the reason for this state of affairs with the "unwritten social contract of nonrelationship" between science and religion (40). Originating at the time of the church's conflict with Galileo in the late seventeenth century, Peck states that the natural world became the province of science, while religion held onto affairs of the supernatural world. He then goes on to say the following:

All this is changing, however. The end result of a science without religious values and verities would appear to be the Strangelovian lunacy of the arms race; the end result of a religion without scientific self-doubt and scrutiny, the Rasputinian lunacy of Jamestown. For a whole variety of factors, the separation of religion and science no longer works. There are many compelling reasons today for their integration—one of them being the problem of evil itself (Peck 1983, 40).

Our discussion here is not about the integration of science and religion. In fact, as we hope to demonstrate, an uninformed "blending" of science (in this case psychology) and religion can be terribly destructive to persons. This is particularly the case when a religious cosmology (or worldview) is hermeneutically imposed in an ill-informed and uncritical fashion upon complex psychological processes and is used as justification for interacting with persons in ways that do added harm to persons already devastated by abuse.

The key to reducing the potential for evil as manifested in entrenched cycles of abuse and violence is in finding ways to promote integration and healthy developmental growth within the mental worlds of people. While some religious worldviews facilitate this endeavor, other religious cosmologies hinder and complicate it. In this regard, the division of the world into the two irreconcilable elements of God and Satan within traditional Western Christian thought is particularly relevant. What we know about the development of human mental structure, more specifically the development and structuralization of the self, and the significant role played in this process by the defense mechanism of splitting is also relevant. The interplay of this split cosmology and the psychological process of splitting is the primary focus of this chapter.

There are two main issues central to this discussion. The first issue is the radically split nature of the cosmology undergirding much of traditional Western Christian theology as it is operative at a practical level within congregations of faith at broad grassroots levels and across denominational lines. The second issue pertains to the detrimental impact theological perspectives based on such a cosmology have on the psychological health of persons not only within particular congregations of faith, but also on all persons living in a culture so profoundly influenced by this theology.

God and Satan: A Split Cosmology

While there is growing interest in integrative processes (e.g., Wheatley 1994), signs point to the continuing tendency of human beings to split the universe. In her historical study entitled *The Origin of Satan*, Elaine Pagels (1995) reminds us that "the worldview of most peoples consists essentially of two pairs of binary opposites: human/not human and we/they" (37).

In this same regard, Peck (1983) describes the "traditional Christian model" as "humanity . . . locked in a titanic struggle between the forces of good and evil, between God and the devil. The battleground of this struggle is the individual human soul. The entire meaning of life revolves around the battle" (37; for a wonderful journey along the path of struggling with this split at a personal level, see Hermann Hesse's novel *Demian: The Story of Emil Sinclair's Youth*). The tremendous power of this particular worldview is described by Pagels (1995) in the following way: "So compelling is this vision of cosmic war that it has pervaded the imagination of millions of people for two thousand years . . ." (182).

Whether one accepts Pagels's compelling historical review or takes the theological position that the universe *is in fact* split as a result of Satan's opposition to God is a matter of personal belief. Even though this subject is one of great importance, it is not our purpose here to enter a theological or philosophical debate on this topic. Rather, we want to look at how a radically split cosmology, whatever its origin and "validity," can interact with psychological processes to do harm to persons.

With regard to the issue of evil, the practical impact of the "traditional Christian model" as described by Peck (1983) is made clear in this statement by him: "This book will concern itself solely with the subject of human evil, and its primary focus will be on 'bad' people" (45). It is our contention that viewing the world as engaged in this type of struggle and using it as a means of focusing attention on "bad people," who are usually "out there," is itself a manifestation of evil as we are defining it. This is because the split and dichotomous worldview described above can lead to an exacerbation of splitting, to a solidifying of differences, and to greater degrees of divisiveness rather than to the reconciliation and healing of divisions within individuals and among groups and diverse peoples of the world.

The "traditional Christian model" of which Peck speaks is particularly relevant to this discussion and is particularly troublesome. From this vantage point, the universe is dichotomously divided into Heaven and Hell, or into "the realm of God" and "the realm of Satan." It normally follows from this way of thinking that "that which is good has come from God" and "that which is bad has come from the Devil." This view has contributed massively to destructive divisions *among* persons. In the words of Pagels (1995) again: "Conflict between groups is . . . nothing new. What may be new in Western Christian tradition . . . is how the use of Satan to represent one's enemies lends to conflict a specific kind of moral and religious interpretation, in which 'we' are God's people and 'they' are God's enemies, and ours as well" (xix). Kathleen Norris (1998) states, "Genocide is justified in the eyes of those who perpetrate it on the grounds that it is not real people who are being killed; rather, something evil is being eliminated from the world by those who are good" (176).

Not only does the radically split cosmology just described contribute to potentially violent divisions *among* persons, but a similar process can occur *within* persons. Within some religious circles, these divisions are also along the lines of traits considered "of God" and those considered "of Satan."

The Tragic Use of the "Of God/Of Satan" Split

The church's traditional way of dealing with what it perceives to be "evil" has been to exorcise it, dispel it, and throw it out. This approach promotes the idea that there is something inside a person that must be gotten rid of. Something alien to a person has gotten inside and must be expelled in order to save the person from greater danger and the potential of hurting someone else or themselves. From this perspective, the goal of "faithful" living is to rid oneself of those aspects of self that can be conceived as being "of Satan" (evil) and to infuse one's self with those attitudes and characteristics considered "of God" (good). In extreme cases, the activity of split-off aspects of oneself that are troublesome or harmful to oneself and/or others has been considered a sign of possession by evil spirits (demons), and exorcism has been used as a way of "ridding one of their presence," i.e., the presence of Satan (evil).

By way of example, it is not uncommon in working with persons suffering from dissociative identity disorder to discover that a person has been pressured by well-meaning people to participate in an exorcism for the purpose of ridding her of persecutory alters which have been labeled "demons." In such cases, these split-off dimensions of the self have typically taken executive control of one's physical body, drawn attention to themselves, succeeded in scaring someone, and/or overtly threatened to harm the individual herself or someone else. Exorcism under these conditions is most often reactive and oppressive.

The impact of such religious views, and the rituals and ceremonies associated specifically with exorcism, can have harmful consequences for persons who have been violated in some profound way, especially those survivors who manifest dissociative symptoms or suffer from dissociative disorders (Fraser 1993). One such consequence has been a furthering of divisions already existing within a person and a reinforcement of an already internalized message that parts of herself are totally unacceptable, dangerous, and unwelcome. In addition, such an experience can increase the level of fear already existent about the presence of powerful and often little-known forces within herself, can increase her felt lack of control over her life, and can make the integrative work with these typically distrustful parts even more difficult.

By virtue of the fact that split-off parts within the self are to a greater or lesser degree dissociated from the self, they frequently take on the quality of feeling alien. They feel like they do not belong to us and are not a part of us. At those times when we are "not ourselves," such split-off parts may be in control of our lives. The more one has dissociated herself from some split-off and troublesome aspect of self or life experience, or from some aspect of self that is incongruent with how she sees herself and wants to be perceived by others, the greater the likelihood she will see that part of herself as alien, and quite often as bad.

And yet these alien feeling aspects of ourselves are generally most in need of reparative work and healing transformation. This is because it is through such work that these split-off parts can become integrated with the rest of the self and in the process lose their destructive powers. Yet these are the very aspects of ourselves we are most reluctant for others to see out of fear that the whole of us will be condemned because of their presence. Such fear plays a major role in a person's resistance to bring into light (and into communal relationship with others) those aspects of herself that are most in need of acceptance and healing. It is within this context that the wisdom of Allen Keith-Lucas (n.d.) is evident when he states that for a helping relationship to be truly helpful a way must be found to "exorcise fear." In his sensitive and conceptually clear way, Stephen Prior (1996) discusses this resistance, or more appropriately this fear, in his discussion of working with sexually abused boys in psychotherapy. In this regard he states the following: "The abused child wants to convey disorganized, frightening, and repulsive feelings, all the while believing that if he does convey them, it will cost him the very relationship that he wants and needs so much" (127).

Prior goes on to discuss how "violent play is the child's way of bringing his issues and fears into treatment, of making real contact with the therapist, and of making the unintegrateable experiences he has lived through tangible for the therapist and himself" (128). While acknowledging the importance of facilitating affect regulation, behavioral containment, and ego building, Prior continues, "If the therapist rejects the primitive, sadomasochistic play, he or she may well *confirm* in the child's mind that the core of the child's self *is* bad, that adults cannot understand or tolerate who he is or what he has experienced, and that if the child conveys who he is, he will be rejected. . . . All too often, this rejection . . . replicates the chronic pattern of the child's life in the family, schools, or treatment system—of being rejected by adults and institutions for aggressive or perverse behavior that he cannot control and that expresses the realities of his life and his feelings. . . . This generates intense guilt and despair that the child suffers completely alone" (129–30). This statement conveys the excruciating dilemma faced by persons struggling with split-off aspects of themselves with which they want assistance, but which also scare, intimidate, and disturb themselves and others. The tragic result is that such persons not only do not get the help they so desperately seek, but their interactions with others are such that people often keep them at a distance, judge them, and even impose legal restraints and restrictions on them. The paradoxical and tragic result of these reactions on the part of others is the ever increasing *loss* of control and power these patients experience over their own lives. It is this series of confounding interchanges that was discussed in chapter four and represented in figures 4 and 5.

By way again of example, a fear of self-exposure is shared by dissociative identity patients at various stages of their treatment. It is common to find such patients fearful of allowing their alters to meet the therapist. This fear is based in part on the lack of control and awareness that often accompanies the process of switching among the radically dissociated ego states and dimensions of the self that alters represent. Overt and intentional switching, in the presence of someone in authority who is attuned, powerful, wanted, and needed, leaves a person seeking help with an intense sense of vulnerability. This vulnerability is based in a lack of knowledge about what a particular alter might say or do, and about how the therapist will respond.

This fear is amplified exponentially if one considers herself possessed and controlled by some evil force. We naturally and defensively want to distance ourselves from that which we are afraid or from that which feels strange and mysterious to us. The view that a person is possessed by some evil force that must be expelled further divides her within herself and increases the self-alienation she already experiences.

Furthermore, the idea that disturbing parts of the self must be "gotten rid of" increases the sense that there *is* some aspect of oneself that others will find repulsive, unacceptable, unforgivable, and unredeemable. This is one of the most common fears among most individuals who start a counseling process—that something about them is so bad that there will be no hope for acceptance and forgiveness if it comes to light. This was the case in the example of the man in chapter nine who lived in constant fear that his criminal record would suddenly be exposed and used perpetually to judge him. Fear such as this is often based on the belief that those personal traits considered by oneself and others as "bad" will be considered as more important and influential than the "good" aspects of oneself, i.e., that the "bad" will forever taint the "good," and forgiveness and wholeness are only wishful illusions.

There may even be aspects of ourselves that we have come to feel so badly about that we have "condemned them to hell." We saw an illustration of this in the student's vision shared at the close of the previous chapter. This fear is exacerbated when someone with perceived authority confirms that one indeed *is* possessed by an evil force, and there is no hope except to cast it out and return it to the hell from which it came. To the extent one remains psychically connected to parts split-off within the self, there is the additional fear that if one part is unredeemable, so must be the whole, and if one part is cast out, the whole self will follow. This perspective contributes to an often already intense internal sense of vileness and evil, and in extreme cases can add to an already present rationale one has worked out to justify harming or even killing oneself.

The Interplay with Splitting

In chapter three, we discussed how a person's sense of self develops, and how the defense mechanism of splitting is a normal process that occurs during the early stages of mental development. The purpose of the splitting defense is to protect the still fragile and developing ego and self from being overwhelmed by negative affect and being confused by an incomprehensible mixture of pleasant and unpleasant experience. We also discussed how splits within the self and object representations interact with and reflect one another. Also in chapter three we presented a figure representing a compilation of the early developmental sequences involving the processes of splitting and differentiation of self from other. Figure 8 is a revision of figure B, which was originally presented in figure 3.

In figure 8, the vertical axis represents the differentiation process by which self and object representations become separated and distinct. The bolded horizontal axis represents an active splitting defense. This is the phase of development in which the splitting defense plays a major role. This defensive process separates the developing self and object representations along the discrimination gradient of comforting and frustrating affective experience, thereby producing good and bad part-self and part-object representations. This same splitting defense then keeps these good and bad part-representations separated from one another.

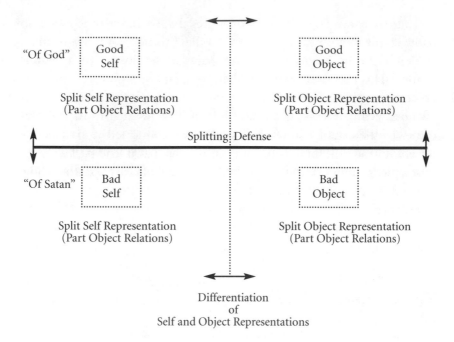

Figure 8: The "Of God"/ "Of Satan" Split

If development proceeds normally, more advanced defense mechanisms become operative, mental capacity for synthesis and integration continues to expand, and these split part-self and part-object representations are eventually integrated into whole self and object representations as was depicted in C of figure 3. Such an integration marks the achievement of the capacity to see self and others in a whole and integrated way and as composed of dimensions that can be nurturing and comforting of self and others (good), as well as frustrating and hurtful to self and others (bad).

The type of integration just described can be blocked and hindered by religious perspectives that are based on a dichotomous view of the universe in which forces of God and forces of Satan do battle. Such a view reinforces and rigidifies the natural splitting defense by normalizing the continual splitting of self and object representations into good and bad parts that are then respectively considered to be "of God" or "of Satan." This is represented in figure 8 by the headings "Of God" and "Of

Satan" that are, respectively, above and below the bold horizontal line representing a rigidified splitting defense.

This way of thinking produces a number of severe consequences. It immediately reinterprets the meaning of "good" and "bad" self and object representations from that which they are—descriptions of the affective feeling states of comfort and frustration, to that which they are not—rigidified moralistic judgments about particular aspects of one's self. In addition, the reinforcement of the natural splitting defense by religious viewpoints essentially "freezes" psychological development at a level where splitting is the major defense.

Lastly, an imposed religious perspective that views the world as divided between the forces of Satan and the forces of God provides little in the way of support and encouragement for persons to develop more integrated, flexible, and holistic perspectives through which to interpret the world and other people. As described in chapter three, when splitting remains a primary defense mechanism, a person's capacity for developing whole object relations suffers. In turn, the development of human qualities such as mercy, grace, and forgiveness that require the capacity to entertain and reconcile opposites and embrace ambiguity is greatly hindered. The danger of a split cosmology of the type we are describing is that it effectively transforms a developmentally appropriate, though transient, psychological defense into a worldview that becomes fixed and supported by religious interpretations and perspectives. In turn, this view becomes a major prism-like lens through which the whole of life is viewed.

Operating at a nearly unconscious level, this lens actively splits the world in a clear and seemingly natural way and provides a well-entrenched rationalization for eliminating any and all elements of life considered "of Satan." One destructive consequence of this view is that it provides the support for what Sam Keen has referred to as "sanctified violence" (Iowa Psychological Association Conference, 1999). At the same time, this religious perspective has so much power because it intuitively feels so congruent with this early and very effective means of making the complexities of life more comprehensibly simple. As a result, the interaction and mutual reinforcement of a split religious cosmology and the primitive and powerful psychological defense mechanism of splitting becomes seemingly unchallengeable.

The Case of Johnny:
Using the Devil to Justify Neglect

The following illustration is presented to point out how a faith perspective that dichotomizes persons and the universe can turn even a little boy against himself and his basic needs and can serve as justification for continued neglect and potential abuse.

A six-year-old boy, Johnny, was presented by his parents for a problem with temper outbursts. The parents described Johnny as "losing it" at times and throwing tantrums in which he would lay on the floor kicking and screaming or at other times would impulsively hit them or his eight-year-old sister. These situations usually occurred in the evening at bedtime when Johnny would make it very clear he was "not ready for bed yet!" They also occurred out in public when he did not get something he wanted or at home when his sister was getting attention from their parents. In one reported incident, Johnny threw a fit when he was ordered out of his "sister's chair" as the family sat down at the kitchen table for dinner. Johnny reported that he did not like acting this way because he felt "unlike" himself at these times, he felt uncomfortably "out of control," and he wanted his parents to "like me," rather than "hate me" as he felt they did.

After meeting with Johnny and his parents separately and together for a few evaluation sessions, the counselor and intake staffing consultants concluded Johnny was protesting a lack of basic care and nurture on the part of his parents. The clearest evidence for this conclusion was that at bedtime mom and dad would not interact with Johnny in the normal rituals associated with getting ready for bed. There was no help offered or parental interaction with Johnny around such activities as taking a bath, brushing his teeth, or cuddling and reading a story together. In short, there was little interaction between the parents and Johnny of a nurturing sort. Rather, the predominant description of their relationship was symbolized by the cool and detached command to "go to bed now!" This pattern seemed characteristic of most interactions between Johnny and his parents.

At the next appointment, the counselor was prepared to offer his conclusions to the parents and recommend a treatment plan, but they precipitously revealed "things were better." When asked what had changed, the parents stated that, because of his unruly behavior, they were concerned their son might be "possessed by the Devil." After the last counseling session, they had taken him to their pastor to be evaluated for "spirit possession." The pastor concluded Johnny *was* possessed and immediately performed an "exorcism." During this process, the pastor reported to the parents that he saw "an evil spirit leave the boy in a cloud of green vapor." He then prayed for the "Spirit of Jesus" to enter Johnny, which they reported did happen.

After revealing this course of events, the parents then informed the counselor there was no reason to pursue further counseling since the problem they were concerned about was solved. When the counselor asked the boy in the presence of his parents how he was feeling, he stated, "I'm not as angry now because Jesus is in my heart and the Devil is gone." He also said he hoped his old behavior would now stop so his parents would "like" him and not "hate" him. There was no reported change in parents' involvement in bedtime routines or the amount of nurturing offered to Johnny at other times, and the family never returned for further counseling.

While it is important to respect the various beliefs people bring with them as they seek help, cases like this are disturbing. They confront us with the realization of how certain religious views contribute to the dichotomous splitting of persons into "good" and "bad" traits. In cases like the one just described, such splitting causes harm. First of all, labeling a child's normal reactions to a lack of care as "bad behavior" is an example of the type of mislabeling discussed in chapter two that not only misleads us but actually revictimizes the victim. Second, attributing these "bad" traits to "the work of the Devil" is an all-too-tempting rationalization that allows persons, in this case primary caretakers, to avoid responsibility and accountability for the impact their own action, or inaction, has on others. Third, the splitting of persons into "good" and "bad" character traits by an imposed and split religious cosmology creates within persons, who are most often susceptible to suggestion and in a less powerful position to begin with, an impression that there are supernatural forces and powers at work within them over which they have no control. Such a perspective can increase and further crystallize one's already present sense of vulnerability, lack of control, and helplessness. In the case just presented, this person was a vulnerable child.

The Devil Outside

Walter Wink (1986) has said, "The issue is not whether there is a metaphysical entity called Satan, but how we are to make sense of our actual experiences of evil" (25). He then goes on to say, "Beliefs about Satan are matters of debate. The experience of Satan is a brute and terrifying fact" (26). The following illustrations are offered to demonstrate how real, tangible, and personified evil can be, and how long-lasting and insidious its effects can be. These are among the clearest and most disturbing examples of evil we have seen in our respective practices.

There are extreme cases of abuse in which the perpetrator tells the victim, and then reinforces the message by means of acts he performs, that he is placing something foreign within her that will remain with her forever as a constant reminder of him. In one particularly vile case, a rapist told a young girl of eight as he penetrated her that he was going to "pump tiny evil germs into her" that would slowly "infect her from the inside and make her totally bad." One day, as an adult woman in therapy, an eight-year-old alter of hers drew a picture of a young girl on her back with a well-contained pool of sperm-shaped "germs" spread throughout her abdominal cavity. While taking the form of a collage composed of differing perceptions stemming from different levels of cognitive development and different pieces of sex information, this picture clearly depicted the rape of this young girl and the continued presence within her of the rapist's description of what he had done to her.

Messages from a perpetrator can be delivered to and taken in by a victim in many ways, and the messages themselves can take many forms. When a perpetrator takes advantage of a developmental process that is occurring within the victim and associates his message and actions with that process, the message's power and damage can increase over time. An example of this was reported by a woman who, as a young girl, was molested at the time her breasts were developing. As he molested her, the perpetrator told her he was fondling her breasts "to help them grow bigger." He then added, "When they are fully developed, they will remind you of me and our special time together. When you get married and your husband does this, you will also think of me."

Expressions of evil similar to those just presented pose a complex set of problems. Occurring at an early age when magical thinking is at its peak, tied to maturational processes that are obvious and cannot be denied, taking advantage of naturally occurring sensations, and associating a perpetrator's actions with a predictable future occurrence, comments and acts such as those just described take on tremendous power and exert continuing influence within a victim's mind (including her developing self-image) for extended periods of time. The massive cognitive, emotional, and structural distortions associated with such expressions of evil contribute substantially to chronic conditions that are extremely difficult to correct. The "Quick-Fix" and short-term focus of the present cultural milieu in which this needed reparative work must be done is incredibly unsupportive of this task.

These case examples are presented to demonstrate how the evil dimension of abuse, violence, and neglect not only produces increased splits within the self-structure and creates a deep sense of self-alienation, but actually results in something alien to the victim becoming "lodged" within her. This occurs as a natural consequence of our internalization of experience. In a very real sense, Satan Outside becomes Satan Inside, and this alien entity then reeks havoc as it interferes with all subsequent developmental processes. As the self on its developmental journey reacts to this actual intrusion, it becomes a complex and entangled Gordian knot-like mixture of that which is inherent, true, and "God given," and that which is in fact "the work of the Devil."

In such cases, it is important to help an individual caught in this dilemma sort out as best she can that which is central and inherent to herself and that which has been formed in reaction to what was diabolically forced upon her and is in fact alien to her. In cases where this can be successfully accomplished, some ritualized way of getting this truly alien element "out of her" or "exorcised" could then be appropriately considered.

The Devil Inside:
Working with Our Bad Objects

Because the psychological mechanism of splitting is such a basic and effective defense, it is always available for use, especially at times of great stress and fear. It is in essence one of our best defensive fallback positions and a familiar place in which to regress when we feel overwhelmed. Thus, it is not surprising that we see it most active and predominant in those times and places where people are confused, fearful, and threatened, and/or fighting for what is most precious to them. It is this fallback position that can be quickly mobilized whenever there is a need to justify or sanctify violence against some perceived or actual threat—whether this be at an individual, relational, institutional, cultural, or even national level.

Because it helps us divide the world into such clearly defined dichotomous categories, splitting can serve an important survival function, especially in those situations that require an immediate response. Splitting enables us to differentiate ourselves succinctly and quickly from our perceived enemies. From such a position, we can envision being securely surrounded by other "good people" like ourselves and aligned with a wholly good and powerful god who is "totally on our side." For all intents and purposes, this would appear to be the most psychologically secure position possible. It is, however, an illusion.

By design, splitting is a process that hinders the entertainment of ambiguity. By its very nature, a psychic structure built around splitting as its major ego defense is not conducive to facilitating the resolution of complex issues requiring sensitivity to varying cultural perspectives, mediation and negotiation, and the reconciliation and healing of apparently opposing positions. These are the very skills, however, that are more and more required by the increasing connectedness of our multicultural societies and world. One of the consequences of a lack of these types of skills, and the psychological maturity and stability they require, can be seen at a public level in the breakdown of public discourse, dialogue, and judgment, which has contributed to the inability to make well-informed decisions about issues of national and global consequence (Yankelovich 1991).

Sooner or later, in one way or another, to be truly secure, we must face and work with our bad objects—those that are outside and those that are inside. Based upon the understanding of evil we have presented, evil acts committed by persons against other persons are in part driven by split-off elements within the self-structures of the perpetrator. Such acts do violence to an individual, create and exacerbate rifts within the victim's self-structure and self-concept, contribute to increased alienation from self and others, and lead to the internalization of bad objects. When professional attitudes, intervention strategies, personal and cultural worldviews, and religious systems of thought amplify, intensify, and rigidify the splits and alienation already existing among persons and within victims and perpetrators, they do more harm than good.

What is needed at religious and psychological levels is an intervention approach that seeks to welcome and embrace those aspects of persons that have become split-off and alienated from the rest of themselves so as to create an environment conducive to a process of reacquaintance, remembering, grieving, reconciliation, healing, and wholeness. Such a process facilitates the transformation and integration of the unintegrated, but internalized, bad objects that have become the demons that haunt us from the inside and make life so destructively difficult for ourselves and others.

From a psychological perspective, such an intervention strategy must proceed slowly and intentionally. In order to preclude the fear and possibility of one's self becoming overwhelmed by those elements that have been defensively split-off, the integrative process must be preceded by and include periodic work that emphasizes the following elements: (1) affirmation and strengthening of a person's true self, (2) the development of higher levels of ego strength and resiliency, (3) the clarification and reframing of cognitive distortions resulting from traumatic events that contributed to the original splits within the self, (4) successful implementation of strategies of containment and the controlled release of affect, (5) the development of strategies for moving out of and staying out of traumatic thinking processes, and (6) active practice and developing competence in an ability to move increasingly closer to, and then away from, those split-off elements of the self.

This type of work brings the therapist, as well as other caregivers working with a particular person, face-to-face with the powerful and disturbing elements that comprise a survivor's internal world. Among the most disturbing of these are unintegrated, internalized bad objects that are mental representations and introjects of persons who have actually abused and neglected an individual. These internal bad objects reflect the actual attributes of abusers as originally experienced by a child (or adult). These attributes are interpreted through the lens of her particular prior life experience and the developmental level operative at the time of the abuse and are embellished by her own fantasies and distortions about these persons (Seinfeld 1990, ix, 19). While working with these internal bad objects is extremely difficult and challenging for therapists, caregivers, and patients alike, it is crucial to healing (Fairbairn 1952).

A survivor's continuing attachments to these internalized bad objects can be intense and represent the tremendous need one has to be attached to *someone* and not be alone. These internalized bad objects form a dyadic relationship with the internal self-representations of the survivor, and the interplay between them takes the form of an internalized and ongoing replication of the original abuse. Thus, what was once perpetrated on the survivor by someone else, she now does to herself. Since this occurs internally and outside of conscious awareness, the unseen but constantly felt havoc these objects wreak upon a survivor are difficult for her and others to comprehend, and provides a constant catalyst for intra- and interpersonal turmoil and misunderstanding. As a result, these objects come to exert unyielding power and control over her life. These internalized bad objects take the form of what Merle Jordan (1986) refers to as "psychic false gods who usurp God's place at the center of the self and oppressively define people's identities" (23). This helps to place in context Fairbairn's view that "the term *salvation* was a more apt designation than that of *cure* for the patient's subjective experience of his need to be rescued from the bad object" (Seinfeld 1990, x).

As touched upon in chapter four, in one of the few references to "demons" (traditionally thought of as evil spirits) within the psychotherapeutic literature, Stephen Johnson (1985) discusses working with schizoid adaptations that result from a child actually being hated by early caretakers. While not necessarily schizoid in character structure, persons subjected to severe and chronic early childhood abuse and neglect do feel hated. In this work, Johnson states that it is necessary to face what he refers to as "the destructive, demonic force" within such persons (67). Elaborating on these "demons," he states they are "typically experienced as completely alien and often completely beyond the control of the individual. Structurally, I believe it is useful to understand this as an unassimilated introject for the mothering figure, as well as the natural response of rage to this rejecting or cold figure" (67).

As we are also suggesting, the approach Johnson (1985) outlines in working with these powerful forces within persons is one of engagement rather than fear and rejection (134). He explains the rationale supporting this approach in the following way: "The demon work is particularly effective because it begins to elicit the aggressive part of the real self and to increase the client's identification with this denied part. . . . In this respect, the demon represents an unlocked window in what may otherwise be a well-locked fortress" (135).

To summarize the process involved in the intrapsychic work with the demons that Johnson (1985) describes, there are four main elements. In a planned and intentional manner, the therapist's role is as follows: (1) engage the survivor's unintegrated internalized bad objects and split-off rage ("demons") as a way of mobilizing and making overt their presence and influence in her intrapsychic world and in her interpersonal interactions with others; (2) help the patient differentiate herself at an intrapsychic level from the "demonic" force possessing her; (3) help her clarify the internal resources she has of her own to deal with it; and (4) clarify with her the external origin of these now internal "demons."

As we saw from the work of Prior (1996), it is important for a therapist to have the capacity and willingness to tolerate and embrace with structure those split-off internalized bad objects or "demons" that are so profoundly disturbing, disruptive, and demanding. This willingness is a necessary element in psychotherapeutic endeavors conducive to the reconciliation and healing of the internal mental worlds of persons ravaged by abuse and violence in our culture. This same capacity and willingness is needed by *all* those who seek to be helpful to survivors.

Looking for the Message Carried by the "Satan"

The tremendous, long-lasting, and insidious impact that evil acts have on persons is well-known and has been amply presented here. The continuing impact these acts have on persons is largely related to the creation and subsequent activity of split-off dimensions of self and life experience (including powerful affects), the internalization of bad objects that are not yet integrated within one's mental world, and the powerfully negative and constant interactive effect these same internalized bad objects have on a person's self-representations and sense of self. Each of these elements has an extremely disruptive effect on the intra- and interpersonal lives of survivors. To the extent these same processes are operative within perpetrators, the impact on them is similar.

These split-off elements within the mental worlds of survivors and perpetrators, including unintegrated and split-off bad part-self and part-object representations, are viewed in many religious circles as things to distance from, cast out, and be rid of. The extent to which this is the case seems to be in direct proportion to whether or not the following criteria are met: (1) these elements make themselves known to others in some manner; (2) they disturb or frighten others; (3) they chronically interfere with one's life in ways obvious to others; (4) they result in actions that others deem repugnant, distasteful, harmful, or fractious to the community-at-large; and (5) the worldviews of the predominant surrounding faith community encourages viewing their presence as "the work of the Devil" or "evil spirits" (demons) within the person. Ironically, these same elements are present in many persons to whom these criteria do not seem to apply because they are more personally adept at keeping such dynamics hidden and are often less socially abrasive than are those persons who are ultimately viewed as "possessed."

As a result of such views, however, *known* perpetrators *and* victims are ostracized and socially isolated from their social and religious communities, thereby effectively removing them from the very social milieu and gospel message that contains the potential for their respective transformation and healing. At the same time, those who remain *unknown* within the community continue to be frightened off by talk of "demon possession," while still others are welcomed and encouraged to reveal the "good" and further hide the "bad" within themselves.

It is within the context of this understanding and the material presented earlier in this chapter concerning the cosmological split between God and Satan that a return to Elaine Pagels's (1995) research becomes fruitful. Based on her historical review, she makes the following observation: "In the Hebrew Bible, as in mainstream Judaism to this day, Satan never appears as Western Christendom has come to know him, as the leader of an 'evil empire,' an army of hostile spirits who make war on God and humankind alike. As he first appears in the Hebrew Bible, Satan is not necessarily evil, much less opposed to God" (39).

She goes on to describe how "the Hebrew term the *satan* describes an adversarial role" and was used by Hebrew storytellers to "help account for unexpected obstacles or reversals of fortune" (Pagels 1995, 39). From this perspective, the *satan* is a messenger of God (angel) that can play an obstructive role that actually prevents us from falling into worse danger. The example of this to which Pagels refers is the biblical account of Balaam and his ass (Numbers 22:23-33).

While not specifically about evil, Pagels's research opens our eyes to the vast historical variations in how the term *satan* has been used over the centuries by religious communities of faith. In so doing, she offers us a plethora of alternatives to the cosmic battle motif we have referred to as "The Tragic Use of the 'Of God/Of Satan' Split." The tragedy here is in the manner with which this radically split and undergirding cosmology is used by some religious persons as justification for perpetrating evil on persons whom we do not understand, or who seem troublesome and harmful to us.

Critically important views of what is needed to heal the rifts within our culture and to help persons might change if we began to view the split-off and unintegrated aspects of ourselves, including our *internalized* bad objects and the pockets of grief and rage associated with them, as *satans* in the original sense—as messengers of God that seek to get our attention. We are *not* suggesting here that those who perpetrate evil and violence on others are "messengers from God." Neither are we wanting to minimize nor "glorify" the suffering of persons, which is always profound and often inconsolable. We *are* suggesting, however, that once we have internalized bad objects and they have become part of *our particular* mental structure, they, like other split-off aspects of ourselves, become a part of us for which *we* must take responsibility. This is a responsibility we cannot be expected to bear alone, however. It is a responsibility that can only be borne within community with others who are willing to share and help us with it.

The disruptions these *satans* produce within individuals and our culture may be God's way of telling us we cannot move on until we hear the unpleasant messages brought to us in the suffering and rage of persons we meet. These *satans* may be alerting us to the need to take shared responsibility for learning how to deal more effectively and empathetically, at individual and cultural/systemic levels, with the issues that they present to us in suffering persons. Prematurely casting them out (the *satans* or the persons), or turning our backs on them without first understanding them and the messages they bring to us, will not work. Such a strategy leaves the broken selves of persons still broken. It also leaves the structures of culture created by broken persons unhealed. The tragic result is that the ground is kept more fertile for the continuing propagation of evil.

Perhaps if we listen with courage and grace, instead of react out of fear with increasing control, power, and oppression, we can hear the vital messages these obnoxious and unsettling elements within ourselves and those around us are offering for our instruction. God does speak in mysterious ways. In addition, as we saw in chapter two, God must constantly search for ways to wake us from the various "sleeps of everyday life" to which we habitually retreat when we become overwhelmed by the massive responsibility of the stewardship God has entrusted to us.

Embracing One Another in Faith and Love: Two Closing Examples

The following two examples lift up for us radically different responses to persons who have hurt other persons. They are presented here as a way of making the preceding discussion more practical and real. Both examples involved males awaiting prosecution for sexually molesting children. In both cases these men were active members of church congregations, and their faith communities were an important part of their lives. Another point of similarity was that in both cases these men's pastors were women.

In the first instance, the man approached his pastor one day to inform her personally of his arrest, which had been publicized heavily in the local news media. In this meeting, he indicated that his faith and church were important to him, and he hoped he would be able to count on her support and prayers through the ordeal he was facing. She responded by reminding him she had a "large flock to take care of." She also informed him it would not be looked upon kindly by a majority of the church membership if she devoted time to pastoral care for him and took time away from others who had "greater needs for her attention." Needless to say, the pastor's response left this man with a deep sense of abandonment and a cynical attitude about the church he had faithfully served for years.

The second instance was quite different. In this case, the congregation discovered that a member of their community had been charged with molesting children and was awaiting trial. It was also learned that this was not the first such incident involving children that resulted from inappropriate and hurtful behavior on his part, although the extent of these incidents was not known. Over the course of several months, the pastor and a few members representing the congregation discussed this situation with him. They made it clear that they wanted to be of support to him and considered him an important part of their community of faith. They also indicated they were concerned for the welfare of the children in the congregation. Together they attempted to agree upon certain conditions and restrictions he would abide by to reduce contact with children at the church. These included the condition that another adult would be present during any interaction he had with children there, and that he would not enter the lower level of the church building where children's programs were held.

Before final agreement could be reached on these matters, the pastor got word that this man had killed himself at home, apparently in anticipation of his trial. Against the judgment of persons she consulted with about the best way to manage this situation in a pastoral manner, this pastor decided there needed to be a memorial service at the church for this man, and she invited his family who lived in another city. Her decision was in part a response to comments she had heard in the congregation at the time of his suicide along the following lines: "He must have felt terribly ashamed, but I don't understand how anyone could kill themselves like that!" and "I can't fathom what leads people like that to hurt others as he did."

The memorial service was held, and the man's family came. During the service there was direct reference made to the perceived dilemma he imposed upon the people of the church—the dilemma of wanting to be supportive and caring while also being concerned for his victims and the protection of potential victims. The fact he had killed himself was also directly addressed. Persons present were encouraged to express freely their own mixed feelings for this man—those aspects of him they had appreciated and those that they found intolerable and unacceptable. Those members of his family who were present did the same. At the conclusion of the service, and for a period of time afterward, gratitude was expressed for the opportunity the service provided to wrestle honestly and openly about all the mixed feelings members had about this man who had been a significant part of their life together in the church.

In reflecting on this experience, the pastor commented that she had been guided by three thoughts throughout this unsettling process. The first was expressed as follows: "I did not want people to believe we could separate him from our community by referring to him as 'one of those people' who did 'things' unrelated to the rest of us. That would be a denial of the community we all shared together." She went on to say, "The danger of idolatry occurs when the covenantal community is not self-critical and fails to value individuals along with the good of the whole." Her second guiding thought was this: "When unresolved stuff directs our response, it is a possible source of evil. Other people help us know what is unresolved for us. How then do we caringly help each other identify our unresolved stuff?" This was the third guiding thought: "If ministry is a magnification of the world, especially of life's traumas, then a minister needs the courage to walk with the faith community while being afraid and unclear."

Summary

From a religious perspective, many potential pitfalls can be avoided by following Wink's reminder that "Cosmology is not gospel" (Wink 1986, 5). The particular worldviews of ourselves and those we care for do entwine with one another, and they respectively color the perceptual and cognitive frameworks through which we each view the world. In these ways they radically affect how we interpret life and make meaning out of it. It is important, therefore, to distinguish these worldviews from the gospel message that offers freedom to the oppressed. As such, the gospel message will always be in tension with any particular and predominant cosmology. It is this complex interplay that at the practical level forms the essence of what Carroll Wise (1966) urged us to understand when he defined pastoral care as the art of communicating "the Gospel to persons at the point of their need" (9).

We can also benefit from the wisdom of persons such as W. R. D. Fairbairn (1955), who recognized the mysterious interplay between the spiritual and psychological dimensions of human beings when he stated: "I consider further that what is sought by the patient who enlists psychotherapeutic aid is not so much health as salvation from his past, from bondage to his 'internal' bad objects, from the burden of guilt and from spiritual death. His search thus corresponds in detail to the religious quest" (156).

Returning to the beginning of the chapter, as caregivers who are committed to our particular faith perspectives and seek guidance from them, our goal is not a blending of psychology (science) and religion. Rather, we feel it is important to recognize and pay homage to the tremendous wisdom each of these worldviews offers us and remain open to be guided by the best that both have to offer. And if we choose to walk in the fuzzy territory composed of the overlap of these two ever evolving bodies of wisdom, a territory that seems so intriguing and beckons for our attention, it is well for us to learn their respective languages. That way we can keep embracing them as the friendly helpmates they are, rather than experience them as the enemies they can be when we misuse one against the other, or remain oblivious to the profound interplay that goes on between them within the minds of those with whom we work. Without a due respect for the integrity of each, we can do irreparable harm to God's human creation, which is, after all, a most miraculous integration of the two.

11

Revisiting the "Wounded Healer"

THIS JOURNEY INTO THE REALM OF EVIL began on a personal note. In the introduction to this book, we reviewed a bit of personal history relative to how each of us became existentially aware of evil in the world and how we came to feel called to respond to evil in some way. In subsequent chapters, our attempt has been to present a perspective on evil that is congruent with our theoretical understandings of human development and traumatic life experience, sensitive to and reflective of the life experience of survivors with whom we have been privileged to work, and true to our respective theological and faith traditions.

The perspectives for understanding how evil works that we have presented derive directly from our work with survivors of abuse and neglect. The essence of our argument has been that abuse and neglect, regardless of whether they are perpetrated at the individual, institutional, or cultural levels of life, set into motion numerous attempts on the part of a victim to protect her self. In the absence of restorative relationships or some type of healing intervention on the part of other persons, and/or in the face of continued abuse and neglect, these adaptations and self defenses gradually become an integral part of one's character structure, continuing to function within a victim and maintaining a perpetual state of internal division.

The resulting alienation from self and others is a manifestation of evil that creates a fertile seedbed for further evil by producing the cleavages that later serve as points of leverage for still greater levels of separation and alienation. In addition, this separation increases the likelihood that future action on the part of a person will be motivated by some aspect of self that is outside conscious awareness and control. If these split-off parts of self and self experience contain reservoirs of affect that the individual has difficulty modulating, contain powerful need states, or if they are comprised of unintegrated and persecutory introjects, the potential for acting against self and others in a destructive and harmful fashion is greatly enhanced.

This scenario suggests that as caregivers we will want to attune ourselves to helping persons integrate within themselves those aspects of their selfs that remain unintegrated and split-off in some fashion. This focus on "healing the divisions within" individuals, while simultaneously working to reform those forces within society that create the need for the types of fragmenting and self-alienating adaptations we have been discussing, are among the best opportunities we have for reducing the self-propagating and rejuvenating power of evil in our world.

Based on this understanding, we have discussed ways caregivers within and outside religious communities can effectively intervene to stop the self-propagating potential for evil that abuse and neglect create. We have not yet discussed the critical role played in this endeavor by the brokenness of caregivers. It is now time to come full circle and look once more at ourselves.

Common Pitfalls

The interchanges that occur during the healing process between a victim of evil and a caregiver are complex. In order to manage this process in a manner that is truly helpful to those seeking help, caregivers must courageously and openly embark upon their own personal journeys into the split-off dimensions of their own selfs. The fruits of this interior journey will be an increased awareness of split-off dimensions of one's self, the increased availability of those dimensions for learning, and the opportunity for deeper levels of personal integration. Such a journey can also serve to reduce the likelihood that split-off dimensions of one's self will become spontaneously activated within the caregiving relationship in a manner that causes harm.

By virtue of the intra/interpersonal processes involved, a successful caregiving relationship will mobilize basic and split-off selfobject needs and reservoirs of affect (e.g., anger, rage, fear, grief, guilt, joy, worry, anxiety, and puzzlement) within a person, which have previously existed outside of awareness. Typically, the person within whom this occurs has no experience dealing with these important yet powerful parts of self. Neither has she/he yet developed the necessary regulatory functions and skills needed to integrate these basic needs and feelings with the rest of her/his self in a manner that will make them an appropriate and integral part of social interactions with others.

Especially in the beginning stages of a caregiving relationship, these unmanageable selfobject needs and affective states can rapidly become activated and are prime candidates for projection onto and into the caregiver. Once lodged within the caregiver, these projections have the potential for activating unintegrated and split-off dimensions within the self of the caregiver about which she/he may or may not have previous knowledge and awareness. If these activated dimensions become disturbing and powerful enough, they themselves can become candidates for projection onto and into the one seeking help. When this happens, the caregiver becomes a reverberating link in an unhelpful and intensifying process, and the caregiving relationship can become precipitously destructive.

The projective identification process is a normal method for communicating a particular dimension of one person's internal world to another person. This process may or may not involve the use of words. Its tremendous effectiveness, as well as its highly confounding quality, rests in its ability to create within the receiver an existential sense of the projector's internal mental and emotional state. It is as if that state becomes transported to the receiver who is then affected by it. This not only helps the projector reestablish internal equilibrium by getting rid of a disturbing element within the self, but it also helps him/her avoid responsibility for dealing with that element of self. Once lodged within the receiver, this projection can also motivate the receiver to act and respond in some way that is frequently impulsive and out of character.

The active use of projective identification within interpersonal relationships can clearly create volatile and destructive exchanges. Such a result is more likely when both parties in an interchange are actively engaged in a projection process and unaware of it. In this context the words of Knight (1985) take on tremendous importance: "the true healer cannot stand outside of the healing experience as a disinterested observer, but must be ready to have his or her own wounds activated and reactivated, but contained within and not projected" (cited in Miller and Baldwin 1987, 147).

Within a caregiving context, the ability of a caregiver to effectively use the projective identification process in a manner that is therapeutic not only requires an awareness of one's own split-off parts and the ability to appropriately manage and/or integrate them, but it also requires the presence of a number of other factors. Chief among these are the following: (1) a theoretical and existentially practiced understanding of projective identification, (2) a willingness and ability on the part of the caregiver to be used as a temporary container for that which the projector wants to get rid of, (3) a communal context that provides the structure, support, and interpretive skills necessary to hold the patient and caregiver as they work together, and (4) a continued openness to exploring and integrating split-off dimensions of self about which one may become aware as a result of fully engaging in caregiving relationships.

In a related matter, the intense affective states that often become mobilized within those seeking help can further heighten the tendency of caregivers to become confused and entrapped within their own countertransference reactions to ever more desperately appearing persons (Barach 1991). One common response to these reactions is that caregivers begin to overfunction. This response not only contributes to caregiver burnout, but also further disempowers a survivor as control and responsibility for her life is usurped by a caregiver who has become ensnared in this destructive process. Other countertransference reactions that can commonly occur within caregivers include voyeuristic fascination with the stories, experiences, and recollections associated with reported traumatic experiences; fear and/or revulsion leading to a desire to avoid the survivor or certain aspects of her life experience; the development of basic fears about their therapeutic effectiveness; and even concerns on the part of caregivers for their own personal safety. These reactions can also lead to such potentially dangerous consequences as intense preoccupation with the person in need, a loss of therapeutic neutrality and objectivity, and a tendency to blur boundaries to the point of engaging in behaviors that retraumatize and further abuse survivors (Wolf 1988, 63). To make matters more complex, caregivers can be overcome by the mobilization within themselves of their own unmet archaic selfobject needs that now also push for recognition and seek satisfaction. This state of affairs can set the stage for caregivers to use their work with survivors to satisfy their own selfobject needs.

The types of reactions just described on the part of caregivers to activated, disturbing, and split-off dimensions of a person seeking help are in and of themselves quite normal. The extent to which we are aware of these reactions within ourselves and manage and respond to them in appropriate and therapeutic ways, however, will largely determine whether the relationships we establish with those seeking our help will be restorative or hurtful. If they turn out to be hurtful, the dynamics involved and the damage done will often replicate the original abuse and neglect in key dimensions.

Because of the repetitive nature of such a hurtful exchange with a person whose role is to be helpful, a survivor's already dwindling hope that such a thing as "help" actually exists is further eroded. Such a destructive outcome is more likely when caregivers are uninformed about these complex processes, when they practice in isolation without the benefit of regular supervision, consultation, and the mutual support of colleagues, and when they remain defensively unaware of their own divided selfs. As Pamela Cooper-White (1995) has stated: "the importance of naming, reflecting upon, and seeking ongoing support for healing of one's own wounds cannot be overemphasized" (196).

Paradoxes within the Wounded-Healer Paradigm

While it is crucial for us caregivers to take responsibility for how our unique wounds affect us and to manage our woundedness in ways that safeguard those who interact with us, perfection is not a requirement or even a goal. What is important, however, is for us to learn to live life to the fullest while simultaneously remaining aware and sensitive to our own pain and the pain and suffering of others. Nouwen (1972) addresses ministers around this critical issue: "For the minister is called to recognize the sufferings of his time in his own heart and make that recognition the starting point of his service. . . . his service will not be perceived as authentic unless it comes from a heart wounded by the suffering about which he speaks. . . . Thus nothing can be written about ministry without a deeper understanding of the ways in which the minister can make his own wounds available as a source of healing" (xvi).

Remaining connected to the pain and suffering of ourselves and others, and making use of our woundedness for service to others, are key ingredients in *all* effective caregiving. It is our belief that this balance is best achieved when caregivers are (1) grounded in a solid theory base that is fully integrated with their personal and professional identities and value/faith commitments (Means 1994, 203), (2) intimately connected within a web of self-restoring and self-sustaining relationships with significant others and the natural world, and (3) nourished by an active and vibrant spiritual faith. Without these resources, caregivers are more prone to being buffeted about by the vicissitudes of prevailing cultural wave trends and the chronic anxiety of the time in ways that are detrimental to their work with vulnerable persons.

For those of us whose faith is rooted within the Judeo-Christian tradition, one of the most remarkable and endearing traits of biblical stories and characters is the fact that they so unabashedly reveal to us both the strengths and weaknesses of persons. The vast depth, breadth, and richness of human personality, life, and experience are shared with us through stories recounting the bold actions and tribulations of real persons struggling to make sense out of life while simultaneously seeking to maintain their covenantal relationship with God and God's call to be faithful. Thus, while our personal wounds may be troublesome, they need not be obstacles to caregiving. Instead, they offer us a medium for the sharing of common human experience that is so crucial to healing and the relevance of therapeutic intervention.

In the *Use of the Self in Therapy*, Miller and Baldwin (1987) "propose that the nature of the helping relationship embodies the basic polarities inherent in the paradigm of the wounded healer . . . the paradox of one who heals and yet remains wounded lies at the heart of the mystery of healing" (140). In the introduction to the first chapter of *The Wounded Healer*, Henri Nouwen (1972) discusses his encounter with a man named Peter: "He came to ask for help, but at the same time he offered a new understanding of my own world!" (3).

These two comments provide a helpful counterbalance to some of the common pitfalls of woundedness just enumerated. Within these comments are two elements that provide the framework for the remainder of this chapter. They are presented together because their helpfulness to us depends up the corrective tension each provides the other. Those elements are the relationship between woundedness and healing and the importance of an ongoing openness to being taught by those we serve.

The Relationship between Woundedness and Healing

All of us are traumatized, broken, and split in some manner as we go about engaging with others and experiencing life. If it were necessary for caregivers to "have it all together" in order to be helpful, the world would be poorer for it. Yet being a "wounded healer" is not a simple or even a natural task. As Nouwen (1972) conceptualized it, a wounded healer is "one who must look after his own wounds but at the same time be prepared to heal the wounds of others" (82). While this concept is currently accepted in many caregiving circles, this has not always been the case. A brief historical excursion will put this into a better context.

In the course of history, natural and culturally endorsed healers, who were also often the spiritual leaders of a community, were gradually replaced by psychotherapists and other human service professionals who turned toward the empirical methods of science for data upon which to build and validate their theories. As Thomas Kuhn (1962) pointed out, "a science needs *esoteric* facts" (cited in Becker 1968, 342). This direction has yielded some critically important findings. Psychoanalysis, for example, provided a fruitful method for the study of the internal mental worlds of human beings. Becker (1968) credited this methodology with giving us "the esoteric data on self-esteem maintenance and anxiety-proneness" (342) that provided the much sought after unifying principle of "human character development" (328) referred to earlier in this book.

In the process, however, the souls of persons were tragically left behind. In addition, the self of the therapist came to be seen as a potentially unfortunate contaminant that needed to be closely managed and controlled. Within the psychoanalytic tradition, the emphasis on "analysis of the transference" and "interpretation" as primary healing agents contributed to the view that therapists were to function as well-tuned instruments and therefore needed to maintain an objective detachment in the therapeutic encounter. It is, therefore, not surprising that psychoanalysts became viewed as "medical technologists" (Becker 1968, 343).

As various psychotherapeutic approaches to helping persons heal became more and more differentiated from psychoanalysis as a scientific method of inquiry, it became easier to return to the practiced awareness that human beings grow and flourish best in caring and sustaining human environments that include real-life, existential interactions between fully engaged persons. As a consequence, the self of the caregiver has been increasingly seen as capable of making a valuable and positive contribution to the therapeutic encounter (Satir 1987) and as a crucial ingredient in a healing process.

The history of the healing professions within Western culture is replete with the dichotomous separation and splitting of one field of inquiry and professional discipline from another. An unfortunate result of this division has been the inclination to split and divide human subjects as if they were "Its" instead of "Thous." This division has not only reinforced the preexisting divisions within persons seeking help, but has also made the journey toward self-integration more difficult for future caregivers. One of the places this has occurred with profound consequences is within the educational systems of our country, including those academic institutions that have historically trained caregivers. In their programs of professional training, these institutions have split students into intellectual and emotional selfs and have then dismissed the emotional dimension as a factor outside the purview of academic education. This approach has not only contributed significantly to a lack of personal integration within the students who have moved through these systems, but it has also hindered the personal integration of caregivers who have relied upon them for their professional training. This situation has existed across professional cognate groups.

This forced separation of the emotional and intellectual dimensions of persons has also resulted in the need for postgraduate internships and residencies to reintroduce graduates in the helping professions to the human dimensions of persons, to the existentially troubling and real problems people bring to caregivers, and to the nurturing of human qualities within themselves that are so crucial to their becoming effective healers. This has meant that those who wish to become caregivers must find ways to involve themselves in processes that help them learn how to move back and forth in an integrated manner between the wounded and healer dimensions of themselves. This also requires a willingness to learn and use a language that aids in this integration process.

Henri Nouwen (1972) emphasized the importance of helping people articulate their inner world and the moving of the Spirit. He indicated that much of the emphasis within ministry in the recent past has been on the organizational level or with what he calls "running the show as a circus director" (37–38). Helping others articulate their inner world and the moving of the Spirit involves caregivers in their own inner journeys of exploration and self-encounter. In Nouwen's words, "As soon as we feel at home in our own house, discover the dark corners as well as the light spots, the closed doors as well as the drafty rooms, our confusion will evaporate, our anxiety will diminish, and we will become capable of creative work" (38).

There are some human qualities that are important to lift up as crucial to caregiving and the developmental formation of caregivers. The first of these is *compassion*. It is this quality that enables us to establish connections between ourselves and those we serve in a way that does not permit the distancing and disconnection between ourselves and others that invites us to view others as strangers who are radically different from us. Nouwen (1972) expresses this in the following way: "Through compassion it is possible to recognize that the craving for love that men feel resides also in our own hearts, that the cruelty that the world knows all too well is also rooted in our own impulses. Through compassion we also sense our hope for forgiveness in our friend's eyes and our hatred in their bitter mouths. When they kill, we know that we could have done it; when they give life, we know that we can do the same. For the compassionate man nothing human is alien: no joy and no sorrow, no way of living and no way of dying" (41). Devoid of compassion, we are more apt to divide the world. Kathleen Norris (1998) puts it this way: "Like a child pulling the covers up to keep at bay the monsters under the bed, we hide behind the mask of the self and say, 'I'm a good person'" (176).

Compassion is a means of bridging the delusional gap we create in our minds between ourselves as "good people" and others as "bad people."

Nouwen not only lifts up for us the *healing* power of compassion, but goes as far as to suggest that compassion provides the base for a new type of *authority*. This authority rests in compassion's ability to break through the pressured fearfulness of in-groups and cliques to establish connections among persons who outwardly seem so different that we feel justified in discounting them (Nouwen 1972, 41). In the wake of an epidemic of school shootings such as witnessed in Littleton, Colorado, an authority built on a base of compassion offers us more hope than one based on a threat of increased power and control through the introduction of law enforcement personnel to our school buildings. A recent example shared by a colleague points out the deep hurt a cliquish culture can inflict on the fragile self of an "outsider" who, like the rest of us, is merely searching for ways to feel accepted and be part of the group.

Heather was a sixteen-year-old junior in high school when prom time came. Since she did not have a date, she asked a few classmates whom she wanted to get to know better if she could join their group for the evening. She was told she could. Heather and her mother shopped for her dress with excitement and enthusiasm. The group had originally planned to have dinner before the dance at one of the nicer restaurants in town. A few days before the prom, one of the girls in the group called Heather. She indicated that everyone was interested in going to a different restaurant than originally planned, and she asked if Heather would call the new restaurant to make the reservations. Heather readily agreed and arranged to meet the group at the new restaurant.

At the appointed time, Heather arrived in her new dress looking forward to the excitement of the evening and the chance to get to know her new friends better. The others never came. After waiting more than forty-five minutes, Heather left in dismay. Upon leaving the restaurant, she heard the group she was supposed to meet shout from a passing van, "Hi, Heather! See you at the dance!" The mixture of anger, rage, humiliation, and profound sadness and abandonment welling up within Heather was so intense there was nothing she could do except go home and cry. While this type of interaction is not that uncommon, the pain and damage it creates within the self-structures of our young people shouts out the need for compassion being taught and modeled in our homes, schools, and faith groups as a basic human quality required for community living.

An equally important concept is *vulnerability*. Virginia Satir (1987) believed that when the self of the therapist and the self of the patient met in significant and deep ways a "context of vulnerability" was created that enhanced the potential for change that is lodged within every patient (24). The capacity to enter into such a "context of vulnerability" is enhanced when the caregiver attends to her/his inner self. This includes becoming attuned to the brokenness, wounds, conflicts, parts, and polarities that exist deep within all of us, but that is easily "overlooked in the glitter of contemporary helper technology" (Miller and Baldwin 1987, 146–48).

Closely related to compassion and vulnerability is *hospitality*. Nouwen (1972) describes hospitality as that which allows us to break through our own fears sufficiently as to "open our houses to the stranger" (89). This process requires that caregivers be at ease and comfortable enough with themselves, the caregiving process, and the setting in which they work so that a "free and fearless place" can be created for "the unexpected traveler" (89). Nouwen is quick to point out that this work is paradoxical in the sense that it requires "the creation of an empty space where the guest can find his own soul" (92). In a similar vein, Carl Rogers was of the belief that "therapy is most effective when the therapist's goals are limited to the process of therapy and not the outcome" (Baldwin 1987, 47). As any experienced caregiver can testify, the creation and maintenance of such a space takes a tremendous amount of energy and constant attention to one's self and one's surroundings. Once created and established, such a space not only leaves room for the revelation of one's true self, but it also creates a welcoming environment that is open to the moving of the Spirit. It is in this sense that such space is *sacred*.

There is nothing as disheartening to some patients in psychotherapy than to feel the imposition of one expectation upon the next with little room to just experience themselves being in relationship with another person in a safe and comfortable place. When caregiver and patient are successful in creating such a place, it becomes a *sanctuary* or "a place to catch one's breath, literally and spiritually" (Ashbrook 1996, 56). In addition to physical and emotional space, a period of time that is free from demands to perform in a certain way according to some externally imposed schedule is also crucial. This is akin to the *Sabbath* experience so vital for the re-creation of our souls as it facilitates the nonconsciously controlled processes of integrating experience and the making of meaning (Ashbrook 1996, 180–97).

An Openness to Being Taught

Throughout this book, we have emphasized the importance of listening to the *messages* our patients bring us about the greater world in which we all live, and not just to the *problems* they bring. There are two major reasons this perspective is so crucial—it keeps us aware of factors existing within our culture and world community that hurt persons and stand in need of reform, and it keeps us in touch with the suffering of the peoples of the world. A brief discussion of each of these follows.

Informing Us about Culture

In chapter nine, we presented the concept of "pastoral counseling as cultural critique" (Means 1997). This concept was originally rooted in the metaphor of patients as scouts, or as persons on the boundaries and frontiers of the culture who get hurt and come to tell us about it (Means 1995).

Theological and faith traditions have historically taken a variety of stances with regard to culture (see Niebuhr 1975). The psychological and social sciences and the human service professions based on them have tended to be less active in critiquing culture. A number of factors have contributed to this stance.

One factor has been the tendency of human service professions to become more easily enmeshed with the culture, thereby losing a transcendent perspective that might otherwise be afforded them by virtue of their particular bases of knowledge. In addition, a reliance on scientific empiricism with its emphasis on the "knowledge of exteriors" has narrowed their vision and has led to a sometimes hostile skepticism regarding the critically important subjective and spiritual dimensions of human life, or the "knowledge of interiors" (see Hinkle 1999). The historical conflict between these equally important perspectives has contributed to an erosion of credibility in the eyes of persons who look to our professions for help.

An additional factor has been the tremendous emphasis on technology within the Western world, especially within the United States. This emphasis encourages an attitude of mastery rather than understanding and misleads us into the untruth that we have the ability to solve all problems quickly with little emotional cost and personal commitment and involvement. When this attitude is coupled with our extreme individualistic orientation and applied to complex human dilemmas, numerous tragic consequences occur as power, control, and manipulation become more highly valued than understanding, cooperation, dialogue, and mediation. In addition to raising complex ethical issues, these same cultural dynamics lead to tremendous paradoxes that further erode credibility and confidence in human service professions and in ourselves. One example is our capacity and willingness to use elaborate and expensive medical procedures to save the life of one person while we are simultaneously unable (and unwilling) to prevent thousands of people from starving (Nouwen 1972, 10–11).

Within the field of psychotherapy, a further difficulty has been the lack of an accepted and unifying theory about what is helpful and not helpful to persons. Increasingly, however, outcome studies looking at the efficacy of psychotherapy services have identified clusters of factors responsible for a large amount of the variance in outcome (Miller et al. 1997, 22–31). The importance of these studies is their identification of factors that cut across particular theoretical orientations and that appear to be necessary ingredients in any helpful caregiving relationship. It is noteworthy that some of these findings support Becker's (1968) conclusion regarding the pivotal role self-esteem maintenance plays in human interactions and the development of human character (328), as well as self psychology's emphasis on the importance of self-development and looking at things from a client's subjective perspective.

There is at present, therefore, a wealth of converging knowledge about what is helpful to people, about the types of environments needed for personal learning, change, and integration, and about the types of interpersonal interactions that are conducive to the development of strong and resilient selfs. Thus, it is time for professional organizations within the human service arena to take a more active and visible role in articulating this information in such a way that it can more fully and persuasively make its way into the normal course of human dialogue. This move will require that we tap into new sources of courage as we move increasingly beyond the role of healers and into the more uncomfortable and threatening role of educators and even prophets. Such a shift may enable us, however, to articulate more assertively our informed perspectives on some of the major human problems that plague us, to push for educational reform that emphasizes the emotional as well as academic development of our children, and to become more involved in formulating public policy. In this regard, one of the criticisms that can be levied against the current emphasis on short-term, problem/solution-focused counseling is that its narrowed attention to presenting symptoms and "solving" problems quickly makes it easier for caregivers to avoid the broader social responsibilities we have to recognize, speak out, and intervene in cultural processes that repetitively harm and devastate persons.

Keeping Us in Touch with Suffering

Not only are we taught by those we serve about aspects of our culture and world that are in need of reform, but in the process hurting persons bring us face-to-face with suffering in the world. They keep us intimately connected to the truth that suffering is not an abstract thing, and that suffering cannot be sanitized and cleansed of its pain and agony without making it something it is not. The tragic suffering presented to us in the stories and lives of those who come to us keeps a human face on suffering and keeps us connected to the vulnerabilities we all share as human beings. As Nouwen (1972) so graciously reminds us, making our own wounds a source of healing is not a matter of us finding ways to share our own personal pains, but rather involves a "constant willingness to see one's own pain and suffering as rising from the depth of the human condition which all men share" (88).

The importance of such an attitude toward our role as caregivers and healers cannot be overstated. Without an ongoing existential connection between us and those who seek our help, we are constantly threatened with complacency and the "sleep of everyday life" discussed in chapter two. Without such a connection, we are more easily seduced and corrupted by the power and prestige of our respectable positions as healers esteemed by the communities in which we live.

It is this theme that is at the center of Khalil Gibran's (1962) haunting tale entitled "Khalil the Heretic." In his unsettling confrontation of fellow monks, the author writes, "Why are you living in the shadow of parasitism, segregating yourselves from the people who are in need of knowledge? Why are you depriving the country of your help? Jesus has sent you as lambs amongst the wolves; what has made you as wolves amongst the lambs? Why are you fleeing from mankind and from God who created you?" (256–57).

Gibran's words are a scathing critique of church hierarchy and the vast crevasse that can separate those in priestly positions from the common people. At the time they were written, they were also partly responsible for his excommunication. But this moving account can also be a message of warning to all "helping professionals." It is an unambiguous reminder of how easily we can become detached from those we serve and how easy it is to hide within the cloistered walls of our offices among the hallowed prestige of degrees and certifications and professional affiliations. One of the many blessings brought to us by those who seek our help is a suffering that offers the potential of reaching in and touching our own hurts and pains. Hour after hour, day after day, and week after week, they offer us this way of connecting intimately with them and the larger world of which we are a part. May God grant us the courage and wisdom to use this precious gift to promote healing and wholeness for all of God's creation.

References

Abrams, Michael. 1996. Interview by Tom Alex. *Des Moines Register*, 11 April, 6A.

Adler, Gerald, and Mark W. Rhine. 1988. "The Selfobject Function of Projective Identification." *Bulletin of the Menninger Clinic* 52: 473–91.

Allen, Jon G. 1995. *Coping with Trauma: A Guide to Self-Understanding.* Washington, D.C.: American Psychiatric Press.

———. 1998. Impact of Trauma on Relationships. Keynote address at the Iowa Psychological Association Conference, April 25, Iowa City, Iowa.

American Psychiatric Association. 1994. *Diagnostic and Statistical Manual of Mental Disorders, Fourth Edition—DSM IV.* Washington, D.C.: American Psychiatric Association.

Anderson, H., and H. Goolishian. 1992. "The Client Is the Expert." In *Therapy as Social Construction*, edited by S. McNamee and K. J. Gergen. Newbury Park, Calif.: Sage.

Anderson, Herbert, and Edward Foley. 1998. *Mighty Stories, Dangerous Rituals: Weaving Together the Human and the Divine.* San Francisco: Josse-Bass.

Ashbrook, James B. 1994. "The Cry for the Other: The Biocultural Womb of Human Development." *Zygon* 29, no. 3 (September): 297–314.

———. 1996. *Minding the Soul: Pastoral Counseling as Remembering.* Minneapolis: Fortress Press.

Ashby, Homer U., Jr. 1997. "Reclaiming the Soul of the Cure of Souls." An address at the American Association of Pastoral Counselors Centers and Training Conference, January 17, at St. Petersburg Beach, Florida.

Atwood, G., and R. Stolorow. 1984. *Structures of Subjectivity: Explorations in Psychoanalytic Phenomenology.* Hillsdale, N.J.: Analytic Press.

Baldwin, DeWitt, Jr. 1987. "Some Philosophical and Psychological Contributions to the Use of Self in Therapy." In *The Use of Self in Therapy,* edited by Michele Baldwin and Virginia Satir. New York: Haworth Press.

Baldwin, Michele. 1987. "Interview with Carl Rogers on the Use of the Self in Therapy." In *The Use of Self in Therapy,* edited by Michele Baldwin and Virginia Satir. New York: Haworth Press.

Barach, Peter M. 1991. "Multiple Personality Disorder as an Attachment Disorder." *Dissociation* 4, no. 3: 117–23.

Becker, Ernest. 1968. *The Structure of Evil: An Essay on the Unification of the Science of Man.* New York: George Braziller.

———. 1973. *The Denial of Death.* New York: The Free Press.

———. 1975. *Escape from Evil.* New York: Macmillan.

Beker, J. Christiaan. 1987. *Suffering and Hope.* Philadelphia: Fortress Press.

———. 1993. Untitled paper presented as part of a series of continuing education events for pastors sponsored by the Presbytery of Des Moines, Iowa.

Bollas, Christopher. 1987. *The Shadow of the Object: Psychoanalysis of the Unthought Known.* London: Free Association Books.

Bollas, Christopher, and David Sundelson. 1995. *The New Informants.* Northvale, N.J.: Jason Aronson.

Bonhoeffer, Dietrich. 1997. *Letters and Papers from Prison.* Edited by Eberhard Bethge. New York: Touchstone.

Borysenko, Joan. 1996. *A Woman's Book of Life: The Biology, Psychology, and Spirituality of the Feminine Life Cycle.* New York: Riverhead Books.

Braun, Bennett G. 1988. "The BASK (Behavior, Affect, Sensation, Knowledge) Model of Dissociation." *Dissociation* 1, no. 1: 4–23.

Brock, Rita Nakashima. 1989. "And a Little Child Will Lead Us: Christology and Child Abuse." In *Christianity, Patriarchy and Abuse: A Feminist Critique,* edited by Joanne Carlson Brown and Carole R. Bohn. New York: Pilgrim Press.

Brueggemann, Walter. 1987. *Hope within History.* Louisville, Ky.: John Knox Press.

———. 1997. "Conversations among Exiles." *Christian Century.* July 2–9: 630–32.

Chu, James A. 1988. "Ten Traps for Therapists in the Treatment of Trauma Survivors." *Dissociation* 1, no. 4: 24–32.

Cooper-White, Pamela. 1995. *The Cry of Tamar: Violence against Women and the Church's Response.* Minneapolis, Minn.: Fortress Press.

Crabtree, Adam. 1992. "Dissociation and Memory: A Two-Hundred-Year Perspective." *Dissociation* 5, no. 3: 150–54.

Crenshaw, Kimberly Williams. 1995. "False Memory Syndrome: Diagnosis, Distortion, or Distraction." An address (5 October) in Des Moines, Iowa.

Crossan, John D. 1975. *The Dark Interval: Towards a Theology of Story.* Niles, Ill.: Argus.

Delany, Sarah I., and A. Elizabeth Delany, with Amy Hill Hearth. 1993. *Having Our Say: The Delany Sisters' First 100 Years.* New York: Dell.

DeMarinis, Valerie M. 1993. *Critical Caring: A Feminist Model for Pastoral Psychology.* Louisville, Ky.: Westminster/John Knox.

Diaz, Tom. 1999. *Making a Killing: The Business of Guns in America.* New York: The New Press.

Doka, Kenneth J. 1998. "Who We Are, How We Grieve." In *Living with Grief: Who We Are, How We Grieve,* edited by Kenneth J. Doka and Joyce D. Davidson. Philadelphia: Brunner/Mazel.

Earl, William L. 1991. "Perceived Trauma: Its Etiology and Treatment." *Adolescence* 26, no. 101: 97–104.

Fairbairn, W. R. D. [1944] 1981. "Endopsychic Structure Considered in Terms of Object-Relations." In *Psychoanalytic Studies of the Personality.* London: Routledge and Kegan Paul, 82–132.

———. 1952. "The Repression and Return of Bad Objects." In *An Object-Relations Theory of the Personality,* edited by W. R. D. Fairbairn. New York: Basic Books.

———. 1955. "Observations in Defense of Object-Relations Theory of the Personality." *British Journal of Medical Psychology* 28.

Figley, Charles. 1985. *Trauma and Its Wake.* New York: Brunner/Mazel.

Flavell, J. H. 1963. *The Developmental Psychology of Jean Piaget.* Princeton: Van Nostrand.

Fraser, George A. 1993. "Exorcism Rituals: Effects on Multiple Personality Disorder Patients." *Dissociation* 6, no. 4: 239–44.

Gazzaniga, M., and J. LeDoux. 1978. *The Integrated Mind.* New York: Plenum Press.

General Assembly of the Presbyterian Church (U.S.A.). 1991. Study Paper on Family Violence presented at the 203rd General Assembly.

Gibran, Khalil. 1962. *A Treasury of Khalil Gibran.* Edited by Martin L. Wolf, translated by Anthony Rizcallah Ferris. New York: Citadel.

Giovacchini, Peter L. 1979. *Treatment of Primitive Mental States.* New York: Jason Aronson.

Goldberg, Susan, Roy Muir, and John Kerr, eds. 1995. *Attachment Theory: Social, Developmental and Clinical Perspectives.* Hillsdale, N.J.: The Analytic Press.

Goldstein, William. 1991. "Clarification of Projective Identification." *American Journal of Psychiatry* 148 (February): 153–61.

Gomes, Peter J. 1996. *The Good Book: Reading the Bible with Mind and Heart.* New York: William Morrow.

Goodman, Ellen. 1995. "She Was Undaunted". *Des Moines Register*, 30 September 9A.

Goodman, Lisa, and Jay Peters. 1995. "Persecutory Alters and Ego States: Protectors, Friends, and Allies." *Dissociation* 8, no. 2: 91–99.

Grotstein, James S. 1985. *Splitting and Projective Identification.* Northvale, N.J.: Jason Aronson.

Guntrip, H. 1969. *Schizoid Phenomena, Object Relations and the Self.* New York: International Universities Press.

Hamilton, N. Gregory. 1990. *Self and Others: Object Relations Theory in Practice.* Northvale, N.J.: Jason Aronson.

Harris, R. L., G. L. Archer, and B. K. Waltke. 1980. *Theological Word Book of the Old Testament.* 2 vols. Chicago: Moody Bible Institute.

Hendrickson, Kate M., Teresita McCarty, and Jean M. Goodwin. 1990. "Animal Alters: Case Reports." *Dissociation* 3, no. 4: 218–21.

Herman, Judith. 1992. *Trauma and Recovery.* New York: Basic Books.

Hesse, Hermann. 1968. *Demian: The Story of Emil Sinclair's Youth.* Translated by Michael Roloff and Michael Lebeck. New York: Bantam Books.

Hessert, Paul. 1993. *Christ and the End of Meaning: The Theology of Passion.* Rockport, Mass.: Element.

Hilberg, Raul. 1987. "Facing Evil with Bill Moyers." Public Affairs Television, Inc., New York. Videotape.

Hinkle, John E., Jr. 1999. "Spirit and Flesh: Prelude to an Epistemology of Interiors." *Aware* (publication of Garrett-Evangelical Theological Seminary, Evanston, Ill.) April: 8–9.

Horner, Althea. 1984. *Object Relations and the Developing Ego in Therapy*. New York: Jason Aronson.

Horowitz, M. J. 1976. *Stress Response Syndromes*. New York: Jason Aronson.

Hsu, Francis. 1977. Class lecture. Northwestern University.

Hulme, William. 1969. "Concern for Corporate Structures or Care for the Individual." *Journal of Pastoral Care* 23, no. 3: 153–63.

Janoff-Bulman, R. 1985. "The Aftermath of Victimization: Rebuilding Shattered Assumptions." In *Trauma and Its Wake*, edited by Charles Figley. New York: Brunner/Mazel.

———. 1989. "Assumptive Worlds and the Stress of Traumatic Events." *Social Cognition* 7: 113–16.

Johnson, Elizabeth A. 1990. *Consider Jesus*. New York: Crossroads.

———. 1992. *She Who Is: The Mystery of God in Feminist Theological Discourse*. New York: Crossroads.

Johnson, Stephen M. 1985. *Characterological Transformation: The Hard Work Miracle*. New York: Norton.

Jordan, Merle R. 1986. *Taking on the Gods: The Task of the Pastoral Counselor*. Nashville, Tenn.: Abingdon Press.

Jory, Brian. 1998. "Intimate Justice Theory in Clinical Practice." Paper read at the Iowa Association of Marriage and Family Therapists (February 28), Ames, Iowa.

Kagan, J. 1982. *Psychological Research on the Human Infant: An Evaluative Summary*. New York: W. T. Grant Foundation.

Kardiner, A. 1941. *The Traumatic Neuroses of War*. New York: P. Hoeber.

Keith-Lucas, Alan. n.d. "The Art and Science of Helping." Unpublished address.

Kernberg, Otto. 1966. "Structural Derivatives of Object Relationships." *International Journal of Psychoanalysis* 47: 236–53.

Kierkegaard, Søren. 1941. *Sickness Unto Death*. Translated by Walter Lowrie. Princeton: Princeton University Press.

Knight, J. A. 1985. "Religio-Psychological Dimensions of Wounded-Healers." Presented at the annual meeting of the American Psychiatric Association, Dallas, Tex., May 20.

Kuhn, Thomas. 1962. *The Structure of Scientific Revolutions.* In the International Encyclopedia of Unified Science Publication. Chicago: University of Chicago Press.

Lee, Ronald R., and J. Colby Martin. 1991. *Psychotherapy after Kohut: A Textbook of Self Psychology.* Hillsdale, N.J.: Analytic Press.

Lindemann, E. 1944. "Symtomatology and Management of Acute Grief." *American Journal of Psychiatry* 101: 141–48.

Mahler, Margaret S. 1968. *On Human Symbiosis and the Vicissitudes of Individuation.* New York: International Universities Press.

Malin, Arthur, and James S. Grotstein. 1966. "Projective Identification in the Therpeutic Process." *International Journal of Psychoanalysis* 47: 26–31.

Masterson, James F. 1976. *Psychotherapy of the Borderline Adult: A Developmental Approach.* New York: Brunner/Mazel.

McDargh, John. 1983. *Psychoanalytic Object Relations Theory and the Study of Religion: On Faith and the Imaging of God.* Lanham, Md.: University Press of America.

———. 1986. "God, Mother and Me: An Object Relational Perspective on Religious Material." *Pastoral Psychology* 34, no. 4.

———. 1993. "Telling Our Stories of God: The Contributions of a Psychoanalytic Perspective." In *Sacred Stories: A Celebration of the Power of Story to Transform and Heal,* edited by Charles and Anne Simpkinson. San Francisco: Harper.

McFarlane, Alexander, and Bessel van der Kolk. 1996. "Conclusions and Future Directions." In *Traumatic Stress: The Effects of Overwhelming Experience on Mind, Body, and Society,* edited by Bessel van der Kolk, Alexaner McFarlene, and Lars Weisaeth. New York: Guilford Press.

McWilliams, Francis C. 1997. "Voices Crying in the Wilderness: Prophetic Ministry in Clinical Pastoral Education." *Journal of Pastoral Care* 51 (spring): 37–47.

Means, J. Jeffrey. 1988. "C. A. Wise Speaks on Professional Education for Ministry." In *At the Point of Need: Living Human Experience: Essays in Honor of Carroll A. Wise,* edited by James B. Ashbrook and John E. Hinkle, Jr. Lanham, Md.: University Press of America.

———. 1995. "Hear No Evil, See No Evil, Speak No Evil: Learning from Our Work with Trauma-Related Disorders, Including Multiple Personality Disorder." *The Journal of Pastoral Care* 49 (fall): 294–305.

———. 1997. "Pastoral Counseling: An Alternative Path in Mental Health." *The Journal of Pastoral Care* 51 (fall): 317–28.

Miller, Grant, and DeWitt Baldwin Jr. 1987. "Implications of the Wounded-Healer Paradigm for the Use of the Self in Therapy." In *The Use of Self in Therapy,* edited by Michele Baldwin and Virginia Satir. New York: Haworth Press.

Miller, Scott, L.; Duncan Barry; and Mark Hubbel. 1997. *Escape from Babel: Toward a Unifying Language for Psychotherapy Practice.* New York: Norton.

Mitchell, Kenneth R., and Herbert Anderson. 1983. *All Our Losses, All Our Griefs: Resources for Pastoral Care.* Philadelphia: Westminster Press.

Modell, Arnold H. 1981. "The Holding Environment and the Therapeutic Action of Psychoanalysis." In *Classics in Psychoanalytic Technique,* edited by Robert Langs. New York: Jason Aronson.

Moore, Dianna. 1995. "Oklahoma Bombing: Reflections on a Tragedy." *Newsletter of the American Association of Pastoral Counselors* (fall): 3, 23.

Moore, Thomas. 1992. *The Care of the Soul: A Guide for Cultivating Depth and Sacredness in Everyday Life.* New York: HarperCollins.

Morgenson, Greg. 1989. *God Is a Trauma.* Dallas, Tex.: Soring Publications.

"Morris Is Remorseful in Interview." 1996. Associated Press, *Des Moines Register,* 24 November, 7A.

Nadeau, J. W. 1997. *Families Making Sense of Death.* Newbury Park, Calif.: Sage.

Nichols, Michael P. 1987. *The Self in the System: Expanding the Limits of Family Therapy.* New York: Brunner/Mazel.

Niebuhr, H. Richard. 1975. *Christ and Culture.* 1951. Reprint, New York: Harper and Row.

Niemeyer, Robert A., and Nancy J. Keese. 1998. "Dimensions of Diversity in the Reconstruction of Meaning." In *Living with Grief: Who We Are, How We Grieve,* edited by Kenneth J. Doka and Joyce D. Davidson. Philadelphia: Brunner/Mazel.

Noddings, Nel. 1989. *Women and Evil.* Berkeley, Calif.: University of California Press.

Norris, Kathleen. 1998. *Amazing Grace: A Vocabulary of Faith.* New York: Riverhead Books.

Nouwen, Henri. 1979. *The Wounded Healer: Ministry in Contemporary Society*. New York: Bantam Doubleday Dell.

———. 1981. *The Living Reminder*. New York: Seabury Press.

Pagels, Elaine. 1995. *The Origin of Satan*. New York: Vintage Books.

Parsons, Talcott. 1970. *Social Structure of Personality*. New York: Free Press.

Peck, M. Scott. 1983. *People of the Lie: The Hope for Healing Human Evil*. New York: Simon and Schuster.

Peters, Ted. 1994. *Sin: Radical Evil in Soul and Society*. Grand Rapids, Mich.: William B. Eerdmans.

Pfafflin, Ursula. 1995. "Displacement and the Yearning for Holding Environments: Visions in Feminist Pastoral Psychology and Theology." *Journal of Pastoral Care* 49 (winter): 391–403.

Piaget, Jean. 1952. *The Origins of Intelligence in Children*. New York: International Universities Press.

Poling, James Newton. 1996. *Deliver Us from Evil: Resisting Racial and Gender Oppression*. Minneapolis, Minn.: Fortress Press.

Price, Donald A. 1996. "Inner Child Work: What Is Really Happening?" *Dissociation* 9, no. 1: 68–73.

Price, Gail M. 1990. "Non-Rational Guilt in Victims of Trauma." *Dissociation* 3, no. 3: 160–64.

Prior, Stephen. 1996. *Object Relations in Severe Trauma: Psychotherapy of the Sexually Abused Child*. Northvale, N.J.: Jason Aronson.

Putnam, Frank. 1988. "The Switch Process in Multiple Personality Disorder and Other State-Change Disorders." *Dissociation* 1, no. 1: 24–32.

Reich, Wilhelm.1972. *Character Analysis*. New York: Farrar, Straus and Giroux.

Resch, Miriam C. 1992. God-Images of Incest Survivors: Implications for Pastoral Psychotherapy. D. Min. field project, Garrett-Evangelical Theological Seminary.

Rizzuto, Ana-Maria. 1979. *The Birth of the Living God: A Psychoanalytic Study*. Chicago: University of Chicago Press.

Ross, Colin A. 1989. *Multiple Personality Disorder: Diagnosis, Clinical Features, and Treatment*. New York: John Wiley and Sons.

———. 1991. "The Dissociated Executive Self and the Cultural Dissociation Barrier." *Dissociation* 4, no. 1: 55–61.

———. 1997. "Treating Trauma Disorders Effectively: Attachment to the Perpetrator." Vol. 1. Ross Institute for Psychological Trauma. Videotape.

Sands, Susan H. 1994. "What Is Dissociated?" *Dissociation* 7, no. 3: 145–52.

Satir, Virginia. 1987. "The Therapist Story." In *The Use of Self in Therapy,* edited by Michele Baldwin and Virginia Satir. New York: Haworth Press.

Scharff, David E., and Jill Savage. 1991. *Object Relations Couple Therapy.* Northvale, N.J.: Jason Aronson.

Schlosser, Eric. 1998. "The Prison-Industrial Complex." *Atlantic Monthly,* December, 51–77.

Seinfelf, Jeffrey. 1990. *The Bad Object: Handling the Negative Therapeutic Reaction in Psychotherapy.* Northvale, N.J.: Jason Aronson.

Shapiro, Francine. 1995. *Eye Movement Desensitization and Reprocessing: Basic Principles, Protocols, and Procedures.* New York: Guilford Press.

Shea, John J. 1997. "Adult Faith, Pastoral Counseling, and Spiritual Direction." *The Journal of Pastoral Care* 51, no. 3: 259–70.

Slipp, Samuel. 1984. *Object Relations: A Dynamic Bridge Between Individual and Family Treatment.* New York: Jason Aronson.

Sorkin, Aaron. *A Few Good Men.* New York: S. French.

Stern, Daniel N. 1985. *The Interpersonal World of the Infant: A View from Psychoanalysis and Developmental Psychology.* New York: Basic Books.

Sullivan, Harry Stack. 1953. *The Interpersonal Theory of Psychiatry.* New York: W. W. Norton.

Tannen, Debra. 1998. *The Argument Culture: Moving from Debate to Dialogue.* New York: Random House.

Tart, Charles. 1987. *Waking Up: Overcoming the Obstacles to Human Potential.* Boston: Shambhala.

Tillich, Paul. 1952. *The Courage to Be.* New Haven, Conn.: Yale University Press.

———. 1957. *The Dynamics of Faith.* New York: Harper and Row.

———. 1967. *Systematic Theology: Three Volumes in One.* Vol. 2. Chicago: University of Chicago Press.

Unger, Michael T., and Judith E. Levene. 1994. "Selfobject Functions of the Family: Implications for Family Therapy." *Clinical Social Work Journal* 22, no. 3 (fall).

van der Kolk, Bessel A. 1987. *Psychological Trauma*. Washington, D.C.: American Psychiatric Press.

VanKatwyk, Peter. 1997. "Healing through Differentiation: A Pastoral Care and Counseling Perspective." *Journal of Pastoral Care* 51, no. 3.

Watkins, John G., and Helen Watkins. 1988. "The Management of Malevolent Ego States." *Dissociation* 1, no. 1: 67–72.

Welsh, Thomas G. 1994. "The Human Problem of Evil." An editorial in the Newsletter of the International Religious Federation for World Peace reporting on the 1994 Seoul Congress of the Federation.

Wheatley, Margaret J. 1994. *Leadership and the New Science: Learning about Organization from an Orderly Universe*. San Francisco: Berrett-Koehler.

Wink, Walter. 1986. *Unmasking the Powers: The Invisible Forces That Determine Human Existence*. Philadelphia: Fortress Press.

Winnicott, D. W. 1965. *The Maturational Processes and the Facilitating Environment*. London: Hogarth Press.

Wipple, Vicky. 1987. "Counseling Battered Women from Fundamentalist Churches." *Journal of Marital and Family Therapy* 13, no. 3: 251–58.

Wise, Carroll A. 1966. *The Meaning of Pastoral Care*. New York: Harper and Row.

Wolf, Ernest S. 1988. *Treating the Self: Elements of Clinical Self Psychology*. New York: Guilford Press.

Yankelovich, Daniel. 1991. *Coming to Public Judgment: Making Democracy Work in a Complex World*. Syracuse, N.Y.: Syracuse University Press.

Young, Walter C. 1988. "Psychodynamics and Dissociation: All That Switches Is Not Split." *Dissociation* 1, no. 1: 33–38.

Index

233